Welcome to

Official GRE® Verbal Reasoning Practice Questions, Volume 1

The book you are holding offers 150 real GRE practice questions directly from the maker of the *GRE®* revised General Test. This book is specially created to give you in-depth practice and accurate test preparation for the Verbal Reasoning measure.

Here's what you will find inside:

- **Authentic GRE Verbal Reasoning test questions** arranged by question type and difficulty level—to help you build your test-taking skills. Plus, mixed practice sets.

- **Answers and explanations** for every question!

- **ETS's own test-taking strategies.** Learn valuable hints and tips that can help you get your best score.

- **Official information on the GRE Verbal Reasoning measure.** Get the facts about the test content, structure, and scoring—straight from ETS.

- **Plus: an overview of the GRE Analytical Writing measure** with writing strategies, sample writing tasks, and sample scored essays.

About ETS

At ETS, we advance quality and equity in education for people worldwide by creating assessments based on rigorous research. ETS serves individuals, educational institutions, and government agencies by providing customized solutions for teacher certification, English language learning, and elementary, secondary, and post-secondary education, as well as conducting educational research, analysis, and policy studies. Founded as a nonprofit in 1947, ETS develops, administers, and scores more than 50 million tests annually—including the *TOEFL®* and *TOEIC®* tests, the *GRE®* tests, and *The Praxis Series™* assessments—in more than 180 countries at over 9,000 locations worldwide. For more information, visit www.ets.org.

IMPORTANT

ETS makes available free test preparation materials for individuals planning to take a GRE test. *POWERPREP® II* software is available for individuals planning to take the computer-delivered GRE revised General Test, and the *Practice Book for the Paper-based GRE revised General Test, Second Edition*, is available for individuals planning to take the paper-delivered test. The information about how to prepare for the Verbal Reasoning measure of the GRE revised General Test, test-taking strategies, question strategies, etc., that is included in the free test preparation is also included in this publication. This publication also provides you with 150 brand new practice questions with answers and explanations.

For more information about the GRE revised General Test, free and low-cost GRE test preparation materials, and other GRE products and services, please visit the GRE website at:

www.ets.org/gre

Inquiries concerning the practice test questions in this book should be sent to the GRE testing program at:

GRETestQuestionInquiries@ets.org

Volume 1

Official
GRE®
VERBAL
REASONING
Practice Questions
with practice for the Analytical Writing measure

Mc
Graw
Hill
Education

New York | Chicago | San Francisco | Athens | London | Madrid
Mexico City | Milan | New Delhi | Singapore | Sydney | Toronto

7 8 9 10   QVS/QVS   1 0 9 8 7 6 5

ISBN 978-0-07-183429-2
MHID 0-07-183429-X

e-ISBN 978-0-07-183430-8
e-MHID 0-07-183430-3

Library of Congress Control Number 2013957256

ETS, the ETS logo, LISTENING, LEARNING, LEADING, E-RATER, GRADUATE RECORD EXAMINATIONS, GRE, POWERPREP, SCORESELECT, TOEFL, and TOEIC are registered trademarks of Educational Testing Service in the United States and other countries and are used under license. THE PRAXIS SERIES is a trademark of Educational Testing Service and is used under license.

McGraw-Hill Education products are available at special quantity discounts to use as premiums and sales promotions or for use in corporate training programs. To contact a representative, please visit the Contact Us pages at www.mhprofessional.com.

Sponsoring Editor: Charles Wall
Interior Designer: Jane Tenenbaum
Typesetters: MPS Limited

Contents

4 Question Type 2: Text Completion 57

5 Question Type 3: Sentence Equivalence 79

6 Mixed Practice Sets 101

7 Overview of the *GRE*® Analytical Writing Measure 179

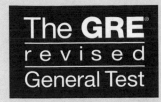

How to Use This Book

This book provides important information about the Verbal Reasoning and Analytical Writing measures of the GRE revised General Test, including the types of questions they include, and the knowledge and skills that they measure. The book will help you:

- Familiarize yourself with the test format and test question types
- Learn valuable test taking-strategies for each question type
- Check your progress with Verbal Reasoning practice questions

The following five-step program has been designed to help you make the best use of this book.

STEP 1 Learn About the GRE Verbal Reasoning Measure

Chapter 1 of this book provides an overview of the GRE Verbal Reasoning measure. Read this chapter to learn about the number of questions, time limits, and the test design features. You will also find valuable test-taking strategies from ETS and important information about how the measure is scored.

STEP 2 Study the Different GRE Verbal Reasoning Question Types

Chapter 2 of this book describes the types of questions you will encounter in the Verbal Reasoning measure. You will learn what the questions are designed to measure, and you will get tips for answering each question type. You will also see samples of each question type, with helpful explanations.

STEP 3 Practice Answering GRE Verbal Reasoning Questions

Chapters 3, 4, and 5 contain sets of Verbal Reasoning practice questions. The question sets are arranged in order of increasing difficulty, from easy to medium to hard. Answer the questions in each set, then read through the explanations to see which question types you found most challenging. Look for patterns. Did specific question types give you trouble? When did you need to guess at the answer? Use the results to identify your weaknesses and to sharpen your test-taking skills.

STEP 4 Test Yourself with the Mixed Practice Tests

Once you have completed the practice sets for each question type, prepare yourself further by practicing with authentic GRE Mixed Practice Sets in Chapter 6 of this book. The Mixed Practice Sets will include all Verbal Reasoning question types in an order similar to the way they will appear on the GRE revised General Test.

STEP 5 Learn About the GRE Analytical Writing Measure

Chapter 7 of this book describes the two types of tasks you will encounter in the Analytical Writing measure. You will learn what the tasks are designed to measure, and you will get tips for answering each task. You will also see samples of each task, with helpful explanations. After you have reviewed the sample questions, you will have the opportunity to write essay responses to two practice questions and you will be able to review scored sample essays with reader commentary.

1 Overview of the GRE® Verbal Reasoning Measure

Your goal for this chapter	⇒ Review basic information on the structure of the *GRE*® Verbal Reasoning measure, test-taking strategies, and scoring

Introduction to the *GRE*® revised General Test

The *GRE*® revised General Test—the most widely accepted graduate admissions test worldwide—measures verbal reasoning, quantitative reasoning, critical thinking, and analytical writing skills that are necessary for success in graduate and business school. Prospective graduate and business school applicants from all around the world take the GRE revised General Test. Applicants come from varying educational and cultural backgrounds, and the GRE revised General Test provides a common measure for comparing candidates' qualifications. GRE scores are used by admissions committees and fellowship panels to supplement undergraduate records, recommendation letters, and other qualifications for graduate-level study.

The GRE revised General Test is available at test centers in more than 160 countries. In most regions of the world, the computer-delivered test is available on a continuous basis throughout the year. In areas of the world where computer-delivered testing is not available, the test is administered in a paper-delivered format up to three times a year.

Before taking the GRE revised General Test, it is important to become familiar with the content and structure of the test, and with each of the three measures—Verbal Reasoning, Quantitative Reasoning, and Analytical Writing. This book provides a close look at the GRE Verbal Reasoning measure and Analytical Writing measure. Chapter 1 provides an overview of the structure and scoring of the GRE Verbal Reasoning measure. In Chapters 2 through 6, you will find information specific to the content of the Verbal Reasoning measure. In Chapter 7, an overview of the Analytical Writing measure is presented. You can use the information in this publication to help you understand the type of material on which you will be tested. For the most up-to-date information about the GRE revised General Test, visit the GRE website at **www.ets.org/gre**.

The Verbal Reasoning Measure of the Computer-delivered GRE revised General Test

Structure of the Verbal Reasoning Measure

Measure	Number of Questions	Allotted Time
Verbal Reasoning (Two sections)	20 questions per section	30 minutes per section

The Verbal Reasoning sections may appear anytime in the test after section 1. The directions at the beginning of each Verbal Reasoning section specify the total number of questions in the section and the time allowed for the section.

Test Design Features

The Verbal Reasoning measure of the computer-delivered GRE revised General Test is section-level adaptive. This means the computer selects the second section of a measure based on your performance on the first section.

The advanced adaptive design also means you can freely move forward and backward throughout an entire section. Specific features include:

- Preview and review capabilities within a section
- "Mark" and "Review" features to tag questions, so you can skip them and return later if you have time remaining in the section
- The ability to change/edit answers within a section

Test-taking Strategies

The questions in the Verbal Reasoning measure are presented in a variety of formats. Some require you to select a single answer choice; others require you to select one or more answer choices. Make sure when answering a question that you understand what response is required.

When taking the Verbal Reasoning measure of the computer-delivered GRE revised General Test, you are free to skip questions that you might have difficulty answering within a section. The testing software has a "Mark" feature that enables you to mark questions you would like to revisit during the time provided to work on that section. The testing software also has a "Review" feature that lets you view a complete list of all the questions in the section on which you are working, indicates whether you have answered each question, and identifies the questions you have marked for review. Additionally, you can review questions you have already answered and change your answers, provided you still have time remaining to work on that section.

A sample review screen appears below. The review screen is intended to help you keep track of your progress on the test. Do not spend too much time on the review screen, as this will take away from the time allotted to read and answer the questions on the test.

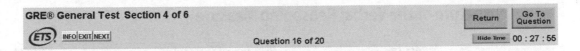

GRE® General Test Section 4 of 6		Return	Go To Question
ETS INFO EXIT NEXT Question 16 of 20		Hide Time 00 : 27 : 55	

Below is the list of questions in the current section. The question you were on is highlighted. Questions you have seen are labeled **Answered**, **Incomplete**, or **Not Answered**. A question is labeled **Incomplete** if the question requires you to select a certain number of answer choices and you have selected more or fewer than that number. Questions you have marked are indicated with a ✔.

To return to the question you were on, click **Return**.

To go to a different question, click on that question to highlight it, then click **Go To Question**.

Question Number	Status	Marked		Question Number	Status	Marked
1	Answered			11	Answered	
2	Answered			12	Incomplete	
3	Answered			13	Incomplete	
4	Answered			14	Incomplete	✔
5	Answered			15	Incomplete	✔
6	Incomplete			16	Answered	
7	Answered	✔		17	Answered	
8	Answered			18	Answered	✔
9	Answered			19	Not seen	
10	Answered			20	Not seen	

Your Verbal Reasoning score will be determined by the number of questions you answer correctly. Nothing is subtracted from a score if you answer a question incorrectly. Therefore, to maximize your scores on the Verbal Reasoning measure, it is best to answer every question.

Work as rapidly as you can without being careless. Since no question carries greater weight than any other, do not waste time pondering individual questions you find extremely difficult or unfamiliar.

You may want to go through each of the Verbal Reasoning sections rapidly first, stopping only to answer questions you can answer with certainty. Then go back and answer the questions that require greater thought, concluding with the difficult questions if you have time.

During the actual administration of the revised General Test, you may work only on one section at a time and only for the time allowed. Once you have completed a section, you may not go back to it.

Scratch Paper

You will receive a supply of scratch paper before you begin the test. You can replenish your supply of scratch paper as necessary throughout the test by asking the test administrator.

How the Verbal Reasoning Measure Is Scored

The Verbal Reasoning measure is section-level adaptive. This means the computer selects the second section of a measure based on your performance on the first section. Within each section, all questions contribute equally to the final score. First a raw score is computed. The raw score is the number of questions you answered correctly. The raw score is then converted to a scaled score through a process known as equating. The equating process accounts for minor variations in difficulty from test to test as well as the differences introduced by the section-level adaptation. Thus a given scaled score reflects the same level of performance regardless of which second section was selected and when the test was taken.

The Verbal Reasoning Measure of the Paper-delivered GRE revised General Test

Structure of the Verbal Reasoning Measure

Measure	Number of Questions	Allotted Time
Verbal Reasoning (Two sections)	25 questions per section	35 minutes per section

The Verbal Reasoning sections may appear in any order after section 2. The directions at the beginning of each section specify the total number of questions in the section and the time allowed for the section.

Test Design Features

- You are free, within any section, to skip questions and come back to them later or change the answer to a question.
- Answers are entered in the test book, rather than a separate answer sheet.

Test-taking Strategies

The questions in the Verbal Reasoning measure have a variety of formats. Some require you to select a single answer choice; others require you to select one or more answer choices. Make sure when answering a question that you understand what response is required.

When taking a Verbal Reasoning section, you are free, within that section, to skip questions that you might have difficulty answering and come back to them later during the time provided to work on that section. Also during that time you may change the answer to any question in that section by erasing it completely and filling in an alternative answer. Be careful not to leave any stray marks in the answer area, as they may be interpreted as incorrect responses. You can, however, safely make notes or perform calculations on other parts of the page. No additional scratch paper will be provided.

Your Verbal Reasoning score will be determined by the number of questions you answer correctly. Nothing is subtracted from a score if you answer a question incorrectly. Therefore, to maximize your score on the Verbal Reasoning measure, it is best to answer every question.

Work as rapidly as you can without being careless. Since no question carries greater weight than any other, do not waste time pondering individual questions you find extremely difficult or unfamiliar.

You may want to go through each of the Verbal Reasoning sections rapidly first, stopping only to answer questions you can answer with certainty. Then go back and answer the questions that require greater thought, concluding with the difficult questions if you have time.

During the actual administration of the revised General Test, you may work only on the section the test center supervisor designates and only for the time allowed. You may *not* go back to an earlier section of the test after the supervisor announces, "Please stop work" for that section. The supervisor is authorized to dismiss you from the center for doing so.

All answers must be recorded in the test book.

How the Verbal Reasoning Measure Is Scored

Scoring of the Verbal Reasoning measure is essentially a two-step process. First a raw score is computed. The raw score is the number of questions answered correctly in the two sections for the measure. The raw score is then converted to a scaled score through a process known as equating. The equating process accounts for minor variations in difficulty among the different test editions. Thus a given scaled score reflects the same level of performance regardless of which edition of the test was taken.

Score Reporting

A Verbal Reasoning score is reported on a 130-170 score scale, in 1-point increments. If you do not answer any questions at all for the measure, you will receive a No Score (NS) for that measure.

The *ScoreSelect®* Option

The *ScoreSelect®* option is available for both the GRE revised General Test and GRE Subject Tests and can be used by anyone with reportable scores from the last five years. This option lets you send institutions your best scores. For your free score reports you can send scores from your Most Recent test administration or scores from All test administrations in your reportable history. After test day, you can send scores from your *Most Recent, All, or Any* specific test administration (s) for a fee when ordering Additional Score Reports. Just remember, scores for a test administration must be reported in their entirety. For more information, visit **www.ets.org/gre/scoreselect**.

Score Reporting Time Frames

Scores from computer-delivered GRE revised General Test administrations are reported approximately 10 to 15 days after the test date. Scores from paper-delivered administrations are reported within six weeks after the test date. If you are applying to a graduate or business school program, be sure to review the appropriate admissions deadlines and plan to take the test in time for your scores to reach the institution.

For more information on score reporting, visit the GRE website at **www.ets.org/gre/scores/get**.

2 Test Content

⇨ Learn the three types of *GRE*® Verbal Reasoning questions
⇨ Get tips for answering each question type
⇨ Study examples of GRE Verbal Reasoning questions

Overview of the Verbal Reasoning Measure

The Verbal Reasoning measure assesses your ability to analyze and evaluate written material and synthesize information obtained from it, to analyze relationships among component parts of sentences, and to recognize relationships among words and concepts.

Verbal Reasoning questions appear in several formats, each of which is discussed in detail below. About half of the measure requires you to read passages and answer questions on those passages. The other half requires you to read, interpret, and complete existing sentences, groups of sentences, or paragraphs. Many, but not all, of the questions are standard multiple-choice questions, in which you are required to select a single correct answer; others ask you to select multiple correct answers; and still others ask you to select a sentence from the passage. The number of choices varies depending on the type of question.

Verbal Reasoning Question Types

The Verbal Reasoning measure contains three types of questions:

- Reading Comprehension
- Text Completion
- Sentence Equivalence

In this section you will study each of these question types in turn, and you'll learn valuable strategies for answering each type. Turn the page to begin.

Reading Comprehension Questions

Reading Comprehension questions are designed to test a wide range of abilities required to read and understand the kinds of prose commonly encountered in graduate school. Those abilities include

- understanding the meaning of individual words
- understanding the meaning of individual sentences
- understanding the meaning of paragraphs and larger bodies of text
- distinguishing between minor and major points
- summarizing a passage
- drawing conclusions from the information provided
- reasoning from incomplete data, inferring missing information
- understanding the structure of a text, how the parts relate to one another
- identifying the author's perspective
- identifying the author's assumptions
- analyzing a text and reaching conclusions about it
- identifying strengths and weaknesses
- developing and considering alternative explanations

As this list implies, reading and understanding a piece of text requires far more than a passive understanding of the words and sentences it contains—it requires active engagement with the text, asking questions, formulating and evaluating hypotheses, and reflecting on the relationship of the particular text to other texts and information.

Each Reading Comprehension question is based on a passage, which may range in length from one paragraph to several paragraphs. The test contains approximately ten passages; the majority of the passages in the test are one paragraph in length, and only one or two are several paragraphs long. Passages are drawn from the physical sciences, the biological sciences, the social sciences, the arts and humanities, and everyday topics, and are based on material found in books and periodicals, both academic and nonacademic.

Typically, about half of the questions on the test will be based on passages, and the number of questions based on a given passage can range from one to six. Questions can cover any of the topics listed above, from the meaning of a particular word to assessing evidence that might support or weaken points made in the passage. Many, but not all, of the questions are standard multiple-choice questions, in which you are required to select a single correct answer; others ask you to select multiple correct answers; and still others ask you to select a sentence from the passage. These question types are presented in more detail below, and you should make sure that you are familiar with the differences among them.

General Advice

Reading passages are drawn from many different disciplines and sources, so you may encounter material with which you are not familiar. Do not be discouraged when this happens; all the questions can be answered on the basis of the information provided in the passage, and you are not expected to rely on any outside knowledge. If, however, you encounter a passage that seems particularly hard or unfamiliar, you may want to save it for last.

- Read and analyze the passage carefully before trying to answer any of the questions and pay attention to clues that help you understand less explicit aspects of the passage.
  - ◆ Try to distinguish main ideas from supporting ideas or evidence.
  - ◆ Try to distinguish ideas that the author is advancing from those he or she is merely reporting.
  - ◆ Similarly, try to distinguish ideas that the author is strongly committed to from those he or she advances as hypothetical or speculative.
  - ◆ Try to identify the main transitions from one idea to the next.
  - ◆ Try to identify the relationship between different ideas. For example:
    - — Are they contrasting? Are they consistent?
    - — Does one support the other?
    - — Does one spell another out in greater detail?
    - — Is one an application of another to a particular circumstance?
- Read each question carefully and be certain that you understand exactly what is being asked.
- Answer each question on the basis of the information provided in the passage and do not rely on outside knowledge. Sometimes your own views or opinions may conflict with those presented in a passage; if this happens, take special care to work within the context provided by the passage. You should not expect to agree with everything you encounter in the reading passages.

Reading Comprehension Multiple-choice Questions: Select One Answer Choice

Description

These are the traditional multiple-choice questions with five answer choices of which you must select one.

Tips for Answering

- **Read all the answer choices before making your selection,** even if you think you know what the answer is in advance.
- **Don't be misled by answer choices that are only partially true or only partially answer the question.** The correct answer is the one that most accurately and most completely answers the question posed. Be careful also not to pick an answer choice simply because it is a true statement.
- **Pay attention to context.** When the question asks about the meaning of a word in the passage, be sure that the answer choice you select correctly represents the way the word is being used in the passage. Many words have quite different meanings in different contexts.

Reading Comprehension Multiple-choice Questions: Select One or More Answer Choices

Description

These provide three answer choices and ask you to select all that are correct; one, two, or all three of the answer choices may be correct. To gain credit for these questions, you must select all the correct answers, and only those; there is no credit for partially correct answers. These questions are marked with square boxes beside the answer choices, not circles or ovals.

Tips for Answering

- **Evaluate each answer choice separately on its own merits.** When evaluating one answer choice, do not take the others into account.
- **Make sure the answer choice you pick accurately and completely answers the question posed.** Be careful not to be misled by answer choices that are only partially true or only partially answer the question. Be careful also not to pick an answer choice simply because it is a true statement.
- **Do not be disturbed if you think all three answer choices are correct.** Questions of this type can have three correct answer choices.

Reading Comprehension Questions: Select-in-Passage

Description

The question asks you to click on the sentence in the passage that meets a certain description. To answer the question, choose one of the sentences and click on it; clicking anywhere on a sentence will highlight it. In longer passages, the question will usually apply to only one or two specified paragraphs, marked by an arrow (➜); clicking on a sentence elsewhere in the passage will not highlight it.

Note. Because this type of question requires the use of the computer, it does not appear in the paper-delivered General Test. Similar multiple-choice questions are used in its place.

Tips for Answering

- **Be careful to evaluate each of the relevant sentences in the passage separately before selecting your answer.** Do not evaluate any sentences that are outside the paragraphs under consideration.
- **Do not select a sentence if the description given in the question only partially applies.** A correct answer choice must accurately match the description in the question. Note, however, that the description need not be complete, that is, there may be aspects of the sentence that are not fully described in the question.

Sample Question Set

Reviving the practice of using elements of popular music in classical composition, an approach that had been in hibernation in the United States during the 1960s, composer Philip Glass (born 1937) embraced the ethos of popular music in his compositions. Glass based two symphonies on music by rock musicians David Bowie and Brian Eno, but the symphonies' sound is distinctively his. Popular elements do not appear out of place in Glass's classical music, which from its early days has shared certain harmonies and rhythms with rock music. Yet this use of popular elements has not made Glass a composer of popular music. His music is not a version of popular music packaged to attract classical listeners; it is high art for listeners steeped in rock rather than the classics.

Line

5

Select only one answer choice.

1. The passage addresses which of the following issues related to Glass's use of popular elements in his classical compositions?
   Ⓐ How it is regarded by listeners who prefer rock to the classics
   Ⓑ How it has affected the commercial success of Glass's music
   Ⓒ Whether it has contributed to a revival of interest among other composers in using popular elements in their compositions
   Ⓓ Whether it has had a detrimental effect on Glass's reputation as a composer of classical music
   Ⓔ Whether it has caused certain of Glass's works to be derivative in quality

Consider each of the three choices separately and select all that apply.

2. The passage suggests that Glass's work displays which of the following qualities?
   Ⓐ A return to the use of popular music in classical compositions
   Ⓑ An attempt to elevate rock music to an artistic status more closely approximating that of classical music
   Ⓒ A long-standing tendency to incorporate elements from two apparently disparate musical styles

3. Select the sentence that distinguishes two ways of integrating rock and classical music.

Explanations

The passage describes in general terms how Philip Glass uses popular music in his classical compositions and explores how Glass can do this without being imitative. Note that there are no opposing views discussed; the author is simply presenting his or her views.

Question 1: One of the important points that the passage makes is that when Glass uses popular elements in his music, the result is very much his own creation (it is "distinctively his"). In other words, the music is far from being derivative. Thus one issue that the passage addresses is the one referred to in answer **Choice E**—it answers it in the negative. The passage does not discuss the impact of Glass's use of popular elements on listeners, on the commercial success of his music, on other composers, nor on Glass's reputation, so none of Choices A through D is correct.

The correct answer is **Choice E.**

Question 2: To answer this question, it is important to assess each answer choice independently. Since the passage says that Glass revived the use of popular music in classical compositions, answer **Choice A** is clearly correct. On the other hand, the passage also denies that Glass composes popular music or packages it in a way to elevate its status, so answer Choice B is incorrect. Finally, since Glass's style has always mixed elements of rock with classical elements, **Choice C** is correct.

Thus the correct answer is **Choice A** and **Choice C**.

Question 3: Almost every sentence in the passage refers to incorporating rock music in classical compositions, but only the last sentence distinguishes two ways of doing so. It distinguishes between writing rock music in a way that will make it attractive to classical listeners and writing classical music that will be attractive to listeners familiar with rock.

Thus the correct answer is **the last sentence of the passage.**

Text Completion Questions

Description

As mentioned above, skilled readers do not simply absorb the information presented on the page; instead, they maintain a constant attitude of interpretation and evaluation, reasoning from what they have read so far to create a picture of the whole and revising that picture as they go. Text Completion questions test this ability by omitting crucial words from short passages and asking the test taker to use the remaining information in the passage as a basis for selecting words or short phrases to fill the blanks and create a coherent, meaningful whole.

Question Structure

- Passage composed of one to five sentences
- One to three blanks
- Three answer choices per blank (five answer choices in the case of a single blank)
- The answer choices for different blanks function independently; that is, selecting one answer choice for one blank does not affect what answer choices you can select for another blank
- Single correct answer, consisting of one choice for each blank; no credit for partially correct answers

Tips for Answering

Do not merely try to consider each possible combination of answers; doing so will take too long and is open to error. Instead, try to analyze the passage in the following way:

- **Read through the passage to get an overall sense of it.**
- **Identify words or phrases that seem particularly significant,** either because they emphasize the structure of the passage (words like *although* or *moreover*) or because they are central to understanding what the passage is about.
- **Think up your own words for the blanks.** Try to fill in the blanks with words or phrases that seem to you to fit and then see if similar words are offered among the answer choices.
- **Do not assume that the first blank is the one that should be filled first.** Perhaps one of the other blanks is easier to fill first. Select your choice for that blank, and then see whether you can complete another blank. If none of the choices for the other blank seem to make sense, go back and reconsider your first selection.
- **Double-check your answers.** When you have made your selection for each blank, check to make sure that the passage is logically, grammatically, and stylistically coherent.

Sample Questions

> **For each blank select one entry from the corresponding column of choices. Fill all blanks in the way that best completes the text.**

1. It is refreshing to read a book about our planet by an author who does not allow facts to be (i)_____ by politics: well aware of the political disputes about the effects of human activities on climate and biodiversity, this author does not permit them to (ii)_____ his comprehensive description of what we know about our biosphere. He emphasizes the enormous gaps in our knowledge, the sparseness of our observations, and the (iii)_____, calling attention to the many aspects of planetary evolution that must be better understood before we can accurately diagnose the condition of our planet.

Blank (i)	Blank (ii)	Blank (iii)
Ⓐ overshadowed	Ⓓ enhance	Ⓖ plausibility of our hypotheses
Ⓑ invalidated	Ⓔ obscure	Ⓗ certainty of our entitlement
Ⓒ illuminated	Ⓕ underscore	Ⓘ superficiality of our theories

Explanation

The overall tone of the passage is clearly complimentary. To understand what the author of the book is being complimented on, it is useful to focus on the second blank. Here, we must determine what word would indicate something that the author is praised for not permitting. The only answer choice that fits the case is "obscure," since enhancing and underscoring are generally good things to do, not things one should refrain from doing. Choosing "obscure" clarifies the choice for the first blank; the only choice that fits well with "obscure" is "overshadowed." Notice that trying to fill blank (i) without filling blank (ii) first is very hard—each choice has at least some initial plausibility. Since the third blank requires a phrase that matches "enormous gaps" and "sparseness of our observations," the best choice is "superficiality of our theories."

Thus the correct answer is **overshadowed** (Choice A), **obscure** (Choice E), and **superficiality of our theories** (Choice I).

2. Vain and prone to violence, Caravaggio could not handle success: the more his (i)_____ as an artist increased, the more (ii)_____ his life became.

Blank (i)	Blank (ii)
Ⓐ temperance	Ⓓ tumultuous
Ⓑ notoriety	Ⓔ providential
Ⓒ eminence	Ⓕ dispassionate

Explanation

In this sentence, what follows the colon must explain or spell out what precedes it. So roughly what the second part must say is that as Caravaggio became more successful, his life got more out of control. When one looks for words to fill the blanks, it becomes clear that "tumultuous" is the best fit for blank (ii), since neither of the other choices suggests being out of control. And for blank (i), the best choice is "eminence," since to increase in eminence is a consequence of becoming more successful. It is true that Caravaggio might also increase in notoriety, but an increase in notoriety as an artist is not as clear a sign of success as an increase in eminence.

Thus the correct answer is **eminence** (Choice C) and **tumultuous** (Choice D).

3. In parts of the Arctic, the land grades into the landfast ice so _____ that you can walk off the coast and not know you are over the hidden sea.

Ⓐ permanently
Ⓑ imperceptibly
Ⓒ irregularly
Ⓓ precariously
Ⓔ relentlessly

Explanation

The word that fills the blank has to characterize how the land grades into the ice in a way that explains how you can walk off the coast and over the sea without knowing it. The word that does that is "imperceptibly"; if the land grades imperceptibly into the ice, you might well not know that you had left the land. Describing the shift from land to ice as permanent, irregular, precarious, or relentless would not help to explain how you would fail to know.

Thus the correct answer is **imperceptibly** (Choice B).

Sentence Equivalence Questions

Description

Like Text Completion questions, Sentence Equivalence questions test the ability to reach a conclusion about how a passage should be completed on the basis of partial information, but to a greater extent they focus on the meaning of the completed whole. Sentence Equivalence questions consist of a single sentence with just one blank, and they ask you to find two choices that both lead to a complete, coherent sentence and that produce sentences that mean the same thing.

Question Structure

- Consists of:
  - ◆ a single sentence
  - ◆ one blank
  - ◆ six answer choices
- Requires you to select two of the answer choices; no credit for partially correct answers.

These questions are marked with square boxes beside the answer choices, not circles or ovals.

Tips for Answering

Do not simply look among the answer choices for two words that mean the same thing. This can be misleading for two reasons. First, the answer choices may contain pairs of words that mean the same thing but do not fit coherently into the sentence, and thus do not constitute a correct answer. Second, the pair of words that do constitute the correct answer may not mean exactly the same thing, since all that matters is that the resultant sentences mean the same thing.

- **Read the sentence to get an overall sense of it.**
- **Identify words or phrases that seem particularly significant,** either because they emphasize the structure of the sentence (words like *although* or *moreover*) or because they are central to understanding what the sentence is about.
- **Think up your own words for the blanks.** Try to fill in the blank with a word that seems to you to fit and then see if two similar words are offered among the answer choices. If you find some word that is similar to what you are expecting but cannot find a second one, do not become fixated on your interpretation; instead, see whether there are other words among the answer choices that can be used to fill the blank coherently.
- **Double-check your answers.** When you have selected your pair of answer choices for the blank, check to make sure that each one produces a sentence that is logically, grammatically, and stylistically coherent, and that the two sentences mean the same thing.

Sample Questions

> **Select the <u>two</u> answer choices that, when used to complete the sentence, fit the meaning of the sentence as a whole <u>and</u> produce completed sentences that are alike in meaning.**

1. Although it does contain some pioneering ideas, one would hardly characterize the work as _____.
    - [A] orthodox
    - [B] eccentric
    - [C] original
    - [D] trifling
    - [E] conventional
    - [F] innovative

Explanation

The word "Although" is a crucial signpost here. The work contains some pioneering ideas, but apparently it is not overall a pioneering work. Thus the two words that could fill the blank appropriately are "original" and "innovative." Note that "orthodox" and "conventional" are two words that are very similar in meaning, but neither one completes the sentence sensibly.

Thus the correct answer is **original** (Choice C) and **innovative** (Choice F).

2. It was her view that the country's problems had been _____ by foreign technocrats, so that to ask for such assistance again would be counterproductive.
    - [A] ameliorated
    - [B] ascertained
    - [C] diagnosed
    - [D] exacerbated
    - [E] overlooked
    - [F] worsened

Explanation

The sentence relates a piece of reasoning, as indicated by the presence of "so that": asking for the assistance of foreign technocrats would be counterproductive because of the effects such technocrats have had already. This means that the technocrats must have bad effects; that is, they must have "exacerbated" or "worsened" the country's problems.

Thus the correct answer is **exacerbated** (Choice D) and **worsened** (Choice F).

Question Type 1: Reading Comprehension

| **Your goals for this chapter** | ⇨ Practice answering GRE Reading Comprehension questions |
| | ⇨ Review answers and explanations, particularly for questions you answered incorrectly |

This chapter contains three sets of practice Reading Comprehension questions. The sets are arranged in order of increasing difficulty; one easy set, one medium, and one hard.

Following the third set are answer keys for quick reference. Then, at the end of the chapter, you will find complete explanations for every question. Passages with more than one associated question are followed by a brief description that outlines the content of the passage. Each question is then presented in turn, together with its explanation, so that you can easily see what was asked and what the various answer choices were.

Sharpen your GRE Verbal Reasoning skills by working your way through these question sets, remembering to use the Tips for Answering given in Chapter 2. Begin with the easy set and then move on to the medium-difficulty and hard sets. Review the answer explanations carefully, paying particular attention to the explanations for questions that you answered incorrectly.

- Were you able to understand the overall meaning of the passage?
- Were you able to understand how the different parts of the passage were related to one another?
- Were you able to identify the parts of the passage relevant to answering each question?

PRACTICE SET 1: Easy

For each of Questions 1 to 9, select <u>one</u> answer choice unless otherwise directed.

Questions 1 and 2 are based on this passage.

Ragwort was accidentally introduced to New Zealand in the late nineteenth century and, like so many invading foreign species, quickly became a pest. By the 1920s, the weed was rampant. What made matters worse was that its proliferation coincided with sweeping changes in agriculture and a massive shift from sheep farming to dairying.
Line
5 Ragwort contains a battery of toxic and resilient alkaloids: even honey made from its flowers contains the poison in dilute form. Livestock generally avoid grazing where ragwort is growing, but they will do so once it displaces grass and clover in their pasture. Though sheep can eat it for months before showing any signs of illness, if cattle eat it they sicken quickly, and fatality can even result.

1. The passage suggests that the proliferation of ragwort was particularly ill-timed because it

   (A) coincided with and exacerbated a decline in agriculture

   (B) took place in conditions that enabled the ragwort to spread faster than it otherwise would have done

   (C) led to an increase in the amount of toxic compounds contained in the plants

   (D) prevented people from producing honey that could be eaten safely

   (E) had consequences for livestock that were more dramatic than they otherwise would have been

For the following question, consider each of the choices separately and select <u>all</u> that apply.

2. The passage implies which of the following about the problems ragwort poses to dairy farmers?

   A Milk produced by cows that eat ragwort causes illness in humans who drink it.

   B Ragwort can supplant the plants normally eaten by cattle.

   C Cattle, unlike sheep, are unable to differentiate between ragwort and healthy grazing.

Question 3 is based on this passage.

Despite the fact that the health-inspection procedures for catering establishments are more stringent than those for ordinary restaurants, more of the cases of food poisoning reported to the city health department were brought on by banquets served by catering services than were brought on by restaurant meals.

3. Which of the following, if true, helps explain the apparent paradox in the statement above?

   (A) A significantly larger number of people eat in restaurants than attend catered banquets in any given time period.

   (B) Catering establishments know how many people they expect to serve, and therefore are less likely than restaurants to have, and serve, leftover food, a major source of food poisoning.

   (C) Many restaurants provide catering services for banquets in addition to serving individual meals.

   (D) The number of reported food-poisoning cases at catered banquets is unrelated to whether the meal is served on the caterer's or the client's premises.

   (E) People are unlikely to make a connection between a meal they have eaten and a subsequent illness unless the illness strikes a group who are in communication with one another.

Questions 4 and 5 are based on this passage.

African American newspapers in the 1930s faced many hardships. For instance, knowing that buyers of African American papers also bought general-circulation papers, advertisers of consumer products often ignored African American publications.
Line
5   Advertisers' discrimination did free the African American press from advertiser domination. Editors could print politically charged material more readily than could the large national dailies, which depended on advertisers' ideological approval to secure revenues. Unfortunately, it also made the selling price of Black papers much higher than that of general-circulation dailies. Often as much as two-thirds of publication costs had to come from subscribers or subsidies from community politicians and other
10   interest groups. And despite their editorial freedom, African American publishers often felt compelled to print a disproportionate amount of sensationalism, sports, and society news to boost circulation.

For the following question, consider each of the choices separately and select all that apply.

4. The passage suggests that if advertisers had more frequently purchased advertising in African American newspapers, then which of the following might have resulted?

   [A] African American newspapers would have given more attention to sports and society news than they did.

   [B] African American newspapers would have been available at lower prices than large national dailies were.

   [C] African American newspapers would have experienced constraints on their content similar to those experienced by large national dailies.

5. The author of the passage suggests which of the following about the "advertisers" (line 3) mentioned in the passage?

(A) They assumed that advertising in African American newspapers would not significantly increase the sales of their products.

(B) They failed to calculate accurately the circulation of African American newspapers.

(C) They did not take African Americans' newspaper reading into account when making decisions about where to advertise.

(D) They avoided African American newspapers partly because of their sensationalism.

(E) They tried to persuade African American newspapers to lower the rates charged for advertising.

Question 6 is based on this passage.

Years ago, consumers in Frieland began paying an energy tax in the form of two Frieland pennies for each unit of energy consumed that came from nonrenewable sources. Following the introduction of this energy tax, there was a steady reduction in the total yearly consumption of energy from nonrenewable sources.

6. If the statements in the passage are true, then which of the following must on the basis of them be true?

(A) There was a steady decline in the yearly revenues generated by the energy tax in Frieland.

(B) There was a steady decline in the total amount of energy consumed each year in Frieland.

(C) There was a steady increase in the use of renewable energy sources in Frieland.

(D) The revenues generated by the energy tax were used to promote the use of energy from renewable sources.

(E) The use of renewable energy sources in Frieland greatly increased relative to the use of nonrenewable energy sources.

Questions 7 to 9 are based on this passage.

In a plausible but speculative scenario, oceanographer Douglas Martinson suggests that temperature increases caused by global warming would not significantly affect the stability of the Antarctic environment, where sea ice forms on the periphery of the continent in the autumn and winter and mostly disappears in the summer. True, less sea ice would form in the winter because global warming would cause temperatures to rise. However, Martinson argues, the effect of a warmer atmosphere may be offset as follows. The formation of sea ice causes the concentration of salt in surface waters to increase; less sea ice would mean a smaller increase in the concentration of salt. Less salty surface waters would be less dense and therefore less likely to sink and stir up deep water. The deep water, with all its stored heat, would rise to the surface at a slower rate. Thus, although the winter sea-ice cover might decrease, the surface waters would remain cold enough so that the decrease would not be excessive.

Line

5

10

7. It can be inferred from the passage that which of the following is true of the surface waters in the current Antarctic environment?

   Ⓐ They are more affected by annual fluctuations in atmospheric temperatures than they would be if they were less salty.

   Ⓑ They are less salty than they would be if global warming were to occur.

   Ⓒ They are more likely to sink and stir up deep waters than they would be if atmospheric temperatures were to increase.

   Ⓓ They are able to offset some of the effects of global warming beyond the Antarctic region.

   Ⓔ They are less affected by the temperature of deep water than they would be if atmospheric temperatures were to increase.

8. The passage suggests that Martinson believes which of the following about deep waters in the Antarctic region?

   Ⓐ They rise to the surface more quickly than they would if global warming were to occur.

   Ⓑ They store heat that will exacerbate the effects of increases in atmospheric temperatures.

   Ⓒ They would be likely to be significantly warmed by an increase in atmospheric temperatures.

   Ⓓ They would be more salty than they currently are if global warming were to occur.

   Ⓔ They are less likely to be stirred up when surface waters are intensely salty than when surface waters are relatively unsalty.

9. According to the passage, which of the following is true about the sea ice that surrounds the Antarctic continent?

   Ⓐ The amount of sea ice that forms in the winter has been declining.

   Ⓑ Most of the sea ice that forms in the winter remains intact in the summer.

   Ⓒ Even small changes in the amount of sea ice dramatically affect the temperature of the surface waters.

   Ⓓ Changes in the amount of sea ice due to global warming would significantly affect the stability of the Antarctic environment.

   Ⓔ Changes in the amount of sea ice affect the degree of saltiness of the surface waters.

PRACTICE SET 2: Medium

> **For each of Questions 1 to 11, select one answer choice unless otherwise directed.**

Question 1 is based on this passage.

That sales can be increased by the presence of sunlight within a store has been shown by the experience of the only Savefast department store with a large skylight. The skylight allows sunlight into half of the store, reducing the need for artificial light. The rest
Line of the store uses only artificial light. Since the store opened two years ago, the depart-
5 ments on the sunlit side have had substantially higher sales than the other departments.

1. Which of the following, if true, most strengthens the argument?
    - (A) On particularly cloudy days, more artificial light is used to illuminate the part of the store under the skylight.
    - (B) When the store is open at night, the departments in the part of the store under the skylight have sales that are no higher than those of other departments.
    - (C) Many customers purchase items from departments in both parts of the store on a single shopping trip.
    - (D) Besides the skylight, there are several significant architectural differences between the two parts of the store.
    - (E) The departments in the part of the store under the skylight are the departments that generally have the highest sales in other stores in the Savefast chain.

Questions 2 to 4 are based on this passage.

While the best sixteenth-century Renaissance scholars mastered the classics of ancient Roman literature in the original Latin and understood them in their original historical
Line context, most of the scholars' educated contemporaries knew the classics only from
5 school lessons on selected Latin texts. These were chosen by Renaissance teachers after much deliberation, for works written by and for the sophisticated adults of pagan Rome were not always considered suitable for the Renaissance young: the central Roman classics refused (as classics often do) to teach appropriate morality and frequently suggested the opposite. Teachers accordingly made students' needs, not textual and historical accu-
10 racy, their supreme interest, chopping dangerous texts into short phrases, and using these to impart lessons extemporaneously on a variety of subjects, from syntax to science. Thus, I believe that a modern reader cannot know the associations that a line of ancient Roman poetry or prose had for any particular educated sixteenth-century reader.

2. The passage is primarily concerned with discussing the
    - (A) unsuitability of the Roman classics for the teaching of morality
    - (B) approach that sixteenth-century scholars took to learning the Roman classics
    - (C) effect that the Roman classics had on educated people in the Renaissance
    - (D) way in which the Roman classics were taught in the sixteenth century
    - (E) contrast between the teaching of the Roman classics in the Renaissance and the teaching of the Roman classics today

3. The information in the passage suggests that which of the following would most likely result from a student's having studied the Roman classics under a typical sixteenth-century teacher?

    (A) The student recalls a line of Roman poetry in conjunction with a point learned about grammar.

    (B) The student argues that a Roman poem about gluttony is not morally offensive when it is understood in its historical context.

    (C) The student is easily able to express thoughts in Latin.

    (D) The student has mastered large portions of the Roman classics.

    (E) The student has a sophisticated knowledge of Roman poetry but little knowledge of Roman prose.

4. Which of the following, if true, would most seriously weaken the assertion made in the passage concerning what a modern reader cannot know?

    (A) Some modern readers are thoroughly familiar with the classics of ancient Roman literature because they majored in classics in college or obtained doctoral degrees in classics.

    (B) Some modern readers have learned which particular works of Roman literature were taught to students in the sixteenth century.

    (C) Modern readers can, with some effort, discover that sixteenth-century teachers selected some seemingly dangerous classical texts while excluding other seemingly innocuous texts.

    (D) Copies of many of the classical texts used by sixteenth-century teachers, including marginal notes describing the oral lessons that were based on the texts, can be found in museums today.

    (E) Many of the writings of the best sixteenth-century Renaissance scholars have been translated from Latin and are available to modern readers.

Questions 5 and 6 are based on this passage.

In humans, the pilomotor reflex leads to the response commonly known as goose bumps, and this response is widely considered to be vestigial—that is, something formerly having a greater physiological advantage than at present. It occurs when the tiny muscle at the base of a hair follicle contracts, pulling the hair upright. In animals with feathers, fur, or quills, this creates a layer of insulating warm air or a reason for predators to think twice before attacking. But human hair is too puny to serve these functions. Goose bumps in humans may, however, have acquired a new role. Like flushing—another thermoregulatory (heat-regulating) mechanism—goose bumps have become linked with emotional responses, notably fear, rage, or the pleasure of, say, listening to beautiful music. They may thus serve as a signal to others.

Line
5

10

5. In explaining the "new role" (line 7) that goose bumps in humans may have acquired, the author assumes which of the following?

    (A) Emotional responses in humans can be triggered by thermoregulatory mechanisms.

    (B) The perceptibility of emotional responses to other humans offers some kind of benefit.

    (C) If human hair were more substantial, goose bumps would not have acquired a new role.

    (D) Goose bumps in animals with feathers, fur, or quills may also be linked to emotional responses.

    (E) In humans, goose bumps represent an older physiological response than flushing.

6. Which of the following best describes the primary function of the next-to-last sentence ("Like . . . music")?

    (A) It makes a distinction between two types of mechanisms.

    (B) It corrects a common misconception about the role of goose bumps in humans.

    (C) It suggests reasons for the connection between emotional responses and goose bumps in humans.

    (D) It suggests that flushing and goose bumps signal the same emotional state.

    (E) It helps explain a possible role played by goose bumps in humans.

Questions 7 to 10 are based on this passage.

This passage is adapted from material published in 2001.

Frederick Douglass was unquestionably the most famous African American of the nineteenth century; indeed, when he died in 1895 he was among the most distinguished public figures in the United States. In his study of Douglass' career as a major figure in the movement to abolish slavery and as a spokesman for Black rights, Waldo Martin has provoked controversy by contending that Douglass also deserves a prominent place in the intellectual history of the United States because he exemplified so many strands of nineteenth-century thought: romanticism, idealism, individualism, liberal humanism, and an unshakable belief in progress. But this very argument provides ammunition for those who claim that most of Douglass' ideas, being so representative of their time, are now obsolete. Douglass' vision of the future as a melting pot in which all racial and ethnic differences would dissolve into "a composite American nationality" appears from the pluralist perspective of many present-day intellectuals to be not only utopian but even wrongheaded. Yet there is a central aspect of Douglass' thought that seems not in the least bit dated or irrelevant to current concerns. He has no rival in the history of the nineteenth-century United States as an insistent and effective critic of the doctrine of innate racial inequality. He not only attacked racist ideas in his speeches and writings, but he offered his entire career and all his achievements as living proof that racists were wrong in their belief that one race could be inherently superior to another.

While Martin stresses Douglass' antiracist egalitarianism, he does not adequately explain how this aspect of Douglass' thought fits in with his espousal of the liberal Victorian attitudes that many present-day intellectuals consider to be naïve and outdated. The fact is that Douglass was attracted to these democratic-capitalist ideals of his time because they could be used to attack slavery and the doctrine of White supremacy. His favorite rhetorical strategy was to expose the hypocrisy of those who, while professing adherence to the ideals of democracy and equality of opportunity, condoned slavery and racial discrimination. It would have been strange indeed if he had not embraced liberal idealism, because it proved its worth for the cause of racial equality during the national crisis that eventually resulted in emancipation and citizenship for African Americans. These points may seem obvious, but had Martin given them more attention, his analysis might have constituted a more convincing rebuttal to those critics who dismiss Douglass' ideology as a relic of the past. If one accepts the proposition that Douglass' deepest commitment was to Black equality and that he used the liberal ideals of his time as weapons in the fight for that cause, then it is hard to fault him for seizing the best weapons at hand.

7. The passage as a whole can best be described as doing which of the following?

    (A) Explaining Douglass' emergence as a major figure in the movement to abolish slavery

    (B) Tracing the origins of Douglass' thought in nineteenth-century romanticism, idealism, and liberal humanism

    (C) Analyzing Douglass' speeches and writings from a modern, pluralist perspective

    (D) Criticizing Martin for failing to stress the contradiction between Douglass' principles and the liberal Victorian attitudes of his day

    (E) Formulating a response to those who consider Douglass' political philosophy to be archaic and irrelevant

8. It can be inferred that the "present-day intellectuals" (line 12) believe that

    (A) although Douglass used democratic-capitalist ideas to attack slavery and racial inequality, he did not sincerely believe in those ideas

    (B) the view that Douglass was representative of the intellectual trends of his time is obsolete

    (C) Douglass' opposition to the doctrine of innate racial inequality is irrelevant to current concerns

    (D) Douglass' commitment to Black equality does not adequately account for his naïve attachment to quaint liberal Victorian political views

    (E) Douglass' goal of ultimately doing away with all racial and ethnic differences is neither achievable nor desirable

9. According to the passage, Douglass used which of the following as evidence against the doctrine of innate racial inequality?

    (A) His own life story

    (B) His vision of a composite American nationality

    (C) The hypocrisy of self-professed liberal idealists

    (D) The inevitability of the emancipation of African Americans

    (E) The fact that most prominent intellectuals advocated the abolition of slavery

10. Each of the following is mentioned in the passage as an element of Douglass' ideology EXCEPT

    (A) idealism

    (B) egalitarianism

    (C) capitalism

    (D) pluralism

    (E) humanism

Question 11 is based on this passage.

The plant called the scarlet gilia can have either red or white flowers. It had long been thought that hummingbirds, which forage by day, pollinate its red flowers and that hawkmoths, which forage at night, pollinate its white flowers. To try to show that this pattern of pollination by colors exists, scientists recently covered some scarlet gilia flowers only at night and others only by day: plants with red flowers covered at night became pollinated; plants with white flowers covered by day became pollinated.

11. Which of the following, if true, would be additional evidence to suggest that hummingbirds are attracted to the red flowers and hawkmoths to the white flowers of the scarlet gilia?

Ⓐ Uncovered scarlet gilia flowers, whether red or white, became pollinated at approximately equal rates.

Ⓑ Some red flowers of the scarlet gilia that remained uncovered at all times never became pollinated.

Ⓒ White flowers of the scarlet gilia that were covered at night became pollinated with greater frequency than white flowers of the scarlet gilia that were left uncovered.

Ⓓ Scarlet gilia plants with red flowers covered by day and scarlet gilia plants with white flowers covered at night remained unpollinated.

Ⓔ In late August, when most of the hummingbirds had migrated but hawkmoths were still plentiful, red scarlet gilia plants produced fruit more frequently than they had earlier in the season.

PRACTICE SET 3: Hard

> For each of Questions 1 to 10, select **one** answer choice unless otherwise directed.

Questions 1 and 2 are based on this passage.

Supernovas in the Milky Way are the likeliest source for most of the cosmic rays reaching Earth. However, calculations show that supernovas cannot produce ultrahigh-energy cosmic rays (UHECRs), which have energies exceeding 10^{18} electron volts. It would seem sensible to seek the source of these in the universe's most conspicuous energy factories: quasars and gamma-ray bursts billions of light-years away from Earth. But UHECRs tend to collide with photons of the cosmic microwave background—pervasive radiation that is a relic of the early universe. The odds favor a collision every 20 million light-years, each collision costing 20 percent of the cosmic ray's energy. Consequently, no cosmic ray traveling much beyond 100 million light-years can retain the energy observed in UHECRs.

Line
5

10

For the following question, consider each of the choices separately and select all that apply.

1. It can be inferred that the author of the passage would agree with which of the following about the origin of UHECRs that reach Earth?

    A The origin is something other than supernovas in the Milky Way.

    B The origin is most likely something other than very distant quasars or gamma-ray bursts.

    C The origin is most likely no more than a little over 100 million light-years away from Earth.

2. In the context of the author's argument, the last sentence performs which of the following functions?

    Ⓐ It explains a criterion that was employed earlier in the argument.

    Ⓑ It shows that an apparently plausible position is actually self-contradictory.

    Ⓒ It is a conclusion drawn in the course of refuting a potential explanation.

    Ⓓ It overturns an assumption on which an opposing position depends.

    Ⓔ It states the main conclusion that the author is seeking to establish.

Questions 3 to 5 are based on this passage.

The massive influx of women cyclists—making up at least a third of the total market—was perhaps the most striking and profound social consequence of the mid-1890s cycling boom. Although the new, improved bicycle had appealed immediately to a few

Line
5 privileged women, its impact would have been modest had it not attracted a greater cross section of the female population. It soon became apparent that many of these pioneer women bicyclists had not taken up the sport as an idle pastime. Rather, they saw cycling as a noble cause to be promoted among all women as a means to improve the general female condition. Not only would cycling encourage healthy outdoor exercise, they reasoned, it would also hasten long-overdue dress reform. To feminists,
10 the bicycle affirmed nothing less than the dignity and equality of women.

For the following question, consider each of the choices separately and select all that apply.

3. Which of the following statements about women cyclists is supported by the passage?

    A The newly improved bicycle of the mid-1890s appealed mostly to women in a privileged position.

    B The great majority of women in the mid-1890s considered cycling an idle pastime.

    C Women bicyclists promoted cycling as a healthy form of outdoor exercise.

For the following question, consider each of the choices separately and select all that apply.

4. Which of the following does the passage suggest about pioneer women cyclists?

    A They saw cycling as a means to promote the advancement of women.

    B They argued that cycling would encourage women to get involved in a variety of noble causes.

    C They provided several reasons for a cross section of the female population to use the bicycle.

5. Which of the following best describes the function of the second sentence ("Although . . . population")?

    Ⓐ It corrects a common misconception regarding the use of the bicycle in the mid-1890s.

    Ⓑ It elaborates on a claim made in the previous sentence regarding a social consequence of the cycling boom.

    Ⓒ It provides a context in which to understand the increased popularity of bicycle riding among privileged women.

    Ⓓ It explains why cycling attracted such a significant cross section of women.

    Ⓔ It describes the demographic characteristics of the consumer market for bicycles in the mid-1890s.

Questions 6 to 9 are based on this passage.

What causes a helix in nature to appear with either a dextral (right-handed, or clockwise) twist or a sinistral (left-handed, or counterclockwise) twist is one of the most intriguing puzzles in the science of form. Most spiral-shaped snail species are
Line predominantly dextral. But at one time, handedness (twist direction of the shell) was
5 equally distributed within some snail species that have become predominantly dextral or, in a few species, predominantly sinistral. What mechanisms control handedness and keep left-handedness rare?

It would seem unlikely that evolution should discriminate against sinistral snails if sinistral and dextral snails are exact mirror images, for any disadvantage that a sinistral
10 twist in itself could confer on its possessor is almost inconceivable. But left- and right-handed snails are not actually true mirror images of one another. Their shapes are noticeably different. Sinistral rarity might, then, be a consequence of possible disadvantages conferred by these other concomitant structural features. In addition, perhaps left- and right-handed snails cannot mate with each other, having
15 incompatible twist directions. Presumably an individual of the rarer form would have relative difficulty in finding a mate of the same hand, thus keeping the rare form rare or creating geographically separated right- and left-handed populations.

But this evolutionary mechanism combining dissymmetry, anatomy, and chance does not provide an adequate explanation of why right-handedness should have
20 become predominant. It does not explain, for example, why the infrequent unions between snails of opposing hands produce fewer offspring of the rarer than the commoner form in species where each parent contributes equally to handedness. Nor does it explain why, in a species where one parent determines handedness, a brood is not exclusively right- or left-handed when the offspring would have the same genetic
25 predisposition. In the European pond snail *Lymnaea peregra*, a predominantly dextral species whose handedness is maternally determined, a brood might be expected to be exclusively right- or left-handed—and this often occurs. However, some broods possess a few snails of the opposing hand, and in predominantly sinistral broods, the incidence of dextrality is surprisingly high.

30 Here, the evolutionary theory must defer to a theory based on an explicit developmental mechanism that can favor either right- or left-handedness. In the case of *Lymnaea peregra*, studies indicate that a dextral gene is expressed during egg formation; i.e., before egg fertilization, the gene produces a protein, found in the cytoplasm of the egg, that controls the pattern of cell division and thus handedness. In
35 experiments, an injection of cytoplasm from dextral eggs changes the pattern of sinistral eggs, but an injection from sinistral eggs does not influence dextral eggs. One explanation for the differing effects is that all *Lymnaea peregra* eggs begin left-handed but most switch to being right-handed. Thus the path to a solution to the puzzle of handedness in all snails appears to be as twisted as the helix itself.

6. Which of the following would serve as an example of "concomitant structural features" (line 13) that might disadvantage a snail of the rarer form?

(A) A shell and body that are an exact mirror image of a snail of the commoner form

(B) A smaller population of the snails of the rarer form

(C) A chip or fracture in the shell caused by an object falling on it

(D) A pattern on the shell that better camouflages it

(E) A smaller shell opening that restricts mobility and ingestion relative to that of a snail of the commoner form

7. The second paragraph of the passage is primarily concerned with offering possible reasons why

   (A) it is unlikely that evolutionary mechanisms could discriminate against sinistral snails

   (B) sinistrality is relatively uncommon among snail species

   (C) dextral and sinistral populations of a snail species tend to intermingle

   (D) a theory based on a developmental mechanism inadequately accounts for the predominance of dextrality across snail species

   (E) dextral snails breed more readily than sinistral snails, even within predominantly sinistral populations

8. Which of the following accurately describes the relationship between the evolutionary and developmental theories discussed in the passage?

   (A) Although the two theories reach the same conclusion, each is based on different assumptions.

   (B) They present contradictory explanations of the same phenomenon.

   (C) The second theory accounts for certain phenomena that the first cannot explain.

   (D) The second theory demonstrates why the first is valid only for very unusual, special cases.

   (E) They are identical and interchangeable in that the second theory merely restates the first in less technical terms.

9. It can be inferred from the passage that a predominantly sinistral snail species might stay predominantly sinistral for each of the following reasons EXCEPT for

   (A) a developmental mechanism that affects the cell-division pattern of snails

   (B) structural features that advantage dextral snails of the species

   (C) a relatively small number of snails of the same hand for dextral snails of the species to mate with

   (D) anatomical incompatibility that prevents mating between snails of opposing hands within the species

   (E) geographic separation of sinistral and dextral populations

Question 10 is based on this passage.

X-ray examination of a recently discovered painting—judged by some authorities to be a self-portrait by Vincent van Gogh—revealed an underimage of a woman's face. Either van Gogh or another painter covered the first painting with the portrait now seen on the
Line surface of the canvas. Because the face of the woman in the underimage also appears on
5 canvases van Gogh is known to have painted, the surface painting must be an authentic self-portrait by van Gogh.

10. The conclusion is properly drawn if which of the following is assumed?

Ⓐ If a canvas already bears a painted image produced by an artist, a second artist who uses the canvas to produce a new painting tends to be influenced by the style of the first artist.

Ⓑ Many painted canvases that can be reliably attributed to van Gogh contain underimages of subjects that appear on at least one other canvas that van Gogh is known to have painted.

Ⓒ Any painted canvas incorrectly attributed to van Gogh would not contain an underimage of a subject that appears in authentic paintings by that artist.

Ⓓ A painted canvas cannot be reliably attributed to an artist unless the authenticity of any underimage that painting might contain can be reliably attributed to the artist.

Ⓔ A painted canvas cannot be reliably attributed to a particular artist unless a reliable x-ray examination of the painting is performed.

ANSWER KEY

PRACTICE SET 1: Easy

1. **Choice E:** had consequences for livestock that were more dramatic than they otherwise would have been
2. **Choice B:** Ragwort can supplant the plants normally eaten by cattle.
3. **Choice E:** People are unlikely to make a connection between a meal they have eaten and a subsequent illness unless the illness strikes a group who are in communication with one another.
4. **Choice C:** African American newspapers would have experienced constraints on their content similar to those experienced by large national dailies.
5. **Choice A:** They assumed that advertising in African American newspapers would not significantly increase the sales of their products.
6. **Choice A:** There was a steady decline in the yearly revenues generated by the energy tax in Frieland.
7. **Choice C:** They are more likely to sink and stir up deep waters than they would be if atmospheric temperatures were to increase.
8. **Choice A:** They rise to the surface more quickly than they would if global warming were to occur.
9. **Choice E:** Changes in the amount of sea ice affect the degree of saltiness of the surface waters.

PRACTICE SET 2: Medium

1. **Choice B:** When the store is open at night, the departments in the part of the store under the skylight have sales that are no higher than those of other departments.
2. **Choice D:** way in which the Roman classics were taught in the sixteenth century
3. **Choice A:** The student recalls a line of Roman poetry in conjunction with a point learned about grammar.
4. **Choice D:** Copies of many of the classical texts used by sixteenth-century teachers, including marginal notes describing the oral lessons that were based on the texts, can be found in museums today.
5. **Choice B:** The perceptibility of emotional responses to other humans offers some kind of benefit.
6. **Choice E:** It helps explain a possible role played by goose bumps in humans.
7. **Choice E:** Formulating a response to those who consider Douglass' political philosophy to be archaic and irrelevant
8. **Choice E:** Douglass' goal of ultimately doing away with all racial and ethnic differences is neither achievable nor desirable
9. **Choice A:** His own life story
10. **Choice D:** pluralism
11. **Choice D:** Scarlet gilia plants with red flowers covered by day and scarlet gilia plants with white flowers covered at night remained unpollinated.

PRACTICE SET 3: Hard

1. **Choice A**: The origin is something other than supernovas in the Milky Way.
   AND
   Choice B: The origin is most likely something other than very distant quasars or gamma-ray bursts.
   AND
   Choice C: The origin is most likely no more than a little over 100 million light-years away from Earth.
2. **Choice C**: It is a conclusion drawn in the course of refuting a potential explanation.
3. **Choice C**: Women bicyclists promoted cycling as a healthy form of outdoor exercise.
4. **Choice A**: They saw cycling as a means to promote the advancement of women.
   AND
   Choice C: They provided several reasons for a cross section of the female population to use the bicycle.
5. **Choice B**: It elaborates on a claim made in the previous sentence regarding a social consequence of the cycling boom.
6. **Choice E**: A smaller shell opening that restricts mobility and ingestion relative to that of a snail of the commoner form
7. **Choice B**: sinistrality is relatively uncommon among snail species
8. **Choice C**: The second theory accounts for certain phenomena that the first cannot explain.
9. **Choice B**: structural features that advantage dextral snails of the species
10. **Choice C**: Any painted canvas incorrectly attributed to van Gogh would not contain an underimage of a subject that appears in authentic paintings by that artist.

Answers and Explanations

PRACTICE SET 1: Easy

> For each of Questions 1 to 9, select <u>one</u> answer choice unless otherwise directed.

Questions 1 and 2 are based on this passage.

Ragwort was accidentally introduced to New Zealand in the late nineteenth century and, like so many invading foreign species, quickly became a pest. By the 1920s, the weed was rampant. What made matters worse was that its proliferation coincided with
Line sweeping changes in agriculture and a massive shift from sheep farming to dairying.
5 Ragwort contains a battery of toxic and resilient alkaloids: even honey made from its flowers contains the poison in dilute form. Livestock generally avoid grazing where ragwort is growing, but they will do so once it displaces grass and clover in their pasture. Though sheep can eat it for months before showing any signs of illness, if cattle eat it they sicken quickly, and fatality can even result.

Description

The passage discusses the introduction of ragwort to New Zealand and explains why the plant had a significant negative impact on New Zealand's agriculture.

1. The passage suggests that the proliferation of ragwort was particularly ill-timed because it
    (A) coincided with and exacerbated a decline in agriculture
    (B) took place in conditions that enabled the ragwort to spread faster than it otherwise would have done
    (C) led to an increase in the amount of toxic compounds contained in the plants
    (D) prevented people from producing honey that could be eaten safely
    (E) had consequences for livestock that were more dramatic than they otherwise would have been

Explanation

The passage mentions that ragwort's impact on New Zealand's agriculture was especially severe because the plant's proliferation "coincided with sweeping changes in agriculture that saw a massive shift from sheep farming to dairying." The severity of the impact was increased because cattle, which were displacing sheep, are much more sensitive than sheep to the toxins contained in ragwort. This points to **Choice E** as the correct answer choice. Nothing in the passage suggests that the proliferation of ragwort coincided with a decline in agriculture (Choice A), occurred faster than it might have done (Choice B), or made the plants more toxic (Choice C). There is a suggestion that ragwort honey might not be safe for humans, but there is no indication that this made the timing of the proliferation particularly unfortunate.

For the following question, consider each of the choices separately and select all that apply.

2. The passage implies which of the following about the problems ragwort poses to dairy farmers?

   [A] Milk produced by cows that eat ragwort causes illness in humans who drink it.

   [B] Ragwort can supplant the plants normally eaten by cattle.

   [C] Cattle, unlike sheep, are unable to differentiate between ragwort and healthy grazing.

Explanation

Choice B is correct. The question asks about the problems ragwort poses to dairy farmers.

Choice A is incorrect: The passage does not mention the effect of ragwort consumption on the milk produced by cows.

Choice B is correct: The passage mentions that livestock will eat ragwort "once it displaces grass and clover in their pasture."

Choice C is incorrect: The passage claims that "livestock generally avoid grazing where ragwort is growing," but does not make a distinction between cattle and sheep.

Question 3 is based on this passage.

Despite the fact that the health-inspection procedures for catering establishments are more stringent than those for ordinary restaurants, more of the cases of food poisoning reported to the city health department were brought on by banquets served by catering services than were brought on by restaurant meals.

3. Which of the following, if true, helps explain the apparent paradox in the statement above?

   (A) A significantly larger number of people eat in restaurants than attend catered banquets in any given time period.

   (B) Catering establishments know how many people they expect to serve, and therefore are less likely than restaurants to have, and serve, leftover food, a major source of food poisoning.

   (C) Many restaurants provide catering services for banquets in addition to serving individual meals.

   (D) The number of reported food-poisoning cases at catered banquets is unrelated to whether the meal is served on the caterer's or the client's premises.

   (E) People are unlikely to make a connection between a meal they have eaten and a subsequent illness unless the illness strikes a group who are in communication with one another.

Explanation

The question calls for an explanation of why more cases of reported food poisoning might be attributed to catering services than to restaurants. Choices A and B both provide reasons why restaurants should account for more cases, so they are incorrect. Choice C would suggest that there would be negligible differences between the likelihood of food poisoning at restaurants and at catered events, so it also sheds no light on the paradox and is therefore incorrect. Since the argument does not pertain to the location of catered banquets, Choice D is incorrect. That leaves Choice E. People who attend banquets are more likely than restaurant patrons to be part of a group that communicates with one another, so **Choice E** would help explain the higher number of reported food poisonings and is the correct answer.

Questions 4 and 5 are based on this passage.

African American newspapers in the 1930s faced many hardships. For instance, knowing that buyers of African American papers also bought general-circulation papers, advertisers of consumer products often ignored African American publications.
Line
5 Advertisers' discrimination did free the African American press from advertiser domination. Editors could print politically charged material more readily than could the large national dailies, which depended on advertisers' ideological approval to secure revenues. Unfortunately, it also made the selling price of Black papers much higher than that of general-circulation dailies. Often as much as two-thirds of publication costs had to come from subscribers or subsidies from community politicians and other
10 interest groups. And despite their editorial freedom, African American publishers often felt compelled to print a disproportionate amount of sensationalism, sports, and society news to boost circulation.

Description

The passage discusses challenges and opportunities faced by African American newspapers in the 1930s.

For the following question, consider each of the choices separately and select <u>all</u> that apply.

4. The passage suggests that if advertisers had more frequently purchased advertising in African American newspapers, then which of the following might have resulted?

    A African American newspapers would have given more attention to sports and society news than they did.

    B African American newspapers would have been available at lower prices than large national dailies were.

    C African American newspapers would have experienced constraints on their content similar to those experienced by large national dailies.

Explanation

Choice C is correct. The question asks about the consequences of more advertising in African American newspapers.

Choice A is incorrect: The passage states that publishers of African American newspapers felt compelled to publish sports and society news even without any pressure from advertisers, so advertising revenue was not a factor in their editorial decisions.

Choice B is incorrect: The passage says that lack of advertising revenue made African American newspapers more expensive than the large national dailies, implying that if advertisers had purchased space, the difference in price would have been smaller; but nothing in the passage supports the claim that African American newspapers would have been cheaper than the large national dailies.

Choice C is correct: The passage states that large newspapers could not readily print politically charged material because they "depended on advertisers' ideological approval to secure revenues," so it can be expected that African American newspapers would have experienced similar constraints if they also had depended on advertisers for revenues.

5. The author of the passage suggests which of the following about the "advertisers" (line 3) mentioned in the passage?

   (A) They assumed that advertising in African American newspapers would not significantly increase the sales of their products.

   (B) They failed to calculate accurately the circulation of African American newspapers.

   (C) They did not take African Americans' newspaper reading into account when making decisions about where to advertise.

   (D) They avoided African American newspapers partly because of their sensationalism.

   (E) They tried to persuade African American newspapers to lower the rates charged for advertising.

Explanation

The second sentence of the passage states that "knowing that buyers of African American newspapers also bought general-circulation papers, advertisers of consumer products often ignored African American publications." This suggests that advertisers believed that the majority of the people who read African American newspapers would see the advertisements when they read general-circulation papers, and that the number of people who read *only* African American newspapers was too small to justify buying advertising space there. Therefore **Choice A** is correct.

Question 6 is based on this passage.

Years ago, consumers in Frieland began paying an energy tax in the form of two Frieland pennies for each unit of energy consumed that came from nonrenewable sources. Following the introduction of this energy tax, there was a steady reduction in the total yearly consumption of energy from nonrenewable sources.

6. If the statements in the passage are true, then which of the following must on the basis of them be true?
    (A) There was a steady decline in the yearly revenues generated by the energy tax in Frieland.
    (B) There was a steady decline in the total amount of energy consumed each year in Frieland.
    (C) There was a steady increase in the use of renewable energy sources in Frieland.
    (D) The revenues generated by the energy tax were used to promote the use of energy from renewable sources.
    (E) The use of renewable energy sources in Frieland greatly increased relative to the use of nonrenewable energy sources.

Explanation

Since the energy tax is based upon the number of units of nonrenewable energy consumed, and since the number of units of nonrenewable energy declined, revenues generated by the energy tax must have declined as well. **Choice A** is therefore the correct answer. The passage gives no information on changes in the total amount of energy consumed, changes in the amount of energy from renewable sources that was used, or what revenues raised by the tax were used for, so all the other choices are incorrect.

> **Questions 7 to 9 are based on this passage.**

In a plausible but speculative scenario, oceanographer Douglas Martinson suggests that temperature increases caused by global warming would not significantly affect the stability of the Antarctic environment, where sea ice forms on the periphery of the
Line continent in the autumn and winter and mostly disappears in the summer. True, less
5 sea ice would form in the winter because global warming would cause temperatures to rise. However, Martinson argues, the effect of a warmer atmosphere may be offset as follows. The formation of sea ice causes the concentration of salt in surface waters to increase; less sea ice would mean a smaller increase in the concentration of salt. Less salty surface waters would be less dense and therefore less likely to sink and stir up deep
10 water. The deep water, with all its stored heat, would rise to the surface at a slower rate. Thus, although the winter sea-ice cover might decrease, the surface waters would remain cold enough so that the decrease would not be excessive.

Description

The passage explains a scenario in which warming would not cause a significant change in Antarctica's environment by detailing the processes triggered by the formation of sea ice, and considering what might occur in the absence of those processes.

7. It can be inferred from the passage that which of the following is true of the surface waters in the current Antarctic environment?

Ⓐ They are more affected by annual fluctuations in atmospheric temperatures than they would be if they were less salty.

Ⓑ They are less salty than they would be if global warming were to occur.

Ⓒ They are more likely to sink and stir up deep waters than they would be if atmospheric temperatures were to increase.

Ⓓ They are able to offset some of the effects of global warming beyond the Antarctic region.

Ⓔ They are less affected by the temperature of deep water than they would be if atmospheric temperatures were to increase.

Explanation

Choice C is correct. The passage states that rising temperatures would decrease the amount of sea ice formed in the winter, and that this change would result in surface water that is less salty, and thus less likely to sink. The current situation, then, results in the opposite: surface waters that are more likely to sink. Choices A and D are incorrect because the passage gives no information about how fluctuating temperatures would affect less salty water or about the relationship between the Antarctic region and the rest of the planet. Choices B and E are incorrect because they are both the opposite of what the passage implies about surface waters in the current environment.

8. The passage suggests that Martinson believes which of the following about deep waters in the Antarctic region?

    (A) They rise to the surface more quickly than they would if global warming were to occur.

    (B) They store heat that will exacerbate the effects of increases in atmospheric temperatures.

    (C) They would be likely to be significantly warmed by an increase in atmospheric temperatures.

    (D) They would be more salty than they currently are if global warming were to occur.

    (E) They are less likely to be stirred up when surface waters are intensely salty than when surface waters are relatively unsalty.

Explanation

Choice A is correct. The passage states that, in Martinson's scenario, the deep water would rise to the surface at a slower rate were warming to occur. He must believe, then, that the water currently rises to the surface more quickly. As for Choice B, while the passage indeed states that deep waters in Antarctica store heat, it also suggests that this heat would be less likely to reach the surface and worsen global warming. Choice B is therefore incorrect. Choice E is incorrect because it contradicts information given in the passage. Choices C and D are incorrect because, while the passage discusses the effects of global warming on the temperature and salinity of *surface* water, it gives no information of warming's effects on the temperature and salinity of *deep* water.

9. According to the passage, which of the following is true about the sea ice that surrounds the Antarctic continent?

    (A) The amount of sea ice that forms in the winter has been declining.

    (B) Most of the sea ice that forms in the winter remains intact in the summer.

    (C) Even small changes in the amount of sea ice dramatically affect the temperature of the surface waters.

    (D) Changes in the amount of sea ice due to global warming would significantly affect the stability of the Antarctic environment.

    (E) Changes in the amount of sea ice affect the degree of saltiness of the surface waters.

Explanation

Choice E is correct: according to the passage, "less sea ice would mean a smaller increase in the concentration of salt." Choices B, C, and D are incorrect because they are all contrary to the information presented in the passage. Choice A is incorrect because the passage does not compare current amounts of sea ice with past quantities; it instead proposes a hypothetical scenario involving a possible future decline of sea ice formation.

PRACTICE SET 2: Medium

> **For each of Questions 1 to 11, select <u>one</u> answer choice unless otherwise directed.**

Question 1 is based on this passage.

That sales can be increased by the presence of sunlight within a store has been shown by the experience of the only Savefast department store with a large skylight. The skylight allows sunlight into half of the store, reducing the need for artificial light. The rest of the store uses only artificial light. Since the store opened two years ago, the departments on the sunlit side have had substantially higher sales than the other departments.

Line

5

1. Which of the following, if true, most strengthens the argument?

    (A) On particularly cloudy days, more artificial light is used to illuminate the part of the store under the skylight.

    (B) When the store is open at night, the departments in the part of the store under the skylight have sales that are no higher than those of other departments.

    (C) Many customers purchase items from departments in both parts of the store on a single shopping trip.

    (D) Besides the skylight, there are several significant architectural differences between the two parts of the store.

    (E) The departments in the part of the store under the skylight are the departments that generally have the highest sales in other stores in the Savefast chain.

Explanation

The passage compares sales of items in the sunlit part of the store with sales of items in the artificially lit part of the store and concludes that since the former are greater than the latter, the presence of sunlight increases sales. The assumption underlying this argument is that the only significant difference between the two parts of the store is the presence of sunlight—otherwise, the inherent popularity of goods sold in different locations, or some other factor, might account for the increased sales. **Choice B** helps rule out the possibility that other factors might be involved, by showing that sales are no greater when the sunlight is taken out of the equation. Therefore it is the correct answer. Choices D and E both suggest that factors besides sunlight might explain the discrepancy between sales; therefore they weaken rather than strengthen the argument, and so are incorrect. Neither Choice A nor Choice C point to differences between the two areas of the store; therefore they are both incorrect as well.

Questions 2 to 4 are based on this passage.

While the best sixteenth-century Renaissance scholars mastered the classics of ancient Roman literature in the original Latin and understood them in their original historical context, most of the scholars' educated contemporaries knew the classics only from
Line school lessons on selected Latin texts. These were chosen by Renaissance teachers after
5 much deliberation, for works written by and for the sophisticated adults of pagan Rome were not always considered suitable for the Renaissance young: the central Roman clas–sics refused (as classics often do) to teach appropriate morality and frequently suggested the opposite. Teachers accordingly made students' needs, not textual and historical accu–racy, their supreme interest, chopping dangerous texts into short phrases, and using these
10 to impart lessons extemporaneously on a variety of subjects, from syntax to science. Thus, I believe that a modern reader cannot know the associations that a line of ancient Roman poetry or prose had for any particular educated sixteenth-century reader.

Description

The passage contrasts the way in which Renaissance scholars studied and contextualized classic Roman texts with the ways in which students of the era were taught snippets of Latin excerpted from them. The methods and motives of Renaissance teachers are explained, and the passage concludes by asserting that this pedagogical practice prevents modern readers from understanding the meanings that such snippets held for most Renaissance readers.

2. The passage is primarily concerned with discussing the
    (A) unsuitability of the Roman classics for the teaching of morality
    (B) approach that sixteenth-century scholars took to learning the Roman classics
    (C) effect that the Roman classics had on educated people in the Renaissance
    (D) way in which the Roman classics were taught in the sixteenth century
    (E) contrast between the teaching of the Roman classics in the Renaissance and the teaching of the Roman classics today

Explanation

The passage focuses primarily on the way Roman classics were taught during the Renaissance, so **Choice D** is the correct answer. The approach that sixteenth-century scholars took is mentioned, but it serves only to introduce and contrast with the pedagogical methods used in schools; therefore Choice B is incorrect. The passage mentions a supposed incompatibility between Roman classics and the teaching of morality as motivating Renaissance teaching methods, but that incompatibility is not the passage's main topic; thus Choice A is incorrect. Choices C and E are also incorrect, since the passage does not discuss the effect of Roman classics on educated Renaissance people or the teaching of Roman classics today.

3. The information in the passage suggests that which of the following would most likely result from a student's having studied the Roman classics under a typical sixteenth-century teacher?

    (A) The student recalls a line of Roman poetry in conjunction with a point learned about grammar.

    (B) The student argues that a Roman poem about gluttony is not morally offensive when it is understood in its historical context.

    (C) The student is easily able to express thoughts in Latin.

    (D) The student has mastered large portions of the Roman classics.

    (E) The student has a sophisticated knowledge of Roman poetry but little knowledge of Roman prose.

Explanation

Choice A is correct. The passage specifically mentions syntax as one of the subjects that the pieces of text served to illustrate; therefore it is logical that students would associate the text with the grammar point it was used to teach. Choices B and D are incorrect because the passage implies that students were not given the context or tools to place Roman classics in context, or to read and master large portions of works. Choices C and E are also incorrect, since the passage makes no mention of Latin composition being taught, or of any differences in the ways in which Roman poetry and prose were treated in schools.

4. Which of the following, if true, would most seriously weaken the assertion made in the passage concerning what a modern reader cannot know?

    (A) Some modern readers are thoroughly familiar with the classics of ancient Roman literature because they majored in classics in college or obtained doctoral degrees in classics.

    (B) Some modern readers have learned which particular works of Roman literature were taught to students in the sixteenth century.

    (C) Modern readers can, with some effort, discover that sixteenth-century teachers selected some seemingly dangerous classical texts while excluding other seemingly innocuous texts.

    (D) Copies of many of the classical texts used by sixteenth-century teachers, including marginal notes describing the oral lessons that were based on the texts, can be found in museums today.

    (E) Many of the writings of the best sixteenth-century Renaissance scholars have been translated from Latin and are available to modern readers.

Explanation

The passage asserts that modern readers cannot know the associations Roman poetry had for Renaissance readers, because those associations arose from the specific ways Roman texts were presented in schools. This assertion assumes that there is no way for modern readers to know how such texts were taught during the Renaissance. **Choice D** shows a way that scholars can recover this pedagogical context and is therefore the correct choice. Since the passage's assertion does not depend on modern readers' familiarity with the classics, with their knowledge of which works were taught in schools, with the inclusion or exclusion by sixteenth-century teachers of specific texts, or with the accessibility of the works of Renaissance scholars, all the other choices are incorrect.

Questions 5 and 6 are based on this passage.

In humans, the pilomotor reflex leads to the response commonly known as goose bumps, and this response is widely considered to be vestigial—that is, something formerly having a greater physiological advantage than at present. It occurs when the

Line
5
tiny muscle at the base of a hair follicle contracts, pulling the hair upright. In animals with feathers, fur, or quills, this creates a layer of insulating warm air or a reason for predators to think twice before attacking. But human hair is too puny to serve these functions. Goose bumps in humans may, however, have acquired a new role. Like flushing—another thermoregulatory (heat-regulating) mechanism—goose bumps have become linked with emotional responses, notably fear, rage, or the pleasure of, say,

10
listening to beautiful music. They may thus serve as a signal to others.

Description

The passage describes the physiological phenomenon of pilomotor reflex (or "goose bumps") and discusses its usefulness in animals and in human beings.

5.   In explaining the "new role" (line 7) that goose bumps in humans may have acquired, the author assumes which of the following?

(A) Emotional responses in humans can be triggered by thermoregulatory mechanisms.

(B) The perceptibility of emotional responses to other humans offers some kind of benefit.

(C) If human hair were more substantial, goose bumps would not have acquired a new role.

(D) Goose bumps in animals with feathers, fur, or quills may also be linked to emotional responses.

(E) In humans, goose bumps represent an older physiological response than flushing.

Explanation

The passage addresses the question of why the pilomotor reflex has survived in human beings despite the fact that its original functions—to insulate and to appear larger to predators—are no longer useful. The suggested reason is that the reflex "has acquired a new role," namely, as a means to signal to others that one is experiencing a strong emotion. This assumes that the ability to send such a signal is useful to human beings; therefore **Choice B** is correct.

6.   Which of the following best describes the primary function of the next-to-last sentence ("Like . . . music")?

(A) It makes a distinction between two types of mechanisms.

(B) It corrects a common misconception about the role of goose bumps in humans.

(C) It suggests reasons for the connection between emotional responses and goose bumps in humans.

(D) It suggests that flushing and goose bumps signal the same emotional state.

(E) It helps explain a possible role played by goose bumps in humans.

Explanation

The next-to-last sentence says that goose bumps in humans now serve as an outward sign of strong emotion. If so, this would explain how they could have taken on another role, so **Choice E** is correct. The sentence does not make a distinction (Choice A), correct a misconception (Choice B), suggest any reason for the connection between emotion and goose bumps (Choice C), or suggest that flushing and goose bumps signal the same state (Choice D).

Questions 7 to 10 are based on this passage.

This passage is adapted from material published in 2001.

Frederick Douglass was unquestionably the most famous African American of the nineteenth century; indeed when he died in 1895 he was among the most distinguished public figures in the United States. In his study of Douglass' career as a major figure in the movement to abolish slavery and as a spokesman for Black rights, Waldo Martin has provoked controversy by contending that Douglass also deserves a prominent place in the intellectual history of the United States because he exemplified so many strands of nineteenth-century thought: romanticism, idealism, individualism, liberal humanism, and an unshakable belief in progress. But this very argument provides ammunition for those who claim that most of Douglass' ideas, being so representative of their time, are now obsolete. Douglass' vision of the future as a melting pot in which all racial and ethnic differences would dissolve into "a composite American nationality" appears from the pluralist perspective of many present-day intellectuals to be not only utopian but even wrongheaded. Yet there is a central aspect of Douglass' thought that seems not in the least bit dated or irrelevant to current concerns. He has no rival in the history of the nineteenth-century United States as an insistent and effective critic of the doctrine of innate racial inequality. He not only attacked racist ideas in his speeches and writings, but he offered his entire career and all his achievements as living proof that racists were wrong in their belief that one race could be inherently superior to another.

While Martin stresses Douglass' antiracist egalitarianism, he does not adequately explain how this aspect of Douglass' thought fits in with his espousal of the liberal Victorian attitudes that many present-day intellectuals consider to be naïve and outdated. The fact is that Douglass was attracted to these democratic-capitalist ideals of his time because they could be used to attack slavery and the doctrine of White supremacy. His favorite rhetorical strategy was to expose the hypocrisy of those who, while professing adherence to the ideals of democracy and equality of opportunity, condoned slavery and racial discrimination. It would have been strange indeed if he had not embraced liberal idealism, because it proved its worth for the cause of racial equality during the national crisis that eventually resulted in emancipation and citizenship for African Americans. These points may seem obvious, but had Martin given them more attention, his analysis might have constituted a more convincing rebuttal to those critics who dismiss Douglass' ideology as a relic of the past. If one accepts the proposition that Douglass' deepest commitment was to Black equality and that he used the liberal ideals of his time as weapons in the fight for that cause, then it is hard to fault him for seizing the best weapons at hand.

Description

The passage discusses the views of the nineteenth-century African American intellectual Frederick Douglass and asserts their continuing relevance to the issues of the modern era. The second paragraph critiques a book about Douglass written by Waldo Martin and faults the author for failing to adequately explain some apparent inconsistencies in Douglass' political views.

7. The passage as a whole can best be described as doing which of the following?

    Ⓐ Explaining Douglass' emergence as a major figure in the movement to abolish slavery

    Ⓑ Tracing the origins of Douglass' thought in nineteenth-century romanticism, idealism, and liberal humanism

    Ⓒ Analyzing Douglass' speeches and writings from a modern, pluralist perspective

    Ⓓ Criticizing Martin for failing to stress the contradiction between Douglass' principles and the liberal Victorian attitudes of his day

    Ⓔ Formulating a response to those who consider Douglass' political philosophy to be archaic and irrelevant

Explanation

The passage discusses the views and intellectual legacy of Frederick Douglass. The key claim in the first paragraph is that while some of Douglass' views are no longer widely accepted, "there is a central aspect of Douglass' thought that seems not the least bit dated or irrelevant to our current concerns" (lines 13–14). The second paragraph critiques a study of Douglass' career by Waldo Martin and claims that Martin has failed to offer a "convincing rebuttal to those critics who dismiss Douglass' ideology as a relic of the past" (lines 30–31). This indicates that **Choice E** is correct.

8. It can be inferred that the "present-day intellectuals" (line 12) believe that

    Ⓐ although Douglass used democratic-capitalist ideas to attack slavery and racial inequality, he did not sincerely believe in those ideas

    Ⓑ the view that Douglass was representative of the intellectual trends of his time is obsolete

    Ⓒ Douglass' opposition to the doctrine of innate racial inequality is irrelevant to current concerns

    Ⓓ Douglass' commitment to Black equality does not adequately account for his naïve attachment to quaint liberal Victorian political views

    Ⓔ Douglass' goal of ultimately doing away with all racial and ethnic differences is neither achievable nor desirable

Explanation

"Present-day intellectuals" are mentioned on line 12; the claim there is that these intellectuals consider Douglass' vision of America as "a melting pot in which all racial and ethnic differences would dissolve" (lines 10–11) as "utopian" and "wrongheaded" (lines 12–13). This points to **Choice E** as correct.

9. According to the passage, Douglass used which of the following as evidence against the doctrine of innate racial inequality?

    (A) His own life story
    (B) His vision of a composite American nationality
    (C) The hypocrisy of self-professed liberal idealists
    (D) The inevitability of the emancipation of African Americans
    (E) The fact that most prominent intellectuals advocated the abolition of slavery

Explanation

One of the claims in the passage is that Frederick Douglass "offered his entire career and all his achievements as living proof that racists were wrong in their belief that one race could be inherently superior to another" (lines 17–18). Thus **Choice A** is correct.

10. Each of the following is mentioned in the passage as an element of Douglass' ideology EXCEPT

    (A) idealism
    (B) egalitarianism
    (C) capitalism
    (D) pluralism
    (E) humanism

Explanation

The passage claims that Douglass "exemplified . . . idealism, . . . liberal humanism" (lines 6–7); it implies that Douglass espoused "antiracist egalitarianism" (line 19) and states that "Douglass was attracted to . . . democratic-capitalist ideals of his time" (line 22). This rules out Choices A, B, C, and E and leaves **Choice D** as correct. Indeed, the mention of "Douglass' vision of the future as a melting pot in which all racial and ethnic differences would dissolve" (lines 10–11) shows that Douglass was not a pluralist, i.e. was not someone who aimed at preserving and celebrating ethnic and cultural differences.

Question 11 is based on this passage.

The plant called the scarlet gilia can have either red or white flowers. It had long been thought that hummingbirds, which forage by day, pollinate its red flowers and that hawkmoths, which forage at night, pollinate its white flowers. To try to show that this pattern of pollination by colors exists, scientists recently covered some scarlet gilia flowers only at night and others only by day: plants with red flowers covered at night became pollinated; plants with white flowers covered by day became pollinated.

Line
5

11. Which of the following, if true, would be additional evidence to suggest that hummingbirds are attracted to the red flowers and hawkmoths to the white flowers of the scarlet gilia?

Ⓐ Uncovered scarlet gilia flowers, whether red or white, became pollinated at approximately equal rates.

Ⓑ Some red flowers of the scarlet gilia that remained uncovered at all times never became pollinated.

Ⓒ White flowers of the scarlet gilia that were covered at night became pollinated with greater frequency than white flowers of the scarlet gilia that were left uncovered.

Ⓓ Scarlet gilia plants with red flowers covered by day and scarlet gilia plants with white flowers covered at night remained unpollinated.

Ⓔ In late August, when most of the hummingbirds had migrated but hawkmoths were still plentiful, red scarlet gilia plants produced fruit more frequently than they had earlier in the season.

Explanation

The results reported in the last sentence of the passage suggest that hummingbirds do pollinate red-flowered plants and that hawkmoths do pollinate white-flowered plants. But to prove that they are attracted preferentially to those colors requires knowing whether they also pollinate flowers of the other color that are uncovered during their respective foraging hours—white flowers uncovered during hummingbirds' daytime hours, and red flowers uncovered during hawkmoths' nocturnal hours. **Choice D** states that such plants remain unpollinated, so it is the correct answer. Of the other options, both Choices C and E could suggest the opposite of what is required, so they are incorrect. Choice A is incorrect because the comparative frequency at which uncovered gilia flowers are pollinated has no bearing on the argument. Likewise, the presence of some quantity of unpollinated flowers of either color does not affect the argument, so Choice B is also incorrect.

PRACTICE SET 3: Hard

For each of Questions 1 to 10, select <u>one</u> answer choice unless otherwise directed.

Questions 1 and 2 are based on this passage.

Supernovas in the Milky Way are the likeliest source for most of the cosmic rays reaching Earth. However, calculations show that supernovas cannot produce ultrahigh-energy cosmic rays (UHECRs), which have energies exceeding 10^{18} electron
Line volts. It would seem sensible to seek the source of these in the universe's most
5 conspicuous energy factories: quasars and gamma-ray bursts billions of light-years away from Earth. But UHECRs tend to collide with photons of the cosmic microwave background—pervasive radiation that is a relic of the early universe. The odds favor a collision every 20 million light-years, each collision costing 20 percent of the cosmic ray's energy. Consequently, no cosmic ray traveling much beyond 100 million
10 light-years can retain the energy observed in UHECRs.

Description

The passage discusses two hypotheses about the origins of ultrahigh-energy cosmic rays (UHECRs) and presents evidence suggesting that both hypotheses are probably false.

For the following question, consider each of the choices separately and select <u>all</u> that apply.

1. It can be inferred that the author of the passage would agree with which of the following about the origin of UHECRs that reach Earth?
    - [A] The origin is something other than supernovas in the Milky Way.
    - [B] The origin is most likely something other than very distant quasars or gamma-ray bursts.
    - [C] The origin is most likely no more than a little over 100 million light-years away from Earth.

Explanation

All three choices are correct. The question asks about claims the author would agree with.

    Choice A is correct: The passage states that supernovas in the Milky Way "cannot produce ultrahigh-energy cosmic rays."

    Choice B is correct: Since very distant quasars and gamma-ray bursts are "billions of light-years away from Earth," they are too far away for a UHECR to reach Earth.

    Choice C is correct: The last sentence of the passage states that "no cosmic ray traveling much beyond 100 million light-years can retain the energy observed in UHECRs."

2. In the context of the author's argument, the last sentence performs which of the following functions?
    - (A) It explains a criterion that was employed earlier in the argument.
    - (B) It shows that an apparently plausible position is actually self-contradictory.
    - (C) It is a conclusion drawn in the course of refuting a potential explanation.
    - (D) It overturns an assumption on which an opposing position depends.
    - (E) It states the main conclusion that the author is seeking to establish.

Explanation

The last sentence is the conclusion of an argument in the last half of the passage; it puts a constraint on the possible origin of UHECRs relative to Earth and thereby rules out the possibility, mentioned earlier in the passage, that distant quasars and gamma-ray bursts could be the origin of UHECRs. Therefore **Choice C** is correct. It is important to note that the last sentence does not show any plausible position to be self-contradictory (Choice B), and that it does not state the author's main conclusion (Choice E), since it is relevant to only one of the two hypotheses considered in the passage.

Questions 3 to 5 are based on this passage.

The massive influx of women cyclists—making up at least a third of the total market—was perhaps the most striking and profound social consequence of the mid-1890s cycling boom. Although the new, improved bicycle had appealed immediately to a few
Line privileged women, its impact would have been modest had it not attracted a greater
5 cross section of the female population. It soon became apparent that many of these pioneer women bicyclists had not taken up the sport as an idle pastime. Rather, they saw cycling as a noble cause to be promoted among all women as a means to improve the general female condition. Not only would cycling encourage healthy outdoor exercise, they reasoned, it would also hasten long-overdue dress reform. To feminists,
10 the bicycle affirmed nothing less than the dignity and equality of women.

Description

The passage discusses the widespread popularity of bicycling among women in the 1890s and mentions several reasons why this activity was seen as beneficial for women.

For the following question, consider each of the choices separately and select <u>all</u> that apply.

3. Which of the following statements about women cyclists is supported by the passage?
    - A The newly improved bicycle of the mid-1890s appealed mostly to women in a privileged position.
    - B The great majority of women in the mid-1890s considered cycling an idle pastime.
    - C Women bicyclists promoted cycling as a healthy form of outdoor exercise.

Explanation

Choice C is correct. The question asks which of three statements about women cyclists are supported by the passage.

Choice A is incorrect: The second sentence of the passage states that the new bicycle appealed to a few privileged women right away, but then implies that it quickly "attracted a greater cross section of the female population."

Choice B is incorrect: The third sentence of the passage explicitly states that many women "had not taken up [bicycling] as an idle pastime."

Choice C is correct: The penultimate sentence of the passage implies that women bicyclists thought that cycling would "encourage healthy outdoor exercise."

For the following question, consider each of the choices separately and select <u>all</u> that apply.

4. Which of the following does the passage suggest about pioneer women cyclists?

    A They saw cycling as a means to promote the advancement of women.

    B They argued that cycling would encourage women to get involved in a variety of noble causes.

    C They provided several reasons for a cross section of the female population to use the bicycle.

Explanation

Choices A and C are correct. The question asks what the passage suggests about pioneer women cyclists.

Choice A is correct: The passage states that pioneer women cyclists saw cycling "as a means to improve the general female condition" and believed that it "affirmed nothing less than the dignity and equality of women."

Choice B is incorrect: The passage states that bicycle pioneers saw cycling itself as a noble cause but does not mention any other noble causes to which cycling would lead.

Choice C is correct. The passage mentions that pioneer women cyclists saw at least two independent reasons for all women to use bicycles: they believed that cycling would "encourage healthy outdoor exercise" as well as "hasten long-overdue dress reform."

5. Which of the following best describes the function of the second sentence ("Although . . . population")?

    (A) It corrects a common misconception regarding the use of the bicycle in the mid-1890s.

    (B) It elaborates on a claim made in the previous sentence regarding a social consequence of the cycling boom.

    (C) It provides a context in which to understand the increased popularity of bicycle riding among privileged women.

    (D) It explains why cycling attracted such a significant cross section of women.

    (E) It describes the demographic characteristics of the consumer market for bicycles in the mid-1890s.

Explanation

The second sentence implies that the bicycle appealed at first only to "a few privileged women" but then "attracted a greater cross section of the female population," thus informing the reader that "the massive influx of women cyclists" mentioned in the previous sentence did not happen all at once. Since the influx of women cyclists *is* the social consequence of the cycling boom mentioned in the previous sentence, the highlighted sentence describes this consequence in more detail. Therefore, **Choice B** is correct. The second sentence does not correct any misconceptions (Choice A), provide help in understanding the appeal of the bicycle to privileged women (Choice C), explain the attraction cycling held for a significant cross section of women (Choice D), or describe demographic characteristics of the consumer market for bicycles (Choice E).

Questions 6 to 9 are based on this passage.

What causes a helix in nature to appear with either a dextral ("right-handed," or clockwise) twist or a sinistral ("left-handed," or counterclockwise) twist is one of the most intriguing puzzles in the science of form. Most spiral-shaped snail species are predominantly dextral. But at one time, handedness (twist direction of the shell) was equally distributed within some snail species that have become predominantly dextral or, in a few species, predominantly sinistral. What mechanisms control handedness and keep left-handedness rare?

It would seem unlikely that evolution should discriminate against sinistral snails if sinistral and dextral snails are exact mirror images, for any disadvantage that a sinistral twist in itself could confer on its possessor is almost inconceivable. But left- and right-handed snails are not actually true mirror images of one another. Their shapes are noticeably different. Sinistral rarity might, then, be a consequence of possible disadvantages conferred by these other concomitant structural features. In addition, perhaps left- and right-handed snails cannot mate with each other, having incompatible twist directions. Presumably an individual of the rarer form would have relative difficulty in finding a mate of the same hand, thus keeping the rare form rare or creating geographically separated right- and left-handed populations.

But this evolutionary mechanism combining dissymmetry, anatomy, and chance does not provide an adequate explanation of why right-handedness should have become predominant. It does not explain, for example, why the infrequent unions between snails of opposing hands produce fewer offspring of the rarer than the commoner form in species where each parent contributes equally to handedness. Nor does it explain why, in a species where one parent determines handedness, a brood is not exclusively right- or left-handed when the offspring would have the same genetic predisposition. In the European pond snail *Lymnaea peregra*, a predominantly dextral species whose handedness is maternally determined, a brood might be expected to be exclusively right- or left-handed—and this often occurs. However, some broods possess a few snails of the opposing hand, and in predominantly sinistral broods, the incidence of dextrality is surprisingly high.

Here, the evolutionary theory must defer to a theory based on an explicit developmental mechanism that can favor either right- or left-handedness. In the case of *Lymnaea peregra*, studies indicate that a dextral gene is expressed during egg formation; i.e., before egg fertilization, the gene produces a protein, found in the cytoplasm of the egg, that controls the pattern of cell division and thus handedness. In experiments, an injection of cytoplasm from dextral eggs changes the pattern of sinistral eggs, but an injection from sinistral eggs does not influence dextral eggs. One explanation for the differing effects is that all *Lymnaea peregra* eggs begin left-handed but most switch to being right-handed. Thus the path to a solution to the puzzle of handedness in all snails appears to be as twisted as the helix itself.

Line appears at line 3 and *5*, *10*, *15*, *20*, *25*, *30*, *35* mark the line numbers.

Description

The passage addresses the question of what determines the dextral (clockwise) or sinistral (counterclockwise) shape of snail shells and discusses two possible explanations of the distributional patterns of shell shapes in snail populations: the evolutionary theory and the developmental theory. Evidence against the evolutionary theory is presented, and the developmental theory is offered as a more plausible explanation.

6. Which of the following would serve as an example of "concomitant structural features" (line 13) that might disadvantage a snail of the rarer form?

    (A) A shell and body that are an exact mirror image of a snail of the commoner form

    (B) A smaller population of the snails of the rarer form

    (C) A chip or fracture in the shell caused by an object falling on it

    (D) A pattern on the shell that better camouflages it

    (E) A smaller shell opening that restricts mobility and ingestion relative to that of a snail of the commoner form

Explanation

Choice A is incorrect: the passage states that "any disadvantage that a sinistral twist in itself could confer on its possessor is almost inconceivable." Choice B is incorrect, as a smaller population would be the consequence of the disadvantage, not the cause of it. Choice C is incorrect, as damage caused by an external object is not a "structural feature" of a snail shell. Choice D is incorrect, as better camouflage is an advantage, not a disadvantage. The correct answer is **Choice E**: an impaired ability to move around and ingest food would be a disadvantage.

7. The second paragraph of the passage is primarily concerned with offering possible reasons why

    (A) it is unlikely that evolutionary mechanisms could discriminate against sinistral snails

    (B) sinistrality is relatively uncommon among snail species

    (C) dextral and sinistral populations of a snail species tend to intermingle

    (D) a theory based on a developmental mechanism inadequately accounts for the predominance of dextrality across snail species

    (E) dextral snails breed more readily than sinistral snails, even within predominantly sinistral populations

Explanation

The first paragraph ends with the question "What mechanisms control handedness and keep left-handedness rare?" The second paragraph attempts to answer this question: perhaps, the paragraph suggests, sinistral rarity is a consequence either of natural selection working on "concomitant structural features," or of difficulties in mating for left-handed snails. Thus **Choice B** is correct. The paragraph starts by dismissing the idea that evolution could be working against left-handedness itself, but Choice A is incorrect because the paragraph is not concerned with offering reasons for that dismissal. The paragraph does not even suggest that opposite-handed populations tend to intermingle (Choice C) or that dextral snails breed more rapidly (Choice E), and it does not discuss developmental mechanisms (Choice D).

8. Which of the following accurately describes the relationship between the evolutionary and developmental theories discussed in the passage?

    Ⓐ Although the two theories reach the same conclusion, each is based on different assumptions.

    Ⓑ They present contradictory explanations of the same phenomenon.

    Ⓒ The second theory accounts for certain phenomena that the first cannot explain.

    Ⓓ The second theory demonstrates why the first is valid only for very unusual, special cases.

    Ⓔ They are identical and interchangeable in that the second theory merely restates the first in less technical terms.

Explanation

The correct answer is **Choice C**. The third paragraph of the passage argues that the evolutionary theory cannot explain "why right-handedness should have become predominant" and lists some specific reproductive outcomes that cannot be accounted for by this theory. The next paragraph offers an alternative theory (developmental) that seems to do a better job of explaining these outcomes.

9. It can be inferred from the passage that a predominantly sinistral snail species might stay predominantly sinistral for each of the following reasons EXCEPT for

    Ⓐ a developmental mechanism that affects the cell-division pattern of snails

    Ⓑ structural features that advantage dextral snails of the species

    Ⓒ a relatively small number of snails of the same hand for dextral snails of the species to mate with

    Ⓓ anatomical incompatibility that prevents mating between snails of opposing hands within the species

    Ⓔ geographic separation of sinistral and dextral populations

Explanation

The question asks about possible reasons why a "sinistral snail species might stay predominantly sinistral"; this would happen if the offspring of a sinistral species is largely sinistral. Choices A, C, D, and E give plausible reasons for why this might happen: either genetic predisposition for sinistrality (Choice A) or lack of reproductive competition from dextral individuals (Choices C, D, and E). Therefore, the correct answer is **Choice B**: having structural features that advantage dextral snails would tend to reduce the number of sinistral individuals in a species and thus to eventually transform a sinistral species into a dextral one.

Question 10 is based on this passage.

X-ray examination of a recently discovered painting—judged by some authorities to be a self-portrait by Vincent van Gogh—revealed an underimage of a woman's face. Either van Gogh or another painter covered the first painting with the portrait now seen on the surface of the canvas. Because the face of the woman in the underimage also appears on canvases van Gogh is known to have painted, the surface painting must be an authentic self-portrait by van Gogh.

10. The conclusion is properly drawn if which of the following is assumed?

(A) If a canvas already bears a painted image produced by an artist, a second artist who uses the canvas to produce a new painting tends to be influenced by the style of the first artist.

(B) Many painted canvases that can be reliably attributed to van Gogh contain underimages of subjects that appear on at least one other canvas that van Gogh is known to have painted.

(C) Any painted canvas incorrectly attributed to van Gogh would not contain an underimage of a subject that appears in authentic paintings by that artist.

(D) A painted canvas cannot be reliably attributed to an artist unless the authenticity of any underimage that painting might contain can be reliably attributed to the artist.

(E) A painted canvas cannot be reliably attributed to a particular artist unless a reliable x-ray examination of the painting is performed.

Explanation

The passage's argument makes a case for the painting's being an authentic van Gogh self-portrait; it cites as evidence the fact that the canvas's painted-over image is that of a woman who appears in other van Gogh paintings. This argument assumes that another artist would not have painted over the original image of the woman, so the correct answer is **Choice C**. Since the argument does not depend upon the painting's stylistic elements or upon the commonalities between this and other van Gogh paintings, Choices A and B are incorrect. Choices D and E establish criteria for attribution beyond the passage's argument, so they are incorrect as well.

Question Type 2: Text Completion

Your goals for this chapter	⇨ Practice answering GRE Text Completion questions ⇨ Review answers and explanations, particularly for questions you answered incorrectly

This chapter contains three sets of practice Text Completion questions. The sets are arranged in order of increasing difficulty, one easy, one medium, and one hard.

Following the third set are answer keys for quick reference. Then, at the end of the chapter, you will find complete explanations for every question. Each explanation is presented with the corresponding question, so that you can easily see what was asked and what the various answer choices were.

Sharpen your GRE Verbal Reasoning skills by working your way through these question sets, remembering to use the Tips for Answering given in Chapter 2. Begin with the easy set and then move on to the medium-difficulty and hard sets. Review the answer explanations carefully, paying particular attention to the explanations for questions that you answered incorrectly. Were you able to

- understand the overall meaning of the passage?
- identify significant words in the passage?
- think up your own words for the blanks?

Turn the page to begin.

PRACTICE SET 1: Easy

> For each of Questions 1 to 9, select **one** entry for each blank from the corresponding column of choices. Fill all blanks in the way that best completes the text.

1. This composer has never courted popularity: her rugged modernism seems to defy rather than to _____ the audience.

Ⓐ	ignore
Ⓑ	discount
Ⓒ	woo
Ⓓ	teach
Ⓔ	cow

2. The sight of a single actor portraying several characters in the same scene is no longer a shock to the average moviegoer, such special-effects trickery having become so _____.

Ⓐ	expensive
Ⓑ	specialized
Ⓒ	sinister
Ⓓ	commonplace
Ⓔ	unreliable

3. Early studies often concluded that the public was _____ the propagandistic influence of mass communications, but one recent study indicates that, on the contrary, mass communications seldom produce marked changes in social attitudes or actions.

Ⓐ	unaware of
Ⓑ	scornful of
Ⓒ	susceptible to
Ⓓ	unimpressed by
Ⓔ	coping with

4. The figure-skating pair's convincing victory last week was particularly (i) _____ to their rivals, who were in peak form and complained privately about the judging. That the pair won when their rivals were (ii) _____ too is also impressive.

Blank (i)		Blank (ii)	
Ⓐ	unsurprising	Ⓓ	terrific
Ⓑ	irksome	Ⓔ	nervous
Ⓒ	gratifying	Ⓕ	inconsistent

5. In his initial works, the playwright made physical disease (i) _____ factor in the action; from this, his early critics inferred that he had a predilection for focusing on (ii) _____ subject matter.

Blank (i)	Blank (ii)
Ⓐ a pivotal	Ⓓ recondite
Ⓑ a nonexistent	Ⓔ uncomplicated
Ⓒ an obscure	Ⓕ morbid

6. We have yet to (i) _____ the assessment of Canada's biodiversity. Most of the vertebrates have been assessed, but our challenge will be the assessment of invertebrates and plants. This task is (ii) _____ not only because of the high number of species, but also because of the diversity, each species requiring a different approach.

Blank (i)	Blank (ii)
Ⓐ initiate	Ⓓ repetitious
Ⓑ complete	Ⓔ trivial
Ⓒ limit	Ⓕ daunting

7. The company's efforts to improve safety were apparently (i) _____, at least according to the company's own data, which showed that the (ii) _____ incidents with the potential to cause a serious accident declined significantly. Nevertheless, independent analysts argue that those statistics are (iii) _____. These analysts maintain that the company has consistently underestimated both the probability and the likely effects of accidents in the sensitive and poorly understood environment in which the company is operating.

Blank (i)	Blank (ii)	Blank (iii)
Ⓐ innovative	Ⓓ frequency of	Ⓖ deceptive
Ⓑ successful	Ⓔ impediments to	Ⓗ testable
Ⓒ frustrated	Ⓕ attention to	Ⓘ consistent

8. Researchers trying to make it possible to trace counterfeit documents to the printer that produced them are (i) _____ the fact that the rotating drums and mirrors inside laser printers are imperfect devices that leave unique patterns of banding in their output. Although these patterns are (ii) _____ to the naked eye, they can be (iii) _____ and analyzed by computer programs that the researchers have spent the past year devising.

Blank (i)	Blank (ii)	Blank (iii)
Ⓐ exploiting	Ⓓ invisible	Ⓖ detected
Ⓑ facing	Ⓔ obvious	Ⓗ implemented
Ⓒ manipulating	Ⓕ unappealing	Ⓘ generated

9. In her startlingly original writing, she went further than any other twentieth-century author in English (perhaps in any language) in (i) _____ literary language and form, (ii) _____ stylistic conventions, and (iii) _____ a rich and diverse structure of meaning.

Blank (i)	Blank (ii)	Blank (iii)
Ⓐ reinventing	Ⓓ undoing	Ⓖ replicating
Ⓑ canonizing	Ⓔ overpraising	Ⓗ borrowing
Ⓒ stabilizing	Ⓕ misunderstanding	Ⓘ introducing

PRACTICE SET 2: Medium

> For each of Questions 1 to 8, select **one** entry for each blank from the corresponding column of choices. Fill all blanks in the way that best completes the text.

1. The media once portrayed the governor as anything but ineffective; they now, however, make her out to be the epitome of _____.

Ⓐ fecklessness
Ⓑ brilliance
Ⓒ dynamism
Ⓓ egoism
Ⓔ punctiliousness

2. For most of the first half of the nineteenth century, science at the university was in _____ state, despite the presence of numerous luminaries.

Ⓐ a scintillating
Ⓑ a pathetic
Ⓒ a controversial
Ⓓ an incendiary
Ⓔ a veracious

3. In a recent history of the Renaissance, by showing how the artistic efflorescence of that era was (i) _____ linked to its commercial vitality, Jardine demonstrated that the spirit of acquisitiveness may be (ii) _____ that of cultural creativity.

Blank (i)	Blank (ii)
Ⓐ questionably	Ⓓ threatened by
Ⓑ intimately	Ⓔ inseparable from
Ⓒ skeptically	Ⓕ comparable to

4. The setting in which the concert took place (i) _____: the group's performance was elegant and polished, but the sound, which seeped across the cold, unresonant high school auditorium, was oddly (ii) _____, given the energy the players seemed to be putting into it.

Blank (i)	Blank (ii)
Ⓐ exacted a toll	Ⓓ clangorous
Ⓑ encouraged nervousness	Ⓔ tepid
Ⓒ solved a dilemma	Ⓕ inviting

5. The governor has long been obsessed with excising the media from the politician-public relationship. That's been the unifying aim of all her seemingly disconnected ventures since entering public life: a determination to (i) _____, and eventually (ii) _____, the media's hold on political communication.

Blank (i)	Blank (ii)
(A) conceal	(D) augment
(B) erode	(E) consolidate
(C) rejuvenate	(F) end

6. Female labor was essential to the growth of eighteenth-century European textile industries, yet it remains difficult to (i) _____. Despite significant (ii) _____ in research about women, the role of female labor remains the single most glaring omission in most economic analyses of the history of European industrialization. Women far outnumbered men as workers in the textile industries, yet wage indices and discussions of growth, cost of living, and the like (iii) _____ about the male labor force.

Blank (i)	Blank (ii)	Blank (iii)
(A) track	(D) advances	(G) incorporate data only
(B) overestimate	(E) gaps	(H) suppress most information
(C) ignore	(F) disinterest	(I) too rarely talk

7. It is a sad but just indictment of some high school history textbooks that they frequently report as (i) _____ claims that historians hotly debate or that are even completely (ii) _____ by (iii) _____ primary sources.

Blank (i)	Blank (ii)	Blank (iii)
(A) factual	(D) resolved	(G) dubious
(B) controversial	(E) corroborated	(H) incomplete
(C) sensational	(F) contradicted	(I) reliable

8. The reason minimum temperatures are going up more rapidly than maximums may involve cloud cover and evaporative cooling. Clouds tend to keep the days cooler by reflecting sunlight, and the nights warmer by (i) _____ loss of heat from Earth's surface. Greater amounts of moisture in the soil from additional precipitation and cloudiness (ii) _____ the daytime temperature increases because part of the solar energy is (iii) _____ the evaporation of that moisture.

Blank (i)	Blank (ii)	Blank (iii)
(A) inhibiting	(D) augment	(G) intensified by
(B) exacerbating	(E) mask	(H) unrelated to
(C) replicating	(F) restrain	(I) used up in

PRACTICE SET 3: Hard

> **For each of Questions 1 to 8, select <u>one</u> entry for each blank from the corresponding column of choices. Fill all blanks in the way that best completes the text.**

1. In searching for norms in the sense of authoritative standards of what ought to be, rather than in the sense of what is average and thus can be considered normal, normative ethics aims to _____.

Ⓐ	predict
Ⓑ	mitigate
Ⓒ	question
Ⓓ	dictate
Ⓔ	personalize

2. When she first came to France from Bulgaria, she was hardly the _____ student she later made herself out to be, since she had access to considerable family wealth.

Ⓐ	naïve
Ⓑ	precocious
Ⓒ	impecunious
Ⓓ	ambitious
Ⓔ	assiduous

3. Researchers have observed chimpanzees feigning injury in order to influence other members of the group, thus showing that the capacity to _____ is not uniquely human.

Ⓐ	cooperate
Ⓑ	instruct
Ⓒ	conspire
Ⓓ	dissemble
Ⓔ	dominate

4. Instant celebrity is often (i) _____ asset because if there is no (ii) _____ to interest the public—no stage or screen triumphs, no interesting books, no heroic exploits—people quickly become bored.

Blank (i)		Blank (ii)	
Ⓐ	a fleeting	Ⓓ	competing attraction
Ⓑ	an incomparable	Ⓔ	continuity of exposure
Ⓒ	an untapped	Ⓕ	real achievement

5. At their best, (i) _____ book reviews are written in defense of value and in the tacit hope that the author, having had his or her (ii) _____ pointed out, might secretly agree that the book could be improved.

Blank (i)	Blank (ii)
Ⓐ abstruse	Ⓓ strengths
Ⓑ adverse	Ⓔ transgressions
Ⓒ hortatory	Ⓕ assumptions

6. The gaps in existing accounts of the playwright's life are not (i) _____, since much of the documentary evidence on which historians have relied is (ii) _____.

Blank (i)	Blank (ii)
Ⓐ trifling	Ⓓ credible
Ⓑ obvious	Ⓔ extant
Ⓒ implicit	Ⓕ incomplete

7. That today's students of American culture tend to (i) _____ classical music is understandable. In our own time, America's musical high culture has degenerated into a formulaic entertainment divorced from the contemporary moment. Thus, to miss out on what our orchestras are up to is not to (ii) _____ much. In the late Gilded Age, however, music was widely esteemed as the "queen of the arts." Classical music was in its American heyday, (iii) _____ the culture at large.

Blank (i)	Blank (ii)	Blank (iii)
Ⓐ promote	Ⓓ sacrifice	Ⓖ antagonistic toward
Ⓑ reinterpret	Ⓔ appreciate	Ⓗ generally rejected by
Ⓒ ignore	Ⓕ malign	Ⓘ centrally embedded in

8. The serious study of popular culture by intellectuals is regularly credited with having rendered obsolete a once-dominant view that popular culture is inherently inferior to high art. Yet this alteration of attitudes may be somewhat (i) _____. Although it is now academically respectable to analyze popular culture, the fact that many intellectuals feel compelled to rationalize their own (ii) _____ action movies or mass-market fiction reveals, perhaps unwittingly, their continued (iii) _____ the old hierarchy of high and low culture.

Blank (i)	Blank (ii)	Blank (iii)
Ⓐ counterproductive	Ⓓ penchant for	Ⓖ aversion to
Ⓑ underappreciated	Ⓔ distaste for	Ⓗ investment in
Ⓒ overstated	Ⓕ indifference to	Ⓘ misunderstanding of

ANSWER KEY

PRACTICE SET 1: Easy

1. **Choice C**: woo
2. **Choice D**: commonplace
3. **Choice C**: susceptible to
4. **Choice B**: irksome; **Choice D**: terrific
5. **Choice A**: a pivotal; **Choice F**: morbid
6. **Choice B**: complete; **Choice F**: daunting
7. **Choice B**: successful; **Choice D**: frequency of; **Choice G**: deceptive
8. **Choice A**: exploiting; **Choice D**: invisible; **Choice G**: detected
9. **Choice A**: reinventing; **Choice D**: undoing; **Choice I**: introducing

PRACTICE SET 2: Medium

1. **Choice A**: fecklessness
2. **Choice B**: a pathetic
3. **Choice B**: intimately; AND **Choice E**: inseparable from
4. **Choice A**: exacted a toll; AND **Choice E**: tepid
5. **Choice B**: erode; AND **Choice F**: end
6. **Choice A**: track; **Choice D**: advances; **Choice G**: incorporate data only
7. **Choice A**: factual; **Choice F**: contradicted; **Choice I**: reliable
8. **Choice A**: inhibiting; **Choice F**: restrain; **Choice I**: used up in

PRACTICE SET 3: Hard

1. **Choice D**: dictate
2. **Choice C**: impecunious
3. **Choice D**: dissemble
4. **Choice A**: a fleeting; AND **Choice F**: real achievement
5. **Choice B**: adverse; AND **Choice E**: transgressions
6. **Choice A**: trifling; AND **Choice F**: incomplete
7. **Choice C**: ignore; **Choice D**: sacrifice; **Choice I**: centrally embedded in
8. **Choice C**: overstated; **Choice D**: penchant for; **Choice H**: investment in

Answers and Explanations

PRACTICE SET 1: Easy

> For each of Questions 1 to 9, select <u>one</u> entry for each blank from the corresponding column of choices. Fill all blanks in the way that best completes the text.

1. This composer has never courted popularity: her rugged modernism seems to defy rather than to _____ the audience.

Ⓐ	ignore
Ⓑ	discount
Ⓒ	woo
Ⓓ	teach
Ⓔ	cow

Explanation

The first part of the sentence asserts that the composer has never sought popularity, while the second part of the sentence explains what the composer's style does instead. The blank, then, must be filled with a verb that is roughly synonymous with "court popularity." The choice that best does this is "woo;" its correctness is confirmed by the fact that it also forms the best contrast with "defy." None of the other choices indicates the desire to be liked by or to win over audiences that a synonym of "court popularity" would require.

Thus the correct answer is **woo** (Choice C).

2. The sight of a single actor portraying several characters in the same scene is no longer a shock to the average moviegoer, such special-effects trickery having become so _____.

Ⓐ	expensive
Ⓑ	specialized
Ⓒ	sinister
Ⓓ	commonplace
Ⓔ	unreliable

Explanation

The blank calls for a term that would explain why the special effects that once astonished moviegoers no longer do so. "Commonplace" does this by suggesting that the technology has become so familiar that it no longer surprises; therefore, it is the correct answer. None of the other options suggests a change that would result in desensitizing moviegoers to the special effects on-screen.

Thus the correct answer is **commonplace** (Choice D).

3. Early studies often concluded that the public was _____ the propagandistic influence of mass communications, but one recent study indicates that, on the contrary, mass communications seldom produce marked changes in social attitudes or actions.

Ⓐ	unaware of
Ⓑ	scornful of
Ⓒ	susceptible to
Ⓓ	unimpressed by
Ⓔ	coping with

Explanation

The recent study found that mass communications had negligible effects on the public. Since the recent study's findings are contrary to those of earlier ones, the earlier studies must have found that the influence of mass communications was significant; thus, the blank must be filled with a word that indicates that the public is swayed by such communications. Of the choices, only "susceptible to" does this. Two of the other choices, "unaware of" and "unimpressed by," indicate the opposite. "Scornful of" also indicates some resistance to mass communications, as does "coping with," so those are incorrect as well.

Thus the correct answer is **susceptible to** (Choice C).

4. The figure-skating pair's convincing victory last week was particularly (i) _____ to their rivals, who were in peak form and complained privately about the judging. That the pair won when their rivals were (ii) _____ too is also impressive.

Blank (i)	Blank (ii)
Ⓐ unsurprising	Ⓓ terrific
Ⓑ irksome	Ⓔ nervous
Ⓒ gratifying	Ⓕ inconsistent

Explanation

The fact that the winning pair's rivals were "in peak physical form" suggests that these rivals had a reasonable expectation of victory; the fact that they "complained about the judging" indicates that they regarded the pair's victory as not completely deserved. These two considerations suggest that the rivals had a negative reaction to the winning pair's victory; the only answer choice for Blank (i) that matches this meaning is "irksome," so it is correct. The second sentence reinforces the implication that the rivals were also strongly deserving of victory, and the word "too" suggests that the performances of the winning pair and of their rivals were comparable in quality. This points to "terrific" as the correct answer choice for Blank (ii).

Thus the correct answer is **irksome** (Choice B) and **terrific** (Choice D).

5. In his initial works, the playwright made physical disease (i) _____ factor in the action; from this, his early critics inferred that he had a predilection for focusing on (ii) _____ subject matter.

Blank (i)	Blank (ii)
Ⓐ a pivotal	Ⓓ recondite
Ⓑ a nonexistent	Ⓔ uncomplicated
Ⓒ an obscure	Ⓕ morbid

Explanation

A writer who has "a predilection for focusing" on a thing makes that thing prominent in his or her work, so the answer to Blank (i) must be synonymous with "prominent" or "significant"; the answer choice that matches this meaning is "pivotal," so it is correct. The answer to Blank (ii) must be a word that describes the subject matter of physical disease, so the correct choice is "morbid."

Thus the correct answer is **a pivotal** (Choice A) and **morbid** (Choice F).

6. We have yet to (i) _____ the assessment of Canada's biodiversity. Most of the vertebrates have been assessed, but our challenge will be the assessment of invertebrates and plants. This task is (ii) _____ not only because of the high number of species, but also because of the diversity, each species requiring a different approach.

Blank (i)	Blank (ii)
Ⓐ initiate	Ⓓ repetitious
Ⓑ complete	Ⓔ trivial
Ⓒ limit	Ⓕ daunting

Explanation

The sentence implies that Canada's invertebrates and plants have not yet been assessed, so the assessment of Canada's biodiversity is not finished; therefore, the correct answer to Blank (i) is "complete." The assessment of invertebrates and plants is described as a "challenge," so the answer to Blank (ii) must be synonymous with "difficult." The only answer choice that matches this meaning is "daunting," so it is correct.

Thus the correct answer is **complete** (Choice B) and **daunting** (Choice F).

7. The company's efforts to improve safety were apparently (i) _____, at least according to the company's own data, which showed that the (ii) _____ incidents with the potential to cause a serious accident declined significantly. Nevertheless, independent analysts argue that those statistics are (iii) _____. These analysts maintain that the company has consistently underestimated both the probability and the likely effects of accidents in the sensitive and poorly understood environment in which the company is operating.

Blank (i)	Blank (ii)	Blank (iii)
Ⓐ innovative	Ⓓ frequency of	Ⓖ deceptive
Ⓑ successful	Ⓔ impediments to	Ⓗ testable
Ⓒ frustrated	Ⓕ attention to	Ⓘ consistent

Explanation

Since the analysts found that the company's statistics underestimated the potential for accidents, the answer to Blank (iii) must reflect the inaccuracy or inapplicability of those statistics. "Deceptive" is the only choice that does so. Blank (i) must then be answered with a choice that reflects the more positive view of accident prevention that deceptive statistics might provide. "Frustrated" efforts would imply the opposite, and while "innovative" has positive connotations, the passage is concerned with the effectiveness of safety measures rather than with their novelty. Thus "successful" is the correct choice. Finally, the word for Blank (ii) describes something related to potentially dangerous incidents that would indicate improved safety if it were to decline. If "impediments to" or "attention to" such incidents were to decline, that would likely have the opposite implication. However, fewer such incidents would presumably be a sign of improved safety; thus "frequency of" is the correct response.

Thus the correct answer is **successful** (Choice B), **frequency of** (Choice D), and **deceptive** (Choice G).

8. Researchers trying to make it possible to trace counterfeit documents to the printer that produced them are (i) _____ the fact that the rotating drums and mirrors inside laser printers are imperfect devices that leave unique patterns of banding in their output. Although these patterns are (ii) _____ to the naked eye, they can be (iii) _____ and analyzed by computer programs that the researchers have spent the past year devising.

Blank (i)	Blank (ii)	Blank (iii)
(A) exploiting	(D) invisible	(G) detected
(B) facing	(E) obvious	(H) implemented
(C) manipulating	(F) unappealing	(I) generated

Explanation

The "although" that begins the second sentence suggests that there is a contrast between the way the naked eye perceives the patterns in question and the way computer programs can view them. The answers to Blank (ii) and Blank (iii) must therefore reflect this contrast. "Invisible" and "detected" are the only pairing that does this. Blank (i) calls for a characterization of the relationship between the researchers and the inevitability of imperfections in printing technology. Since the passage asserts that researchers are using computers to analyze these imperfections, "exploiting" is the best choice for Blank (i). "Facing" does not imply the level of engagement detailed in the passage, while "manipulating" suggests that the researchers' focus might be on changing the imperfections themselves, rather than analyzing them.

Thus the correct answer is **exploiting** (Choice A), **invisible** (Choice D), and **detected** (Choice G).

9. In her startlingly original writing, she went further than any other twentieth-century author in English (perhaps in any language) in (i) _____ literary language and form, (ii) _____ stylistic conventions, and (iii) _____ a rich and diverse structure of meaning.

Blank (i)	Blank (ii)	Blank (iii)
(A) reinventing	(D) undoing	(G) replicating
(B) canonizing	(E) overpraising	(H) borrowing
(C) stabilizing	(F) misunderstanding	(I) introducing

Explanation

The writer's work is described as startlingly original, and the sentence specifies three ways in which the author achieved this originality. Therefore each blank must be filled with a word that reflects innovative rather than conventional ways of writing. For Blank (i), the choice must be "reinventing," because neither "canonizing" nor "stabilizing" would indicate a break with traditional forms or language. Blank (ii) must contain a word that describes the writer's relationship with convention; "undoing" is the only one that reflects originality. Blank (iii) likewise requires a word that conveys the novelty of the writer's work. Both "replicating" and "borrowing" suggest a derivative approach to writing, so they are incorrect. "Introducing" implies that the writer's structure is new; therefore it is the correct choice.

Thus the correct answer is **reinventing** (Choice A), **undoing** (Choice D), and **introducing** (Choice I).

PRACTICE SET 2: Medium

> For each of Questions 1 to 8, select <u>one</u> entry for each blank from the corresponding column of choices. Fill all blanks in the way that best completes the text.

1. The media once portrayed the governor as anything but ineffective; they now, however, make her out to be the epitome of _____.

Ⓐ	fecklessness
Ⓑ	brilliance
Ⓒ	dynamism
Ⓓ	egoism
Ⓔ	punctiliousness

Explanation

The sentence contrasts the media's former and current depictions of the governor. Since the governor was once presented as "anything but ineffective," the media once saw her as extremely competent. It follows that the phrase completed by the blank will have the opposite meaning. To be the epitome of something is to be representative of that trait, so the blank must be filled with a word that implies incompetence. "Brilliance," "dynamism," and "punctiliousness" are all positive traits, so they do not work in this context. "Egoism," while often thought of as a negative trait, does not imply incompetence. That leaves "fecklessness," whose meaning includes ineffectiveness, making it a very good contrast with the first half of the sentence.

Thus, the correct answer is **fecklessness** (Choice A).

2. For most of the first half of the nineteenth century, science at the university was in _____ state, despite the presence of numerous luminaries.

Ⓐ	a scintillating
Ⓑ	a pathetic
Ⓒ	a controversial
Ⓓ	an incendiary
Ⓔ	a veracious

Explanation

Since the presence of numerous luminaries, a positive thing, is portrayed as a factor that runs counter to the general state of science at the university, that general state must be negative. Therefore the word that fills the blank must describe a generally negative atmosphere. "Pathetic" certainly does. Of the other answers, "scintillating," meaning brilliant, is just the opposite of what is called for, while "veracious" is similarly too positive. "Controversial" and "incendiary" both describe an argumentative or explosive environment that would not necessarily be mitigated by the presence of numerous luminaries.

Thus the correct answer is **a pathetic** (Choice B).

3. In a recent history of the Renaissance, by showing how the artistic efflorescence of that era was (i) _____ linked to its commercial vitality, Jardine demonstrated that the spirit of acquisitiveness may be (ii) _____ that of cultural creativity.

Blank (i)	Blank (ii)
Ⓐ questionably	Ⓓ threatened by
Ⓑ intimately	Ⓔ inseparable from
Ⓒ skeptically	Ⓕ comparable to

Explanation

The sentence talks about Jardine's demonstrating a certain general relation between two social phenomena ("spirit of acquisitiveness" and "cultural creativity") by showing that this relation was held between two particular historical instances of these phenomena ("commercial vitality" and "artistic efflorescence" of the Renaissance). Therefore, the phrase "(i)_____ linked to" and the answer to Blank (ii) must be identical or very similar in meaning. The only answer choices that are related in this way are "intimately" and "inseparable from": if two things are "intimately linked," then they are very plausibly "inseparable from" each other.

Thus the correct answer is **intimately** (Choice B) and **inseparable from** (Choice E).

4. The setting in which the concert took place (i) _____: the group's performance was elegant and polished, but the sound, which seeped across the cold, unresonant high school auditorium, was oddly (ii) _____, given the energy the players seemed to be putting into it.

Blank (i)	Blank (ii)
Ⓐ exacted a toll	Ⓓ clangorous
Ⓑ encouraged nervousness	Ⓔ tepid
Ⓒ solved a dilemma	Ⓕ inviting

Explanation

The "but" in the sentence suggests that there is a contrast between the group's overall performance and the quality of the sound; since the former is given a positive description ("elegant and polished"), the description of the latter in Blank (ii) must be negative. Furthermore, the quality of the sound must be in contrast with the apparent energy of the performers. The only answer choice for Blank (ii) that meets these conditions is "tepid," so it is correct. The sentence as a whole suggests that the setting of the concert had a negative effect on the performance; the answer choice for Blank (i) that best fits this meaning is "exacted a toll," so it is correct.

Answer Choice B for Blank (i), "encouraged nervousness," is also negative in meaning, but it is incorrect, because the sentence does not talk about the psychological state of the musicians or the audience.

Thus the correct answer is **exacted a toll** (Choice A) and **tepid** (Choice E).

5. The governor has long been obsessed with excising the media from the politician-public relationship. That's been the unifying aim of all her seemingly disconnected ventures since entering public life: a determination to (i) _____, and eventually (ii) _____, the media's hold on political communication.

Blank (i)	Blank (ii)
Ⓐ conceal	Ⓓ augment
Ⓑ erode	Ⓔ consolidate
Ⓒ rejuvenate	Ⓕ end

Explanation

Blanks (i) and (ii) must describe what the governor wants to do to "the media's hold on political communication." From the first sentence, it is clear that the governor's goal is to "excise" or eliminate the media as an intermediary between politicians and the public; this must be the meaning of the answer to Blank (ii), which describes the governor's eventual, or long-term, goal. The only answer choice for Blank (ii) that has this meaning is "end," so it is correct. The answer to Blank (i) must be a word that denotes the initial phase of a gradual process that ends with the complete elimination of the media's influence; the answer choice that fits this meaning is "erode," so it is correct.

Thus the correct answer is **erode** (Choice B) and **end** (Choice F).

6. Female labor was essential to the growth of eighteenth-century European textile industries, yet it remains difficult to (i) _____. Despite significant (ii) _____ in research about women, the role of female labor remains the single most glaring omission in most economic analyses of the history of European industrialization. Women far outnumbered men as workers in the textile industries, yet wage indices and discussions of growth, cost of living, and the like (iii) _____ about the male labor force.

Blank (i)	Blank (ii)	Blank (iii)
Ⓐ track	Ⓓ advances	Ⓖ incorporate data only
Ⓑ overestimate	Ⓔ gaps	Ⓗ suppress most information
Ⓒ ignore	Ⓕ disinterest	Ⓘ too rarely talk

Explanation

The second sentence asserts that the role of women is generally left out from most analyses of industrialization. Given this omission, it follows that data about female labor would be hard to come by, making it difficult to measure its growth; therefore "track" is the correct answer for Blank (i). As for the other choices, since the author asserts that the role of female labor has routinely been overlooked, "ignore" cannot be correct. The conjunction "yet" in the first sentence indicates that the phrase containing Blank (i) contrasts with the importance of female labor; since "overestimate" emphasizes this importance, it also cannot be correct. The second sentence places research about female labor during industrialization into the larger context of research about women; the word "despite" that begins the sentence indicates that the latter runs counter to trends in the larger field. Neither "gaps" nor "disinterest" would provide the necessary contrast between the two, since "gaps" in the larger field of research about women would mirror the omission of the role of female labor and "disinterest" would explain such omissions.

"Advances" does provide a contrast, and is thus the correct answer. In the sentence containing Blank (iii), "yet" indicates a contrast between the makeup of the workforce and the availability of data about the workforce. Because the author says that women outnumbered men in the workforce, the contrast would likely require data that mostly concerned men. Of the three choices for Blank (iii), "incorporate data only" conveys this sense. The other two options can be ruled out because of the previous sentence's assertion that female labor is ignored by economic analyses. With women being excluded from the data, it follows that it is mostly about men; therefore it does not make sense to assert that information about male labor is suppressed or too infrequently discussed.

Thus the correct answer is **track** (Choice A), **advances** (Choice D), and **incorporate data only** (Choice G).

7. It is a sad but just indictment of some high school history textbooks that they frequently report as (i) _____ claims that historians hotly debate or that are even completely (ii) _____ by (iii) _____ primary sources.

Blank (i)	Blank (ii)	Blank (iii)
(A) factual	(D) resolved	(G) dubious
(B) controversial	(E) corroborated	(H) incomplete
(C) sensational	(F) contradicted	(I) reliable

Explanation

The use of the word "indictment," meaning a charge of wrongdoing, indicates that the sentence is sharply criticizing the textbooks in question and that the blanks must be completed with words that support this critique. Blank (i) describes how such textbooks characterize historical claims that are hotly debated. Since such claims are in fact controversial, it would not be surprising or inaccurate for textbooks to report them as such, so "controversial" is not correct. Of the other two responses, "sensational" has some merit, suggesting that the textbooks resort to a melodramatic presentation of historical debate; however, "factual" is the better choice, implying as it does gross inaccuracies. That the critique of the textbooks centers upon accuracy rather than tone is confirmed by the rest of the sentence, which deals with the relationship between the textbooks' claims and the primary sources upon which historical scholarship is based. The "even" that precedes Blank (ii) calls for a word that is yet further away from factual than "hotly debated." Of the choices, only "contradicted" fits this criterion; the other two options are the opposite of what is needed. Finally, Blank (iii) calls for a word that describes the primary sources. Since the critique of the textbooks' accuracy rests upon their divergence from these sources, the sources themselves must be characterized as authoritative. "Reliable" does exactly that, while "dubious" and "incomplete" suggest the opposite.

Thus the correct answer is **factual** (Choice A), **contradicted** (Choice F), and **reliable** (Choice I).

8. The reason minimum temperatures are going up more rapidly than maximums may involve cloud cover and evaporative cooling. Clouds tend to keep the days cooler by reflecting sunlight, and the nights warmer by (i) _____ loss of heat from Earth's surface. Greater amounts of moisture in the soil from additional precipitation and cloudiness (ii) _____ the daytime temperature increases because part of the solar energy is (iii) _____ the evaporation of that moisture.

Blank (i)	Blank (ii)	Blank (iii)
Ⓐ inhibiting	Ⓓ augment	Ⓖ intensified by
Ⓑ exacerbating	Ⓔ mask	Ⓗ unrelated to
Ⓒ replicating	Ⓕ restrain	Ⓘ used up in

Explanation

The second sentence asserts that clouds make for warmer nights by doing something to the loss of heat from Earth. Since less heat lost means more warmth, a word that means preventing or slowing heat loss is required for Blank (i). "Inhibiting" is therefore the answer. "Exacerbating" has the opposite meaning, while "replicating" makes no sense in this context. Since the first sentence asserts that daytime highs are increasing less rapidly than nighttime lows, Blank (ii) calls for a verb that indicates a moderation in rises in temperature during the day, and "restrain" has this sense. "Augment," meaning to increase, has the opposite meaning, while "mask" would indicate that measurements are not reflecting actual increases in temperature, an idea not supported by the rest of the passage. The "because" in the last sentence indicates that the second clause explains how daytime temperature increases are restrained; it does so by making reference to solar energy and the evaporation of moisture. Because solar energy is responsible for increases in daytime temperature, the answer to Blank (iii) requires a word that explains how evaporation can lessen or divert that energy for other purposes. "Used up in" does this because it indicates that less solar energy is available to warm the Earth's surface when a portion of it is instead devoted to evaporation. Neither "intensified by" nor "unrelated to" indicate a connection between solar energy and evaporation that would lessen warming.

Thus the correct answer is **inhibiting** (Choice A), **restrain** (Choice F), and **used up in** (Choice I).

PRACTICE SET 3: Hard

> **For each of Questions 1 to 8, select <u>one</u> entry for each blank from the corresponding column of choices. Fill all blanks in the way that best completes the text.**

1. In searching for norms in the sense of authoritative standards of what ought to be, rather than in the sense of what is average and thus can be considered normal, normative ethics aims to _____.

Ⓐ	predict
Ⓑ	mitigate
Ⓒ	question
Ⓓ	dictate
Ⓔ	personalize

Explanation

The sentence defines normative ethics by specifying the sense of the "norms" for which it searches. Since these are authoritative ethical standards, the word that fills the blank must describe the act of establishing those standards. The choice that does this is "dictate." Of the other choices, "predict" suggests that normative ethics merely attempts to describe future behavior rather than establish what guidelines should shape it, while "personalize" suggests a concern with individual circumstances that is not otherwise addressed in the sentence. "Mitigate" (to moderate or alleviate) is likewise incongruent with the rest of the sentence, while "question" does not address normative ethics' concern with establishing rather than questioning norms.

   Thus the correct answer is **dictate** (Choice D).

2. When she first came to France from Bulgaria, she was hardly the _____ student she later made herself out to be, since she had access to considerable family wealth.

Ⓐ	naïve
Ⓑ	precocious
Ⓒ	impecunious
Ⓓ	ambitious
Ⓔ	assiduous

Explanation

The student's considerable family wealth is cited as proof that her later depiction of herself was false; the word that fills the blank describes this later depiction, so it must be an adjective that is incompatible with wealth. "Impecunious," meaning penniless, is therefore the correct choice. None of the other responses is dependent on wealth—her family's finances would have no bearing on whether the student was actually naïve, precocious (advanced for her age), ambitious, or assiduous (diligent)—so they are incorrect.

   Thus the correct answer is **impecunious** (Choice C).

3. Researchers have observed chimpanzees feigning injury in order to influence other members of the group, thus showing that the capacity to _____ is not uniquely human.

Ⓐ	cooperate
Ⓑ	instruct
Ⓒ	conspire
Ⓓ	dissemble
Ⓔ	dominate

Explanation

The words "thus showing" suggest that the capacity that is not unique to humans was demonstrated by the activity the researchers observed. Since that activity—feigning injury to influence others—requires the capacity to transmit false information, "dissemble" is the correct answer. Because there is no indication that the chimpanzees worked together to feign injury, "conspire" is incorrect. None of the other options— "dominate," "instruct," or "cooperate"—suggests the pretense involved in feigning an injury, so they are all incorrect.

Thus the correct answer is **dissemble** (Choice D).

4. Instant celebrity is often (i) _____ asset because if there is no (ii) _____ to interest the public—no stage or screen triumphs, no interesting books, no heroic exploits—people quickly become bored.

Blank (i)	Blank (ii)
Ⓐ a fleeting	Ⓓ competing attraction
Ⓑ an incomparable	Ⓔ continuity of exposure
Ⓒ an untapped	Ⓕ real achievement

Explanation

The sentence says that people quickly become bored with those who achieve sudden fame in the absence of the condition named by Blank (ii), implying that instant celebrity often does not last long; among the answer choices for Blank (i) only "a fleeting" matches this meaning, so it is correct. The answer to Blank (ii) must be an umbrella term for things listed in the second part of the sentence as defeaters of boredom: "screen triumphs," "interesting books," "heroic exploits." The answer choice that best matches this meaning is "real achievement," so it is correct. "Competing attraction" also seems a plausible choice for Blank (ii), but it is incorrect because the sentence does not mention competition between attractions.

Thus the correct answer is **a fleeting** (Choice A) and **real achievement** (Choice F).

5. At their best, (i) _____ book reviews are written in defense of value and in the tacit hope that the author, having had his or her (ii) _____ pointed out, might secretly agree that the book could be improved.

Blank (i)	Blank (ii)
Ⓐ abstruse	Ⓓ strengths
Ⓑ adverse	Ⓔ transgressions
Ⓒ hortatory	Ⓕ assumptions

Explanation

The second part of the sentence talks about the author agreeing that the book can be improved after the things named by Blank (ii) are pointed out; therefore, the answer to Blank (ii) must denote something negative whose presence calls for improvement. The only answer choice for Blank (ii) that is negative in meaning is "transgressions," so it is correct. Book reviews that point out the author's transgressions are negative in nature, so the answer to Blank (i) must be negative in meaning; the only answer choice that meets this condition is "adverse," so it is correct.

Thus the correct answer is **adverse** (Choice B) and **transgressions** (Choice E).

6. The gaps in existing accounts of the playwright's life are not (i) _____, since much of the documentary evidence on which historians have relied is (ii) _____.

Blank (i)	Blank (ii)
(A) trifling	(D) credible
(B) obvious	(E) extant
(C) implicit	(F) incomplete

Explanation

The sentence focuses on the relationship between the gaps in existing accounts of a life and the evidence used to produce those accounts. Since "gaps" implies a concern with completeness, the characterization of that evidence that makes the most sense for Blank (ii) is "incomplete." The other choices, "credible" or "extant," could explain the accuracy or verifiability of the accounts in question but nothing about the gaps themselves. Once it is determined that "incomplete" is the best choice for characterizing the evidence, it follows that the gaps in the accounts based on that evidence would likely be considerable, so the opposite of considerable, "trifling," is the correct answer for Blank (i).

Thus the correct answer is **trifling** (Choice A) and **incomplete** (Choice F).

7. That today's students of American culture tend to (i) _____ classical music is understandable. In our own time, America's musical high culture has degenerated into a formulaic entertainment divorced from the contemporary moment. Thus, to miss out on what our orchestras are up to is not to (ii) _____ much. In the late Gilded Age, however, music was widely esteemed as the "queen of the arts." Classical music was in its American heyday, (iii) _____ the culture at large.

Blank (i)	Blank (ii)	Blank (iii)
(A) promote	(D) sacrifice	(G) antagonistic toward
(B) reinterpret	(E) appreciate	(H) generally rejected by
(C) ignore	(F) malign	(I) centrally embedded in

Explanation

The "however" of the next-to-last sentence indicates that the author's characterization of the relationship between classical music and popular culture during the Gilded Age contrasts with the current state of affairs. Since music was widely esteemed during the Gilded Age, it follows that it is viewed more negatively, or disregarded, during the current era. Of the choices for Blank (i), "ignore" is the only choice that conveys this sentiment; "promote" connotes the opposite, while "reinterpret" suggests a different sort of positive engagement with classical music that is otherwise unmentioned in the passage. The author characterizes the current disconnection between music and culture as understandable, and uses pejorative language ("degenerated," "formulaic") to describe current classical music. Of the three choices for Blank (ii), "sacrifice" best conveys this dismissive attitude; "appreciate" would convey that those who forego orchestral concerts are indeed missing something worthwhile, while "malign" overstates the presumed level of feeling and activity of one who simply does not attend concerts. Since the lack of a connection between culture and classical music must contrast with the relationship during the Gilded Age, the answer to Blank (iii) is "centrally embedded in." Of the other two choices, "generally rejected by" would provide no contrast, while "antagonistic toward" suggests a relationship that would not explain why music was so widely esteemed.

Thus the correct answer is **ignore** (Choice C), **sacrifice** (Choice D), and **centrally embedded in** (Choice I).

8. The serious study of popular culture by intellectuals is regularly credited with having rendered obsolete a once-dominant view that popular culture is inherently inferior to high art. Yet this alteration of attitudes may be somewhat (i) _____. Although it is now academically respectable to analyze popular culture, the fact that many intellectuals feel compelled to rationalize their own (ii) _____ action movies or mass-market fiction reveals, perhaps unwittingly, their continued (iii) _____ the old hierarchy of high and low culture.

Blank (i)	Blank (ii)	Blank (iii)
(A) counterproductive	(D) penchant for	(G) aversion to
(B) underappreciated	(E) distaste for	(H) investment in
(C) overstated	(F) indifference to	(I) misunderstanding of

Explanation

The sentence discusses a purported change in how popular culture and high art are relatively valued; the author is scrutinizing the notion that the academic study of the former has significantly raised its once lowly status. In the last sentence, Blank (iii) is preceded by the word "continued," indicating that something about intellectuals' view of the hierarchy of culture has remained unchanged. Since the author states in the first sentence that this hierarchy was once dominant, "investment in" the hierarchy would indicate that sense of continuity. Neither of the other two options is supported by the passage because there is no indication the author believes that intellectuals have a long-held aversion to or misunderstanding of that hierarchy. The "although" that begins the last sentence indicates that the phrase completed by Blank (ii) will contrast the respectability of analyses of popular culture with something that nonetheless reveals a continued allegiance to the hierarchy. A need to explain away a "distaste for" or an "indifference to" action movies or pulp fiction would not indicate any such allegiance, so those choices must be incorrect. However, a need to justify one's penchant or liking for popular culture would indicate an adherence to the high-low culture hierarchy. Thus "penchant for" is the correct choice for Blank (ii). Finally, since the author is suggesting that the hierarchy given to high and low culture is not obsolete as some claim, it follows that the shift in attitudes is exaggerated; thus, the correct answer to Blank (i) is "overstated." "Underappreciated" implies the opposite, and "counterproductive" implies a judgment about the value of the hierarchy, whereas the passage is primarily concerned with its existence.

Thus the correct answer is **overstated** (Choice C), **penchant for** (Choice D), and **investment in** (Choice H).

5 Question Type 3: Sentence Equivalence

Your goals for this chapter	⇒ Practice answering GRE Sentence Equivalence questions ⇒ Review answers and explanations, particularly for questions you answered incorrectly

This chapter contains three sets of practice Sentence Equivalence questions. The sets are arranged in order of increasing difficulty, one easy, one medium, and one hard.

Following the third set are answer keys for quick reference. Then, at the end of the chapter, you will find complete explanations for every question. Each explanation is presented with the corresponding question, so that you can easily see what was asked and what the various answer choices were.

Sharpen your GRE Verbal Reasoning skills by working your way through these question sets, remembering to use the Tips for Answering given in Chapter 2. Begin with the easy set and then move on to the medium-difficulty and hard sets. Review the answer explanations carefully, paying particular attention to the explanations for questions that you answered incorrectly. Were you able to

- understand the overall meaning of the passage?
- identify significant words in the passage?
- think up your own words for the blanks?
- identify suitable matching words to fill the blanks?

Turn the page to begin.

PRACTICE SET 1: Easy

> For each of Questions 1 to 5, select the <u>two</u> answer choices that, when used to complete the sentence, fit the meaning of the sentence as a whole <u>and</u> produce completed sentences that are alike in meaning.

1. Retrofitted with stabilizing devices, some of which _____ its aesthetics, the bridge has been reopened, no longer prone to excessive swaying but not quite the breathtaking structure it originally was.

   A impair
   B resist
   C improve
   D enhance
   E restore
   F compromise

2. Although cosmic objects have struck Earth since the planet's very formation, humanity has only recently become aware of these events: two centuries ago the idea that objects orbiting the Sun could collide with Earth was widely _____.

   A ridiculed
   B doubted
   C disseminated
   D promulgated
   E marginalized
   F disbelieved

3. That people _____ the musical features of birdsongs suggests that despite the vast evolutionary gulf between birds and mammals, songbirds and humans share some common auditory perceptual abilities.

   A mimic
   B recognize
   C relish
   D are confounded by
   E can make out
   F are puzzled by

4. Torpey's study has turned a seemingly _____ topic, the passport, into a fascinating one by making an original contribution to the sociology of the state.

    A ironic
    B banal
    C provocative
    D witty
    E insipid
    F stimulating

5. Britain is attractive to worldwide advertisers because it is _____ market, so there is no need to tailor advertisements for different parts of the country.

    A a global
    B an uncomplicated
    C a vast
    D a homogeneous
    E a uniform
    F an immense

PRACTICE SET 2: Medium

> **For each of Questions 1 to 8, select the <u>two</u> answer choices that, when used to complete the sentence, fit the meaning of the sentence as a whole <u>and</u> produce completed sentences that are alike in meaning.**

1. The band's long-standing strategy of laying leisurely explorations atop a steady funk beat has proven to be surprisingly _____: a concert in Cologne from 1972 sounds as if it could have taken place today.

    A fortuitous
    B foresighted
    C prescient
    D popular
    E serendipitous
    F lucrative

2. Factory production made an absence of imperfections so blandly commonplace that the _____ of hand-produced goods were now cherished where they once might have been shunned.

    A advantages
    B revivals
    C benefits
    D pretensions
    E blemishes
    F defects

3. Through its state associations, the American Medical Association controlled who could become a physician and dominated _____ professions like nursing and occupational therapy.

    A commensurate
    B proportionate
    C kindred
    D affiliated
    E imperative
    F voluntary

4. In a strong indication of the way the entire party is _____ the candidate with moderate credentials, the outspokenly conservative former mayor of a major city has promised to raise a substantial amount of money for the candidate's campaign.

    A rallying behind
    B incensed over
    C undecided about
    D mortified over
    E embarrassed about
    F coalescing around

5. Mr. Hirsch says he will aim to preserve the foundation's support of _____ thinkers, individuals who are going against the trends in a field or an acknowledged set of opinions.

    A iconoclastic
    B integrative
    C doctrinaire
    D heterodox
    E dogmatic
    F synthesizing

6. In France cultural subsidies are _____: producers of just about any film can get an advance from the government against box-office receipts, even though most such loans are never fully repaid.

    A ubiquitous
    B invaluable
    C sporadic
    D scanty
    E questionable
    F omnipresent

7. The problem of avoiding duplicate names—such as for Internet domain names or for e-mail accounts—is particularly _____ when the name has to fit into a format that allows only a finite number of possibilities.

    A meager
    B acute
    C agreeable
    D severe
    E beneficial
    F productive

8. At nearly 450 pages, the novel is _____: the author does not often resist the temptation to finish off a chapter, section, or even paragraph with some unnecessary flourish.

    A instructive
    B complex
    C prolix
    D educational
    E long-winded
    F explicit

PRACTICE SET 3: Hard

> For each of Questions 1 to 7, select the <u>two</u> answer choices that, when used to complete the sentence, fit the meaning of the sentence as a whole <u>and</u> produce completed sentences that are alike in meaning.

1. If researchers can determine exactly what is wrong with people who suffer from this condition, they may be able to suggest drug therapies or other treatments that could _____ the effects of the damage.

   A mitigate
   B exacerbate
   C specify
   D identify
   E ameliorate
   F stabilize

2. Some analysts worry about consumers' perception that the electronics industry is always on the verge of major breakthroughs; that perception could hurt the industry by making consumers reluctant to buy products they believe will soon be _____.

   A incompatible
   B devalued
   C obsolete
   D ubiquitous
   E everywhere
   F outmoded

3. After people began to make the transition from gathering food to producing food, human societies followed markedly _____ courses; some adopted herding, others took to tillage, and still others stuck to foraging.

   A divergent
   B rural
   C novel
   D unfamiliar
   E disparate
   F quotidian

4. In *The Simple Soybean*, the author is much less restrained in his enthusiasm for the bean's medical efficacy than he is in his technical writings, but he still cautions against treating soy as a _____.

    A staple
    B supplement
    C herald
    D panacea
    E cure-all
    F harbinger

5. Parkin's characterization of the movement as neoscholastic is too _____ to be accepted without further investigation.

    A cursory
    B detailed
    C perfunctory
    D biased
    E self-evident
    F complete

6. A recent study suggests that vitamin E supplements, despite widespread belief in their _____, are no better than sugar pills for delaying the onset of the degenerative disease.

    A potential
    B misuse
    C popularity
    D efficacy
    E prevalence
    F usefulness

7. Despite her relaxed and flexible style, Ms. de la Fressange is _____ businesswoman who knows how to market her brand: herself.

    A a ruthless
    B a creative
    C a canny
    D an industrious
    E a shrewd
    F an effective

ANSWER KEY

PRACTICE SET 1: Easy

1. **Choice A**: impair; AND **Choice F**: compromise
2. **Choice B**: doubted; AND **Choice F**: disbelieved
3. **Choice B**: recognize; AND **Choice E**: can make out
4. **Choice B**: banal; AND **Choice E**: insipid
5. **Choice D**: a homogeneous; AND **Choice E**: a uniform

PRACTICE SET 2: Medium

1. **Choice B**: foresighted; AND **Choice C**: prescient
2. **Choice E**: blemishes; AND **Choice F**: defects
3. **Choice C**: kindred; AND **Choice D**: affiliated
4. **Choice A**: rallying behind; AND **Choice F**: coalescing around
5. **Choice A**: iconoclastic; AND **Choice D**: heterodox
6. **Choice A**: ubiquitous; AND **Choice F**: omnipresent
7. **Choice B**: acute; AND **Choice D**: severe
8. **Choice C**: prolix; AND **Choice E**: long-winded

PRACTICE SET 3: Hard

1. **Choice A**: mitigate; AND **Choice E**: ameliorate
2. **Choice C**: obsolete; AND **Choice F**: outmoded
3. **Choice A**: divergent; AND **Choice E**: disparate
4. **Choice D**: panacea; AND **Choice E**: cure-all
5. **Choice A**: cursory; AND **Choice C**: perfunctory
6. **Choice D**: efficacy; AND **Choice F**: usefulness
7. **Choice C**: a canny; AND **Choice E**: a shrewd

Answers and Explanations

PRACTICE SET 1: Easy

> For each of Questions 1 to 5, select the <u>two</u> answer choices that, when used to complete the sentence, fit the meaning of the sentence as a whole <u>and</u> produce completed sentences that are alike in meaning.

1. Retrofitted with stabilizing devices, some of which _____ its aesthetics, the bridge has been reopened, no longer prone to excessive swaying but not quite the breathtaking structure it originally was.

   A impair
   B resist
   C improve
   D enhance
   E restore
   F compromise

Explanation

The sentence suggests that the addition of devices to make the bridge more stable has consequently lessened its previous aesthetic impact as a "breathtaking structure." The words "restore," "improve," and "enhance" do not describe the appropriate qualitative direction of the change caused by the retrofitting as "impair" and "compromise" do. Though "resist" makes some sense when inserted into the blank, it does not produce a sentence with the same meaning as either of these.

   Thus the correct answer is **impair** (Choice A) and **compromise** (Choice F).

2. Although cosmic objects have struck Earth since the planet's very formation, humanity has only recently become aware of these events: two centuries ago the idea that objects orbiting the Sun could collide with Earth was widely _____.

   A ridiculed
   B doubted
   C disseminated
   D promulgated
   E marginalized
   F disbelieved

Explanation

The colon introduces an example that explains or demonstrates the former lack of awareness about cosmic collisions with Earth. Because people were not aware of the existence of events of this type, the idea of their possibility would not have been "disseminated" or "promulgated." Although "ridiculed" and "marginalized" make sense when inserted into the blank, they do not produce sentences with the same meaning, which "doubted" and "disbelieved" do.

   Thus the correct answer is **doubted** (Choice B) and **disbelieved** (Choice F).

3. That people _____ the musical features of birdsongs suggests that despite the vast evolutionary gulf between birds and mammals, songbirds and humans share some common auditory perceptual abilities.

    A mimic
    B recognize
    C relish
    D are confounded by
    E can make out
    F are puzzled by

Explanation

According to the sentence, some human ability or other suggests that humans share a perceptual ability with songbirds. The words that fill the blank must allow for the existence of this ability in humans, which "are confounded by" and "are puzzled by" do not. Although both "mimic" and "relish" make sense when inserted into the blank, they each designate more than just perception, and they both lack another word that would create a sentence similar in meaning.

Thus the correct answer is **recognize** (Choice B) and **can make out** (Choice E).

4. Torpey's study has turned a seemingly _____ topic, the passport, into a fascinating one by making an original contribution to the sociology of the state.

    A ironic
    B banal
    C provocative
    D witty
    E insipid
    F stimulating

Explanation

The adjective "seemingly" indicates that the words that fill the blank will contrast with "fascinating." Of the responses, "banal" and "insipid" are both opposites of "fascinating," and they yield sentences alike in meaning, so they are the correct response. While "provocative" and "stimulating" are near in meaning, they do not provide any contrast to "fascinating," so they are incorrect. Neither of the other responses has a near synonym among the choices, nor do they provide any opposition to the characterization of the passport as a fascinating topic.

Thus the correct answer is **banal** (Choice B) and **insipid** (Choice E).

5. Britain is attractive to worldwide advertisers because it is _____ market, so there is no need to tailor advertisements for different parts of the country.

    A a global
    B an uncomplicated
    C a vast
    D a homogeneous
    E a uniform
    F an immense

Explanation

The sentence describes a country whose different parts share a similarity that does not require differential action (tailoring for different parts) by advertisers. The blank must designate this sameness. While the words "vast" and "immense" produce sentences with the same meaning—and "global" less so—they all describe size, not similarity. Being "uncomplicated" might also attract advertisers, but it suggests a different virtue than similarity, and there is no other word that produces a sentence with the same meaning.

Thus the correct answer is **a homogenous** (Choice D) and **a uniform** (Choice E).

PRACTICE SET 2: Medium

> **For each of Questions 1 to 8, select the <u>two</u> answer choices that, when used to complete the sentence, fit the meaning of the sentence as a whole <u>and</u> produce completed sentences that are alike in meaning.**

1. The band's long-standing strategy of laying leisurely explorations atop a steady funk beat has proven to be surprisingly _____: a concert in Cologne from 1972 sounds as if it could have taken place today.

   A fortuitous
   B foresighted
   C prescient
   D popular
   E serendipitous
   F lucrative

Explanation

The colon indicates that the second part of the sentence supports the assertion made in the first part. Since this second part emphasizes the modern sound of the 1972 concert, the blank calls for choices that refer to the similarities between the band's 1972 sound and music characteristic of more recent times. Both "foresighted" and "prescient" suggest that the band's musical strategy anticipated the trends of the coming decades, so they are the correct choice. Of the other responses, "fortuitous" and "serendipitous" are similar in meaning, but they do not fit well with the word "surprisingly," nor with the emphasis on the band's having a long-term strategy. Neither "popular" nor "lucrative" have a synonym among the other choices; moreover, they too go beyond the sentence's emphasis on the band's seemingly timeless style.

   Thus the correct answer is **foresighted** (Choice B) and **prescient** (Choice C).

2. Factory production made an absence of imperfections so blandly commonplace that the _____ of hand-produced goods were now cherished where they once might have been shunned.

    A advantages
    B revivals
    C benefits
    D pretensions
    E blemishes
    F defects

Explanation

The sentence suggests a contrast between the quality of factory-produced goods, marked by an absence of imperfections, with that of hand-produced goods, which must possess such imperfections. The words "blemishes" and "defects" are the only ones that connote imperfection. While "advantages" and "benefits" produce sentences with the same meaning, they neither connote imperfection nor make sense as one would not necessarily shun a product with such positive attributes. The word "revivals" also does not connote imperfection, and there is no other word that would produce a sentence with the same meaning.

    Thus the correct answer is **blemishes** (Choice E) and **defects** (Choice F).

3. Through its state associations, the American Medical Association controlled who could become a physician and dominated _____ professions like nursing and occupational therapy.

    A commensurate
    B proportionate
    C kindred
    D affiliated
    E imperative
    F voluntary

Explanation

The blank calls for words that will describe professions such as nursing and occupational therapy as they relate to physicians. These professions are also in the health-care field; the answer choices "kindred" and "affiliated" both suggest this close relationship and produce completed sentences that are similar in meaning. Of the other choices, both "commensurate" and "proportionate" suggest some sort of comparative measurement between the professions mentioned, something unsupported by the rest of the sentence. Neither "imperative" nor "voluntary" would typically be used to describe "profession" nor does either have a word close in meaning among the other choices with which it could be paired.

    Thus the correct answer is **kindred** (Choice C) and **affiliated** (Choice D).

4. In a strong indication of the way the entire party is _____ the candidate with moderate credentials, the outspokenly conservative former mayor of a major city has promised to raise a substantial amount of money for the candidate's campaign.

    A rallying behind
    B incensed over
    C undecided about
    D mortified over
    E embarrassed about
    F coalescing around

Explanation

The former mayor's promise to raise funds is used as an example of the party's attitude or actions toward the candidate. Since raising funds is a way of supporting a candidate, the words filling the blank must be positive rather than negative. Only two of the choices given, "rallying behind" and "coalescing around," indicate a positive attitude toward the candidate; moreover, they also produce similar meanings, so they are the correct answer. The other four choices indicate negative or indifferent attitudes toward the candidate that would not be exemplified by promises of fund-raising.

Thus the correct answer is **rallying behind** (Choice A) and **coalescing around** (Choice F).

5. Mr. Hirsch says he will aim to preserve the foundation's support of _____ thinkers, individuals who are going against the trends in a field or an acknowledged set of opinions.

    A iconoclastic
    B integrative
    C doctrinaire
    D heterodox
    E dogmatic
    F synthesizing

Explanation

The portion of the sentence following the comma defines the type of thinkers characterized by the words that will fill the blank. The challenge posed by this item, then, is mainly one of vocabulary: the answers must be words that describe individuals who go against the trends in a field or against a set of opinions. "Iconoclastic" and "heterodox" mean exactly that, with both words describing people whose opinions run counter to established norms. Of the other choices, "doctrinaire" and "dogmatic" both mean the opposite—adhering to established principles—while "integrative" and "synthesizing" both refer to a willingness to bring together disparate points of view.

Thus the correct answer is **iconoclastic** (Choice A) and **heterodox** (Choice D).

6. In France cultural subsidies are _____: producers of just about any film can get an advance from the government against box-office receipts, even though most such loans are never fully repaid.

    Ⓐ ubiquitous
    Ⓑ invaluable
    Ⓒ sporadic
    Ⓓ scanty
    Ⓔ questionable
    Ⓕ omnipresent

Explanation

The colon signals that the second part of the sentence provides an example of the first part, so the blank must characterize the idea that *just about any* film (as an instance of subsidized culture) gets an advance. This rules out "sporadic" and "scanty" neither of which suggest the pervasiveness of the subsidies. While "invaluable" and "questionable" may make some sense, they do not produce sentences with the same meaning.

Thus the correct answer is **ubiquitous** (Choice A) and **omnipresent** (Choice F).

7. The problem of avoiding duplicate names—such as for Internet domain names or for e-mail accounts—is particularly _____ when the name has to fit into a format that allows only a finite number of possibilities.

    Ⓐ meager
    Ⓑ acute
    Ⓒ agreeable
    Ⓓ severe
    Ⓔ beneficial
    Ⓕ productive

Explanation

The blank must be filled with a word that describes the challenge of ensuring unique names under certain limitations. Since these limitations add to the difficulty of avoiding duplication, the blank must be filled with choices that reflect the arduousness of this task. To characterize the problem as particularly "acute" or "severe" would do this nicely; both adjectives indicate the added difficulty of the problem under the circumstances described, and the pairing renders sentences with similar meanings. None of the other responses describe the difficulty of the problem that the rest of the sentence emphasizes.

Thus the correct answer is **acute** (Choice B) and **severe** (Choice D).

8. At nearly 450 pages, the novel is _____: the author does not often resist the temptation to finish off a chapter, section, or even paragraph with some unnecessary flourish.

A instructive
B complex
C prolix
D educational
E long-winded
F explicit

Explanation

The words that fill the blank in must convey that the novel is not merely long but also contains numerous portions deemed unnecessary. While it may be "instructive" and "educational" these do not properly describe the novel's length. While "complex" and "explicit" may correlate with (though not characterize) length, they do not produce sentences with the same meaning.

Thus the correct answer is **prolix** (Choice C) and **long-winded** (Choice E).

PRACTICE SET 3: Hard

> **For each of Questions 1 to 7, select the <u>two</u> answer choices that, when used to complete the sentence, fit the meaning of the sentence as a whole <u>and</u> produce completed sentences that are alike in meaning.**

1. If researchers can determine exactly what is wrong with people who suffer from this condition, they may be able to suggest drug therapies or other treatments that could _____ the effects of the damage.

   [A] mitigate
   [B] exacerbate
   [C] specify
   [D] identify
   [E] ameliorate
   [F] stabilize

Explanation

The sentence suggests that more information about a damaging condition will allow researchers to lessen future negative effects. While "specify" and "identify" create sentences with approximately the same meaning, the sentence also suggests that the researchers are seeking to control effects that are already known rather than needing further specificity or identification. Even in this limited context, it is unreasonable that researchers would wish to "exacerbate" or increase the negative effects of damage, and there is no other word that creates a sentence with the same meaning. "Stabilize" implies that the negative effects would simply be controlled, rather than lessened, and likewise there is no other word that produces a sentence with the same meaning.

   Thus the correct answer is **mitigate** (Choice A) and **ameliorate** (Choice E).

2. Some analysts worry about consumers' perception that the electronics industry is always on the verge of major breakthroughs; that perception could hurt the industry by making consumers reluctant to buy products they believe will soon be _____.

   [A] incompatible
   [B] devalued
   [C] obsolete
   [D] ubiquitous
   [E] everywhere
   [F] outmoded

Explanation

The blank characterizes products that consumers fear will be superseded in quality as a result of industry breakthroughs. While "ubiquitous" and "everywhere" produce sentences with the same meaning, they assume an increase in volume or sales that is not necessarily implied by innovatory breakthroughs. And while "devalued" makes for a coherent sentence, there is no other word that would produce a sentence with the same meaning.

   Thus the correct answer is **obsolete** (Choice C) and **outmoded** (Choice F).

3. After people began to make the transition from gathering food to producing food, human societies followed markedly _____ courses; some adopted herding, others took to tillage, and still others stuck to foraging.

    A divergent
    B rural
    C novel
    D unfamiliar
    E disparate
    F quotidian

Explanation

The sentence describes the variable courses of three different societies after the beginning of a transition, and the blank characterizes the differences among these courses. While "rural" and "quotidian" may describe a common quality of each course, they do not emphasize their variability. And while the words "novel" and "unfamiliar" are alike in meaning, they do not fit the context, since one of the paths taken (sticking to foraging) is precisely neither novel nor unfamiliar.

Thus the correct answer is **divergent** (Choice A) and **disparate** (Choice E).

4. In *The Simple Soybean*, the author is much less restrained in his enthusiasm for the bean's medical efficacy than he is in his technical writings, but he still cautions against treating soy as a _____.

    A staple
    B supplement
    C herald
    D panacea
    E cure-all
    F harbinger

Explanation

The blank characterizes the medical efficacy or effectiveness of soy. While the words "herald" and "harbinger" are similar in meaning, they do not characterize medical effectiveness as "panacea" and "cure-all" do. Nor do "staple" and "supplement," each of which may refer to a medical regime or a dosage but not to efficacy.

Thus the correct answer is **panacea** (Choice D) and **cure-all** (Choice E).

5. Parkin's characterization of the movement as neoscholastic is too _____ to be accepted without further investigation.

   A cursory
   B detailed
   C perfunctory
   D biased
   E self-evident
   F complete

Explanation

The blank describes Parkin's characterization as demanding further investigation. If the characterization is too "complete" or too "self-evident," there is nothing further to investigate; if it is too "detailed" but not flawed, there is no reason to investigate further. The word "biased" does suggest that further investigation is necessary, but there is no other word that produces a sentence alike in meaning.

   Thus the correct answer is **cursory** (Choice A) and **perfunctory** (Choice C).

6. A recent study suggests that vitamin E supplements, despite widespread belief in their _____, are no better than sugar pills for delaying the onset of the degenerative disease.

   A potential
   B misuse
   C popularity
   D efficacy
   E prevalence
   F usefulness

Explanation

The sentence suggests that vitamin E supplements are ineffective in deterring the disease, and the use of the word "despite" indicates that this ineffectiveness contrasts with how they are widely viewed. The words that fill the blank, then, must mean the opposite of "ineffectiveness." Among the answer choices, the words that do so are "efficacy" and "usefulness." Of the other choices, "potential" is tempting, but it does not contrast as directly with "ineffectiveness," nor does it have a near synonym among the other answers with which it could be paired. "Prevalence" and "popularity" might be initially attractive because the passage suggests that these words might describe the use of vitamin E supplements, but the blank calls for a word that characterizes how they are viewed rather than how they are used.

   Thus the correct answer is **efficacy** (Choice D) and **usefulness** (Choice F).

7. Despite her relaxed and flexible style, Ms. de la Fressange is _____ businesswoman who knows how to market her brand: herself.

    A a ruthless
    B a creative
    C a canny
    D an industrious
    E a shrewd
    F an effective

Explanation

The sentence describes Ms. de la Fressange as a businesswoman but none of the words besides "canny" and "shrewd" provide sentences that are alike in meaning.

Thus the correct answer is **a canny** (Choice C) and **a shrewd** (Choice E).

Mixed Practice Sets

Your goals for this chapter	⇨ Practice answering all three types of GRE Verbal Reasoning questions ⇨ Review answers and explanations, particularly for questions you answered incorrectly

This chapter contains three practice sets of 25 questions. Each set contains a representative mixture of all three question types: Reading Comprehension, Text Completion, and Sentence Equivalence. Following each set of questions is an answer key for quick reference. After the answer key, you will find complete explanations for every question. Each explanation is presented with the corresponding question for easy reference. Review the answers and explanations carefully, paying particular attention to explanations for questions that you answered incorrectly.

To use these practice sets most effectively, take them under actual test conditions. Find a quiet place to work, and set aside enough time to work on one set without being disturbed. You should allow 35 minutes to work through one set. Work only on one set at a time, and use a watch or timer to keep track of your time.

Please note that these sets of questions are structured like individual Verbal Reasoning sections in the paper-delivered test. If you are taking the computer-delivered GRE revised General Test, the sections will contain only 20 questions and you will be given 30 minutes to answer them. If you can successfully complete each practice set in this book in 35 minutes, you will be well prepared for the actual test, but for a more realistic experience of the computer-delivered test, you should also use the practice tests in the free *POWERPREP® II* software.

PRACTICE SET 1

For each question, indicate the best answer, using the directions given.

> **For each of Questions 1 to 8, select <u>one</u> entry for each blank from the corresponding column of choices. Fill all blanks in the way that best completes the text.**

1. The name of the Sloane Matthew Library has long been _____ ; even longtime city residents assume it is a run-of-the-mill library, never suspecting what art treasures it contains.

Ⓐ	revered
Ⓑ	proposed
Ⓒ	misleading
Ⓓ	elevated
Ⓔ	intriguing

2. Although economic growth has conventionally been viewed as the _____ for poverty in underdeveloped regions, this prescription's negative environmental side effects are becoming a concern.

Ⓐ	culprit
Ⓑ	recipe
Ⓒ	panacea
Ⓓ	explanation
Ⓔ	refuge

3. Even as the economy struggled, the secretary stood by his _____ long-term outlook, saying that technology was allowing businesses to make deep-rooted improvements in their productivity, the best indicator of an economy's ability to grow.

Ⓐ	arcane
Ⓑ	sanguine
Ⓒ	equivocal
Ⓓ	ambivalent
Ⓔ	irresolute

4. The villas and compounds that proliferated during the building boom of the 1990s were (i) _____, far too (ii) _____ for people of average means.

Blank (i)		Blank (ii)	
Ⓐ	opulent	Ⓓ	bucolic
Ⓑ	eclectic	Ⓔ	expensive
Ⓒ	enigmatic	Ⓕ	mundane

5. The governor has considerable political talents, but as a speaker he is far less
    (i) _____ than his opponent, whose oratorical skills are (ii) _____.

Blank (i)	Blank (ii)
(A) adroit	(D) unpretentious
(B) unconvincing	(E) spurious
(C) prolix	(F) breathtaking

6. There is no point in combing through the director's work for hints of ideological
    significance. It is unnecessary: his ideology—Marxist, anti-imperialist, aligned
    with the perceived interests of the powerless and the marginal—is the (i) _____
    of his films. The clarity and force of that ideology are considerable, but its
    (ii) _____ sometimes bothers critics, who often scold the director for lacking
    (iii) _____.

Blank (i)	Blank (ii)	Blank (iii)
(A) hidden focus	(D) bluntness	(G) lucidity
(B) chief impetus	(E) obscurity	(H) subtlety
(C) murky lesson	(F) feebleness	(I) courage

7. As the finances of the energy-trading firm began unraveling, what eventually
    became (i) _____ was that the company had been concocting "value" out of
    thin air, thanks not to the trading strategies it promoted as visionary but to
    financial (ii) _____ that turned a once-solid entity into the most notorious
    (iii) _____ in an era of corporate scandals.

Blank (i)	Blank (ii)	Blank (iii)
(A) vindicated	(D) redemption	(G) omission
(B) unmistakable	(E) responsibilities	(H) boon
(C) unverifiable	(F) games	(I) debacle

8. Kept (i) _____ by cloying commercial radio and clueless record executives, the
    American popular music scene has frequently depended on cities at the edges of
    the cultural map to provide a much-needed shot of (ii) _____. The momentary
    (iii) _____ what the next big thing is seems to come out of nowhere—as if
    someone blows a whistle only those in the know can hear, and suddenly record
    executives and journalists are crawling all over what had previously been an
    obscure locale.

Blank (i)	Blank (ii)	Blank (iii)
(A) hidebound	(D) originality	(G) consensus about
(B) liberated	(E) truth	(H) indifference to
(C) obligated	(F) orthodoxy	(I) guarantee of

For each of Questions 9 to 14, select <u>one</u> answer choice unless otherwise directed.

Questions 9 and 10 are based on this passage.

Despite hypotheses ranging from armed conflict to climate change, the abandonment of more than 600 Pueblo cliff dwellings in Mesa Verde by A.D. 1300 still puzzles archaeologists. Researchers analyzing refuse from one Pueblo community found
Line remains of maize—a Pueblo crop—in 44 percent of samples from years when the
5 community flourished, but in only 10 percent of samples from years near the time of depopulation, while the remains of wild plants increased significantly.

Bones found in the samples showed that the consumption of domesticated turkeys—which were fed maize—decreased from 55 to 14 percent, while there was a marked increase in wild-animal bones. These data suggest that near the end of the
10 site's occupation, villagers experienced substantial food shortages and adopted hunting-and-gathering strategies to compensate for crop failure.

9. According to the passage, which of the following is likely true regarding the consumption of wild plants in the Pueblo community investigated by researchers?

   (A) It decreased dramatically as the settlement began to decline.
   (B) It significantly affected the food supply of wild animals living nearby.
   (C) It increased as domesticated sources of food declined.
   (D) It represented a continuation of centuries-old traditions.
   (E) It fell markedly as the consumption of wild animals increased.

10. The research described in the passage most clearly supports which of the following claims about the abandonment of Mesa Verde?

    (A) It likely resulted from factors affecting crop viability.
    (B) It was more extensive than had previously been documented.
    (C) It may have been hastened by the abundance of wild animals in the area.
    (D) It has been misdated by previous archaeological research.
    (E) It happened more rapidly in certain Pueblo communities than in others.

Questions 11 and 12 are based on this passage.

Although it is intuitively clear that an increase in antipredator behavior lowers an animal's risk of predation when predators are present, such benefits are not easily demonstrated. One study that did so found that well-fed guppies are more alert for predators and are consequently less likely to be killed than are their hungry counterparts, which feed with greater intensity. It is also well documented that a decrease in activity lowers an animal's risk of predation by reducing the probability of being detected or encountered by a predator. This effect was convincingly demonstrated by a study in which it was found that partially anesthetized tadpoles were less likely to be captured by dragonfly larvae than were unanesthetized tadpoles.

Line

5

For the following question, consider each of the choices separately and select <u>all</u> that apply.

11. It can be inferred that the guppy study and the tadpole study, as they are described in the passage, differed in which of the following ways?

    A The animals less likely to become the victims of predators were the more active ones in the guppy study but were the less active ones in the tadpole study.

    B The animals less likely to become the victims of predators were those more alert to their surroundings in the guppy study but were the less alert ones in the tadpole study.

    C The situation created experimentally for the guppy study would be more likely to occur in the wild than would the situation created for the tadpole study.

12. In the context indicated, "demonstrated" (line 3) most nearly means

    (A) explained
    (B) presented
    (C) shown
    (D) protested
    (E) justified

Questions 13 and 14 are based on this passage.

Since the 1980s, experts have been claiming that the skill demands of today's jobs have outstripped the skills workers possess. Moss and Tilly counter that worker deficiencies lie less in job-specific skills than in such attributes as motivation, interpersonal skills, and appropriate work demeanor. However, Handel suggests that these perceived deficiencies are merely an age effect, arguing that workers pass through a phase of early adulthood characterized by weak attachment to their jobs. As they mature, workers grow out of casual work attitudes and adjust to the workplace norms of jobs that they are more interested in retaining. Significantly, complaints regarding younger workers have persisted for over two decades, but similar complaints regarding older workers have not grown as the earlier cohorts aged.

Line 5

10

13. The passage suggests that Moss and Tilly are most likely to disagree with the "experts" (line 1) about which of the following?

Ⓐ Whether the skills demanded by jobs in the labor market have changed since the 1980s

Ⓑ Whether employers think that job-specific skills are as important as such attributes as motivation and appropriate work demeanor

Ⓒ Whether workers in today's labor market generally live up to the standards and expectations of employers

Ⓓ Whether adequate numbers of workers in the labor market possess the particular skills demanded by various different jobs

Ⓔ Whether most workers are motivated to acquire new skills that are demanded by the labor market

14. The last sentence serves primarily to

Ⓐ suggest that worker deficiencies are likely to become more pronounced in the future

Ⓑ introduce facts that Handel may have failed to take into account

Ⓒ cite evidence supporting Handel's argument about workers

Ⓓ show that the worker deficiencies cited by Handel are more than an age effect

Ⓔ distinguish certain skills more commonly possessed by young workers from skills more commonly found among mature workers

---

For each of Questions 15 to 19, select the <u>two</u> answer choices that, when used to complete the sentence, fit the meaning of the sentence as a whole <u>and</u> produce completed sentences that are alike in meaning.

---

15. Family photos of the author suggest that she was _____ child: she seemed to wear a permanent frown.

A a sullen

B an amiable

C a surly

D a beautiful

E a prudent

F a stunning

16. Biologists agree that snakes descended from lizards, but exactly where this first happened has been a matter of debate since the 1800s, when two _____ theories emerged.

    A complex
    B competing
    C dubious
    D conclusive
    E contending
    F irrefutable

17. A particular bacterium that has never encountered a particular virus will usually succumb to it, a _____ that may, surprisingly, be beneficial to the colony in which the bacterium lives.

    A susceptibility
    B theory
    C characteristic
    D juxtaposition
    E collision
    F hypothesis

18. The remarkable thing about the mayoral race, in retrospect, is that so many people wanted the job of managing a municipality so obviously about to _____.

    A materialize
    B disintegrate
    C crumble
    D prosper
    E flourish
    F scuffle

19. It is a testimony to Roth's _____ that he could not quite bring himself to write a book as dull and flat as his original conception for his novel *Everyman* seemed to demand.

    A persistence
    B deterioration
    C talent
    D ambition
    E decline
    F genius

Questions 20 to 23 are based on this passage.

In the early twentieth century, the idea that pianists should be musician-scholars whose playing reflected the way composers wanted their music to sound replaced the notion that pianists should be virtuosos whose performances thrilled audiences
Line
with emotional daring and showy displays of technique. One important figure to
5 emerge in the period, though a harpsichordist rather than a pianist, was Wanda Landowska (1879–1959). She demonstrated how the keyboard works of Baroque composers such as Bach, Handel, Scarlatti, and Couperin probably sounded in their own times. It would be a mistake to consider Landowska a classicist, however. She had been born in an age of Romantic playing dominated by Liszt, Leschetizky,
10 and their pupils. Thus she grew up with and was influenced by certain Romantic traditions of performance, whatever the stringency of her musical scholarship; Landowska knew how to hold audiences breathless, and when she gave recitals, they responded with deathlike silence and rapt attention.

Her playing was Romantic, but it was at least as close in spirit to the style of playing
15 intended by composers of the Baroque (1600–1750) and Classical (1750–1830) eras, as have been the more exacting but less emotionally resonant interpretations of most harpsichordists since Landowska. She had a miraculous quality of touch, a seemingly autonomous left hand; no artist in her generation could clarify with such deftness the polyphonic writing of the Baroque masters. And none could make their music so
20 spring to life.

Her achievements were the result of a lifetime of scholarship, truly remarkable physical gifts, and resilient rhythm, all combined with excellent judgment about when not to hold the printed note sacrosanct. Of course, developing such judgment demanded considerable experience and imagination. She was a genius at underlining the dramatic and emotional
25 content of a piece, and to do so, she took liberties, all kinds of liberties, while nevertheless preserving the integrity of a composer's score. In short, her entire musical approach was Romantic: intensely personal, full of light and shade, never pedantic.

Thanks to Landowska, Bach's music (originally composed for the harpsichord) now sounded inappropriately thick when played on the piano. One by one, pianists stopped
30 playing Bach's music as adapted for the piano by Liszt or by Tausig. Then they gradually stopped performing any kind of Baroque music on the piano, even Scarlatti's. The piano repertoire, it began to be felt, was extensive enough without reverting to transcriptions of Baroque music originally written for the harpsichord—and piano performances of Bach and Scarlatti were, despite the obvious similarities between the harpsichord and
35 the piano, transcriptions, no matter how faithfully the original notes were played. In accordance with this kind of purism came an emphasis on studying composers' manuscript notations, a relatively new field of musicology that is flourishing even today.

20. The passage suggests that Landowska's playing embodied a rejection of which of the following?

    (A) Emotionally resonant interpretations of musical works.

    (B) An audience's complete silence during a performance.

    (C) Performances of previously obscure Baroque works.

    (D) The idea that a performer can correctly judge when not to hold the printed note sacrosanct.

    (E) Performances emphasizing showy displays of technique that compromise the integrity of a composer's original score.

21. Which of the following can be inferred from the passage about the compositions of Scarlatti?

    (A) They were adapted by Liszt and Tausig.

    (B) They have not been transcribed faithfully.

    (C) They were not composed during the Baroque period.

    (D) They were composed for instruments other than piano.

    (E) They fell out of favor with most musicians in the early twentieth century.

22. The passage suggests that Landowska would probably have objected most strongly to which of the following?

    (A) A performance of a Bach keyboard piece played on the harpsichord.

    (B) A performance of a Handel organ piece on a Baroque pipe organ.

    (C) A modern composition written for a harpsichord and two pianos.

    (D) A piano solo in which the performer occasionally departs from the tempo indicated by the composer.

    (E) A performance of a piano and violin sonata in which the piano part is played on the harpsichord.

23. The author's assertion that Landowska should not be considered a classicist serves primarily to emphasize which of the following?

    (A) Landowska specialized in playing the works of composers of the Baroque era.

    (B) Landowska's repertoire included orchestral music only.

    (C) Landowska's musical performances were not devoid of emotion.

    (D) Landowska's repertoire emphasized works of long-lasting interest and value.

    (E) Landowska advocated the study of Classical style or form.

Scientists formerly believed that the rocky planets—Earth, Mercury, Venus, and Mars—were created by the rapid gravitational collapse of a dust cloud, a deflation giving rise to a dense orb. That view was challenged in the 1960s, when studies of Moon craters revealed that these craters were caused by the impact of objects that were in great abundance about 4.5 billion years ago but whose number appeared to have quickly decreased shortly thereafter. This observation rejuvenated Otto Schmidt's 1944 theory of accretion. According to this theory, cosmic dust gradually lumped into ever-larger conglomerates: particulates, gravel, small and then larger balls, planetesimals (tiny planets), and, ultimately, planets. As the planetesimals became larger, their numbers decreased. Consequently, the number of collisions between planetesimals decreased.

Line

5

10

For the following question, consider each of the choices separately and select all that apply.

24. The passage provides evidence that Schmidt would be likely to <u>disagree</u> with the theory presented in the first sentence over

   A the length of time it took for the rocky planets to form.

   B the most likely causes of the Moon's impact craters.

   C the importance of cosmic dust as a seminal material in planetary formation.

25. Which of the following best describes the "observation" (line 6) referred to in the passage?

   Ⓐ The rocky planets were created by the rapid gravitational collapse of a dust cloud.

   Ⓑ Certain features on the Moon's surface are impact craters caused by collisions with objects such as planetesimals.

   Ⓒ The rocky planets were formed by a slow accretion of cosmic dust into increasingly larger bodies.

   Ⓓ The number of objects colliding with the Moon appears to have been high for a while and then rapidly diminished.

   Ⓔ There are far fewer planetesimals in existence today than there were about 4.5 billion years ago.

ANSWER KEY

PRACTICE SET 1

1. **Choice C**: misleading
2. **Choice C**: panacea
3. **Choice B**: sanguine
4. **Choice A**: opulent; **Choice E**: expensive
5. **Choice A**: adroit; **Choice F**: breathtaking
6. **Choice B**: chief impetus; **Choice D**: bluntness; **Choice H**: subtlety
7. **Choice B**: unmistakable; **Choice F**: games; **Choice I**: debacle
8. **Choice A**: hidebound; **Choice D**: originality; **Choice G**: consensus about
9. **Choice C**: It increased as domesticated sources of food declined.
10. **Choice A**: It likely resulted from factors affecting crop viability.
11. **Choice B**: The animals less likely to become the victims of predators were those more alert to their surroundings in the guppy study but were the less alert ones in the tadpole study.
    AND
    Choice C: The situation created experimentally for the guppy study would be more likely to occur in the wild than would the situation created for the tadpole study.
12. **Choice C**: shown
13. **Choice D**: Whether adequate numbers of workers in the labor market possess the particular skills demanded by various different jobs
14. **Choice C**: cite evidence supporting Handel's argument about workers
15. **Choice A**: a sullen; AND **Choice C**: a surly
16. **Choice B**: competing; AND **Choice E**: contending
17. **Choice A**: susceptibility; AND **Choice C**: characteristic
18. **Choice B**: disintegrate; AND **Choice C**: crumble
19. **Choice C**: talent; AND **Choice F**: genius
20. **Choice E**: Performances emphasizing showy displays of technique that compromise the integrity of a composer's original score
21. **Choice D**: They were composed for instruments other than piano.
22. **Choice E**: A performance of a piano and violin sonata in which the piano part is played on the harpsichord
23. **Choice C**: Landowska's musical performances were not devoid of emotion.
24. **Choice A**: the length of time it took for the rocky planets to form
25. **Choice D**: The number of objects colliding with the Moon appears to have been high for a while and then rapidly diminished.

Answers and Explanations

PRACTICE SET 1

For each question, indicate the best answer, using the directions given.

> **For each of Questions 1 to 8, select <u>one</u> entry for each blank from the corresponding column of choices. Fill all blanks in the way that best completes the text.**

1. The name of the Sloane Matthew Library has long been _____; even longtime city residents assume it is a run-of-the-mill library, never suspecting what art treasures it contains.

(A) revered
(B) proposed
(C) misleading
(D) elevated
(E) intriguing

Explanation

The second half of the sentence contrasts the art treasures actually housed in the Sloane Matthew Library with city residents' perceptions of the institution. The semicolon that separates the first half of the sentence from the second half suggests that this contrast explains the assertion made in the first half. The blank, then, calls for a word that indicates the disparity between the public's image of the library and its actual contents. "Misleading" does this, suggesting that it is the name of the institution that leads residents to view it as a run-of-the-mill library rather than an art museum. "Revered," "elevated," and even "intriguing" would all suggest that the public sees the library as an extraordinary institution. "Proposed" suggests that the institution is still in the process of being named, an idea not supported by anything else in the sentence.

Thus the correct answer is **misleading** (Choice C).

2. Although economic growth has conventionally been viewed as the _____ for poverty in underdeveloped regions, this prescription's negative environmental side effects are becoming a concern.

(A) culprit
(B) recipe
(C) panacea
(D) explanation
(E) refuge

Explanation

The use of the word "prescription" suggests that the word that fills the blank will imply that economic growth is a cure for poverty. "Panacea," meaning a universal remedy, fits this sense exactly. Of the other choices, "culprit" and "recipe" would provide the opposite sense by implying that economic growth causes poverty in underdeveloped regions. Neither "refuge" nor "explanation" conveys the sense of remediation implied by the word "prescription," so they are both incorrect.

Thus the correct answer is **panacea** (Choice C).

3. Even as the economy struggled, the secretary stood by his _____ long-term outlook, saying that technology was allowing businesses to make deep-rooted improvements in their productivity, the best indicator of an economy's ability to grow.

Ⓐ	arcane
Ⓑ	sanguine
Ⓒ	equivocal
Ⓓ	ambivalent
Ⓔ	irresolute

Explanation

The sentence contrasts the economy's current struggles with the secretary's predictions for its long-term prospects. Since the secretary believes that technology will lead to economic growth, the secretary's outlook is an optimistic one. Thus the correct answer is "sanguine," which can mean optimistic. Since there is no indication that the secretary's view has wavered or is open to alternate interpretations, "irresolute," "ambivalent," and "equivocal" are all incorrect. The straightforward explanation of the rationale for the secretary's out-look suggests that it is not an "arcane" one, making that choice incorrect as well.

Thus the correct answer is **sanguine** (Choice B).

4. The villas and compounds that proliferated during the building boom of the 1990s were (i) _____, far too (ii) _____ for people of average means.

Blank (i)		Blank (ii)	
Ⓐ	opulent	Ⓓ	bucolic
Ⓑ	eclectic	Ⓔ	expensive
Ⓒ	enigmatic	Ⓕ	mundane

Explanation

The sentence talks about "villas and compounds," which are high-end properties, so the intuitive answer to Blank (ii) must be a word denoting a quality that makes these properties unsuitable or out of reach for people of average means. The answer choice that best matches this meaning is "expensive," so it is correct. The answer to Blank (i) must name the quality of the properties that makes them too expensive for people of average means; the answer choice that best meets this requirement is "opulent."

"Bucolic" may also seem a plausible choice for Blank (ii), as it denotes a quality that may not normally be associated with "people of average means." However, it is incorrect, as none of the qualities named in Blank (i) would make a property bucolic.

Thus the correct answer is **opulent** (Choice A) and **expensive** (Choice E).

5. The governor has considerable political talents, but as a speaker he is far less (i) _____ than his opponent, whose oratorical skills are (ii) _____.

Blank (i)		Blank (ii)	
Ⓐ	adroit	Ⓓ	unpretentious
Ⓑ	unconvincing	Ⓔ	spurious
Ⓒ	prolix	Ⓕ	breathtaking

Explanation

The "but" in the sentence suggests that there is a contrast between the governor's political talents and his speaking ability. Since the former is described in positive terms ("considerable"), the description of the latter must be negative. The governor is described as "far less (i)_____ than his opponent" as a speaker; since this whole phrase must have a negative meaning, the answer to Blank (i) must be positive. The only answer choice for Blank (i) that is positive is "adroit," so it is correct. Given this, the opponent's speaking ability must be much better than the governor's, so the answer to Blank (ii) has to be positive. The only positive choice for Blank (ii) is "breathtaking," so it is correct.

Thus the correct answer is **adroit** (Choice A) and **breathtaking** (Choice F).

6. There is no point in combing through the director's work for hints of ideological significance. It is unnecessary: his ideology—Marxist, anti-imperialist, aligned with the perceived interests of the powerless and the marginal—is the (i) _____ of his films. The clarity and force of that ideology are considerable, but its (ii) _____ sometimes bothers critics, who often scold the director for lacking (iii) _____.

Blank (i)	Blank (ii)	Blank (iii)
(A) hidden focus	(D) bluntness	(G) lucidity
(B) chief impetus	(E) obscurity	(H) subtlety
(C) murky lesson	(F) feebleness	(I) courage

Explanation

The colon in the second sentence indicates that the second half of the sentence will explain the first, so Blank (i) must contain a phrase that explains why it is needless to search the director's work for hints of ideology. "Chief impetus" does so, since it implies that the director's ideology is so obvious that "combing through" it for hints is not needed. The other two choices are incorrect because they suggest on the contrary a need for deeper analysis to detect what is "hidden" or "murky" in the films. Blank (ii) calls for an aspect of the director's ideology that bothers critics. The first part of the sentence mentions the considerable force and clarity of that ideology, so neither "feebleness" nor "obscurity" makes sense. "Bluntness" is therefore correct. Blank (iii) must then be a word whose lack characterizes bluntness. Since "subtlety" is the opposite of "bluntness," it is the correct answer.

Thus the correct answer is **chief impetus** (Choice B), **bluntness** (Choice D), and **subtlety** (Choice H).

7. As the finances of the energy-trading firm began unraveling, what eventually became (i) _____ was that the company had been concocting "value" out of thin air, thanks not to the trading strategies it promoted as visionary but to financial (ii) _____ that turned a once-solid entity into the most notorious (iii) _____ in an era of corporate scandals.

Blank (i)	Blank (ii)	Blank (iii)
(A) vindicated	(D) redemption	(G) omission
(B) unmistakable	(E) responsibilities	(H) boon
(C) unverifiable	(F) games	(I) debacle

Explanation

The characterization of the company's activities as "concocting 'value' out of thin air" strongly suggests that its transactions have been fraudulent. The word that completes Blank (ii) must reflect this financial trickery; "games" does so, whereas both "redemption" and "responsibilities" both reflect more upstanding behavior than the sentence ascribes to the firm. The word that completes Blank (iii) should reflect the company's fall from respectability and have a sense opposite to the "once-solid entity" with which it is contrasted. "Debacle" does this nicely, while the other two choices lack the necessary pejorative meaning. For Blank (i), "vindicated" suggests that there had been previous warnings about the firm's practices that were eventually borne out, something indicated nowhere else in the passage. "Unverifiable" is at odds with the sentence's surety about the firm's wrongdoing; that assurance is best conveyed by "unmistakable."

Thus the correct answer is **unmistakable** (Choice B), **games** (Choice F), and **debacle** (Choice I).

8. Kept (i) _____ by cloying commercial radio and clueless record executives, the American popular music scene has frequently depended on cities at the edges of the cultural map to provide a much-needed shot of (ii) _____. The momentary (iii) _____ what the next big thing is seems to come out of nowhere—as if someone blows a whistle only those in the know can hear, and suddenly record executives and journalists are crawling all over what had previously been an obscure locale.

Blank (i)	Blank (ii)	Blank (iii)
Ⓐ hidebound	Ⓓ originality	Ⓖ consensus about
Ⓑ liberated	Ⓔ truth	Ⓗ indifference to
Ⓒ obligated	Ⓕ orthodoxy	Ⓘ guarantee of

Explanation

The second sentence provides a clue for Blank (iii): the whistle metaphor and the talk about record executives and journalists "crawling all over" a location bring up the image of a race that involves a large number of people; this, and the fact that all these people congregate in one place, point to "consensus about" as the right answer choice for Blank (iii). The search for "the next big thing" suggests that the American popular music scene is looking for something new; this points to "originality" as the correct answer for Blank (ii). Finally, someone who needs a "shot of originality" is unwilling or unable to let go of the past; therefore, "hidebound" is the correct answer choice for Blank (i).

Thus, the correct answer choices are **hidebound** (Choice A), **originality** (Choice D) and **consensus about** (Choice G).

For each of Questions 9 to 14, select <u>one</u> answer choice unless otherwise directed.

Questions 9 and 10 are based on this passage.

Despite hypotheses ranging from armed conflict to climate change, the abandonment of more than 600 Pueblo cliff dwellings in Mesa Verde by A.D. 1300 still puzzles archaeologists. Researchers analyzing refuse from one Pueblo community found
Line remains of maize—a Pueblo crop—in 44 percent of samples from years when the
5 community flourished, but in only 10 percent of samples from years near the time of depopulation, while the remains of wild plants increased significantly.

Bones found in the samples showed that the consumption of domesticated turkeys—which were fed maize—decreased from 55 to 14 percent, while there was a marked increase in wild-animal bones. These data suggest that near the end of the
10 site's occupation, villagers experienced substantial food shortages and adopted hunting-and-gathering strategies to compensate for crop failure.

Description

The passage presents a puzzle—why did the Pueblo abandon their dwellings in Mesa Verde?—and provides some evidence about food remains that suggests a possible explanation.

9. According to the passage, which of the following is likely true regarding the consumption of wild plants in the Pueblo community investigated by researchers?

(A) It decreased dramatically as the settlement began to decline.

(B) It significantly affected the food supply of wild animals living nearby.

(C) It increased as domesticated sources of food declined.

(D) It represented a continuation of centuries-old traditions.

(E) It fell markedly as the consumption of wild animals increased.

Explanation

The passage presents four developments that accompanied the decline of one Pueblo community: consumption of maize and domesticated turkeys fell, while that of wild plants and wild animals increased. This summary shows that answer Choices A and E are incorrect, since both refer to a drop in the consumption of wild plants. Since the passage says nothing about whether the consumption of wild plants affected nearby wildlife nor about whether it was a long-standing tradition, Choices B and D are incorrect. **Choice C is correct**, however: consumption of wild plants rose as that of maize and domesticated turkeys fell.

10. The research described in the passage most clearly supports which of the following claims about the abandonment of Mesa Verde?

　(A) It likely resulted from factors affecting crop viability.

　(B) It was more extensive than had previously been documented.

　(C) It may have been hastened by the abundance of wild animals in the area.

　(D) It has been misdated by previous archaeological research.

　(E) It happened more rapidly in certain Pueblo communities than in others.

Explanation

The research strongly suggests that when the Pueblo community was flourishing, maize and maize-fed turkey formed a substantial part of the inhabitants' diet, but that just before the abandonment of Mesa Verde, maize had become a much scarcer commodity. This decline in what had been a dietary mainstay supports the claim that the villagers were experiencing difficulty growing crops. Thus **Choice A** is correct. Nothing in the passage suggests that the extent or date of the abandonment should be revised (Choices B and D), nor that the rate of the abandonment was affected by wild animals or varied from one community to another (Choices C and E).

Questions 11 and 12 are based on this passage.

Although it is intuitively clear that an increase in antipredator behavior lowers an animal's risk of predation when predators are present, such benefits are not easily demonstrated. One study that did so found that well-fed guppies are more alert for predators and are consequently less likely to be killed than are their hungry counterparts, which feed with greater intensity. It is also well documented that a decrease in activity lowers an animal's risk of predation by reducing the probability of being detected or encountered by a predator. This effect was convincingly demonstrated by a study in which it was found that partially anesthetized tadpoles were less likely to be captured by dragonfly larvae than were unanesthetized tadpoles.

Line

5

Description

The passage mentions two factors that can plausibly lower an animal's risk of predation and discusses experiments that confirm these hypotheses.

For the following question, consider each of the choices separately and select all that apply.

11. It can be inferred that the guppy study and the tadpole study, as they are described in the passage, differed in which of the following ways?

　A　The animals less likely to become the victims of predators were the more active ones in the guppy study but were the less active ones in the tadpole study.

　B　The animals less likely to become the victims of predators were those more alert to their surroundings in the guppy study but were the less alert ones in the tadpole study.

　C　The situation created experimentally for the guppy study would be more likely to occur in the wild than would the situation created for the tadpole study.

Explanation

Choices B and C are correct. The question asks how the two studies differed.

Choice A is incorrect: In the guppy study, the more likely victims are the hungry guppies who "feed with greater intensity" and are, therefore, more active than well-fed guppies.

Choice B is correct: The passage states that "well-fed guppies are more alert for predators and are consequently less likely to be killed" and that "anesthetized," or less alert, tadpoles "were less likely to be captured by dragonfly larvae."

Choice C is correct: In the guppy study the subjects were well fed, while in the tadpole study the subjects were anesthetized; this latter condition is much less unlikely to occur in the wild.

12. In the context indicated, "demonstrated" (line 3) most nearly means

   (A) explained

   (B) presented

   (C) shown

   (D) protested

   (E) justified

Explanation

The passage states that benefits of increased antipredator behavior "are not easily demonstrated"; in this context, "shown" is the closest synonym, so **Choice C** is correct.

Questions 13 and 14 are based on this passage.

Since the 1980s, experts have been claiming that the skill demands of today's jobs have outstripped the skills workers possess. Moss and Tilly counter that worker deficiencies lie less in job-specific skills than in such attributes as motivation, interpersonal skills, and appropriate work demeanor. However, Handel suggests that these perceived deficiencies are merely an age effect, arguing that workers pass through a phase of early adulthood characterized by weak attachment to their jobs. As they mature, workers grow out of casual work attitudes and adjust to the workplace norms of jobs that they are more interested in retaining. Significantly, complaints regarding younger workers have persisted for over two decades, but similar complaints regarding older workers have not grown as the earlier cohorts aged.

Line

5

10

Description

The passage discusses various perceived inadequacies of contemporary workers for their jobs and focuses on inadequacies stemming from lack of motivation and from poor workplace attitudes. A hypothesis is presented that attributes these deficiencies to worker youth and immaturity.

13. The passage suggests that Moss and Tilly are most likely to disagree with the "experts" (line 1) about which of the following?

   Ⓐ Whether the skills demanded by jobs in the labor market have changed since the 1980s

   Ⓑ Whether employers think that job-specific skills are as important as such attributes as motivation and appropriate work demeanor

   Ⓒ Whether workers in today's labor market generally live up to the standards and expectations of employers

   Ⓓ Whether adequate numbers of workers in the labor market possess the particular skills demanded by various different jobs

   Ⓔ Whether most workers are motivated to acquire new skills that are demanded by the labor market

Explanation

According to the passage, the "experts" on the one hand, and Moss and Tilly on the other, disagree about the specific kinds of deficiencies possessed by today's workers: the "experts" claim that workers are deficient because of the lack of job skills, while Moss and Tilly believe that the deficiencies stem from the lack of motivation and poor attitude. This means that the two sides would disagree about whether the skills of today's workers are adequate for their jobs; thus **Choice D** is correct.

14. The last sentence serves primarily to

   Ⓐ suggest that worker deficiencies are likely to become more pronounced in the future

   Ⓑ introduce facts that Handel may have failed to take into account

   Ⓒ cite evidence supporting Handel's argument about workers

   Ⓓ show that the worker deficiencies cited by Handel are more than an age effect

   Ⓔ distinguish certain skills more commonly possessed by young workers from skills more commonly found among mature workers

Explanation

If Handel's account is correct, it would not be surprising that a high level of perceived skill deficiencies in young workers at one time translates into a relatively low level of perceived deficiencies among older workers some twenty years later. If the deficiencies in young workers are in job-related skills, however, some trace of those deficiencies would still be noticeable twenty years later. Since the last sentence presents data that support the first prediction rather than the second, **Choice C** is correct.

> **For each of Questions 15 to 19, select the <u>two</u> answer choices that, when used to complete the sentence, fit the meaning of the sentence as a whole <u>and</u> produce completed sentences that are alike in meaning.**

15. Family photos of the author suggest that she was _____ child: she seemed to wear a permanent frown.

   A a sullen
   B an amiable
   C a surly
   D a beautiful
   E a prudent
   F a stunning

Explanation

The second part of the sentence explains the first, so the blank describes someone who is best characterized by wearing a permanent frown. This disallows "an amiable," "a beautiful," "a prudent," and "a stunning," none of which demand or allow for such a characterization. While "a sullen" and "a surly" do not mean exactly the same thing, they create sentences with the same meaning.

Thus the correct answer is **a sullen** (Choice A) and **a surly** (Choice C).

16. Biologists agree that snakes descended from lizards, but exactly where this first happened has been a matter of debate since the 1800s, when two _____ theories emerged.

   A complex
   B competing
   C dubious
   D conclusive
   E contending
   F irrefutable

Explanation

The "but" that connects the two parts of the sentence indicates that the second part contrasts in some way with the first part. In this case, the contrast is between the biologists' agreement on a central fact (snakes' descent from lizards) and a disagreement over the details (which have long been a matter of debate). The words that best complete the blank, then, must somehow emphasize this disagreement. Of the choices, "competing" and "contending" best do so because they imply that the two theories are what the long-running debate has centered upon. Of the other choices, "conclusive" and "irrefutable" are roughly synonymous, but neither suggests a matter worthy of a long-running debate. "Dubious," in addition to having no near-synonym among the choices, would also not explain why the emergence of the two theories triggered the debate. While "complex" might well describe a theory, it too has no obvious pair among the choices, and it also does not foreground biologists' disagreement regarding the two theories.

Thus the correct answer is **competing** (Choice B) and **contending** (Choice E).

17. A particular bacterium that has never encountered a particular virus will usually succumb to it, a _____ that may, surprisingly, be beneficial to the colony in which the bacterium lives.

- [A] susceptibility
- [B] theory
- [C] characteristic
- [D] juxtaposition
- [E] collision
- [F] hypothesis

Explanation

The blank calls for words that can refer to the tendency of a bacterium to be killed by an unfamiliar virus. "Susceptibility" and "characteristic," although not synonyms, can both be used to indicate this trait, and because it is clear that they are both referring to the same behavior, they produce sentences alike in meaning. The other choices contain a pair of synonyms—"theory" and "hypothesis"—that might at first seem tempting. But these, along with the other two choices, cannot aptly be used to characterize the typical behavior of bacteria, so they are all incorrect.

Thus the correct answer is **susceptibility** (Choice A) and **characteristic** (Choice C).

18. The remarkable thing about the mayoral race, in retrospect, is that so many people wanted the job of managing a municipality so obviously about to _____.

- [A] materialize
- [B] disintegrate
- [C] crumble
- [D] prosper
- [E] flourish
- [F] scuffle

Explanation

The sentence expresses surprise that the job of mayor was seen as desirable, given the state of the municipality. Thus the phrase containing the blank likely expresses something negative about the municipality. Of the choices, three—"disintegrate," "crumble," and "scuffle"—are negative. Of these, two—"disintegrate" and "crumble"—are synonyms that would yield sentences alike in meaning, so they are the correct choices. Of the other three possibilities, one pairing, "prosper" and "flourish," are synonyms, but the mayorship of a municipality on the verge of prosperity would be a desirable job, so that pairing does not fit the meaning of the sentence.

Thus the correct answer is **disintegrate** (Choice B) and **crumble** (Choice C).

19. It is a testimony to Roth's _____ that he could not quite bring himself to write a book as dull and flat as his original conception for his novel *Everyman* seemed to demand.

- [A] persistence
- [B] deterioration
- [C] talent
- [D] ambition
- [E] decline
- [F] genius

Explanation

The sentence suggests that both Roth's original conception and his execution were negative, but it relies on the contrast between these to create irony. While the "deterioration" and "decline" produce sentences alike in meaning, they do not capture the irony demanded by the use of the word "quite." While "ambition" and "persistence" may each capture that irony, there are no other words that when paired with them would produce sentences alike in meaning.

Thus the correct answer is **talent** (Choice C) and **genius** (Choice F).

For each of Questions 20 to 25, select <u>one</u> answer choice unless otherwise directed.

Questions 20 to 23 are based on this passage.

In the early twentieth century, the idea that pianists should be musician-scholars whose playing reflected the way composers wanted their music to sound replaced the notion that pianists should be virtuosos whose performances thrilled audiences
Line with emotional daring and showy displays of technique. One important figure to
5 emerge in the period, though a harpsichordist rather than a pianist, was Wanda Landowska (1879–1959). She demonstrated how the keyboard works of Baroque composers such as Bach, Handel, Scarlatti, and Couperin probably sounded in their own times. It would be a mistake to consider Landowska a classicist, however. She had been born in an age of Romantic playing dominated by Liszt, Leschetizky,
10 and their pupils. Thus she grew up with and was influenced by certain Romantic traditions of performance, whatever the stringency of her musical scholarship; Landowska knew how to hold audiences breathless, and when she gave recitals, they responded with deathlike silence and rapt attention.

Her playing was Romantic, but it was at least as close in spirit to the style of playing
15 intended by composers of the Baroque (1600–1750) and Classical (1750–1830) eras, as have been the more exacting but less emotionally resonant interpretations of most harpsichordists since Landowska. She had a miraculous quality of touch, a seemingly autonomous left hand; no artist in her generation could clarify with such deftness the polyphonic writing of the Baroque masters. And none could make their music so
20 spring to life.

Her achievements were the result of a lifetime of scholarship, truly remarkable physical gifts, and resilient rhythm, all combined with excellent judgment about when not to hold the printed note sacrosanct. Of course, developing such judgment demanded considerable experience and imagination. She was a genius at underlining the dramatic and emotional
25 content of a piece, and to do so, she took liberties, all kinds of liberties, while nevertheless preserving the integrity of a composer's score. In short, her entire musical approach was Romantic: intensely personal, full of light and shade, never pedantic.

Thanks to Landowska, Bach's music (originally composed for the harpsichord) now sounded inappropriately thick when played on the piano. One by one, pianists stopped
30 playing Bach's music as adapted for the piano by Liszt or by Tausig. Then they gradually stopped performing any kind of Baroque music on the piano, even Scarlatti's. The piano repertoire, it began to be felt, was extensive enough without reverting to transcriptions of Baroque music originally written for the harpsichord—and piano performances of Bach and Scarlatti were, despite the obvious similarities between the harpsichord and
35 the piano, transcriptions, no matter how faithfully the original notes were played. In accordance with this kind of purism came an emphasis on studying composers' manuscript notations, a relatively new field of musicology that is flourishing even today.

Description

The passage describes the career, performing style, and influence of the musician Wanda Landowska in the context of a general shift in attitudes among early-twentieth-century pianists and the emergence of the belief that music should be performed in a way that fits the composer's original vision most faithfully.

20. The passage suggests that Landowska's playing embodied a rejection of which of the following?

     (A) Emotionally resonant interpretations of musical works
     (B) An audience's complete silence during a performance
     (C) Performances of previously obscure Baroque works
     (D) The idea that a performer can correctly judge when not to hold the printed note sacrosanct
     (E) Performances emphasizing showy displays of technique that compromise the integrity of a composer's original score

Explanation

Choice E is correct because throughout the passage Wanda Landowska's playing serves as the embodiment of the historical change described in the passage's first sentence: the replacement of "showy displays of technique" in favor of playing that "reflected the way composers wanted their music to sound." The passage later describes Landowska's playing as "preserving the integrity of the composer's original score."

21. Which of the following can be inferred from the passage about the compositions of Scarlatti?

     (A) They were adapted by Liszt and Tausig.
     (B) They have not been transcribed faithfully.
     (C) They were not composed during the Baroque period.
     (D) They were composed for instruments other than piano.
     (E) They fell out of favor with most musicians in the early twentieth century.

Explanation

In the last paragraph, the passage states that pianists gradually stopped playing Scarlatti's music on the piano because they felt that the piano repertoire was extensive enough and that they had no need to resort to transcriptions of harpsichord pieces. It follows from this that Scarlatti's music was not written for the piano, so **Choice D** is correct.

22. The passage suggests that Landowska would probably have objected most strongly to which of the following?

     (A) A performance of a Bach keyboard piece played on the harpsichord
     (B) A performance of a Handel organ piece on a Baroque pipe organ
     (C) A modern composition written for a harpsichord and two pianos
     (D) A piano solo in which the performer occasionally departs from the tempo indicated by the composer
     (E) A performance of a piano and violin sonata in which the piano part is played on the harpsichord

Explanation

The passage tells us that Landowska was an adherent of the idea that performers of other people's musical works should play "the way composers wanted their music to sound" (line 2). In the context of the passage, this means that performers should use the instrument for which the music was originally written. This rules out Choices B, C, and D, as they are not examples of this kind of deviation from the composers' intentions. Choice A is incorrect, since the passage tells us that Bach's music was "originally composed for the harpsichord" (line 28). This leaves **Choice E** as the only correct option: Landowska would object to the music originally intended for the piano being performed on a harpsichord.

23. The author's assertion that Landowska should not be considered a classicist serves primarily to emphasize which of the following?

    (A) Landowska specialized in playing the works of composers of the Baroque era.

    (B) Landowska's repertoire included orchestral music only.

    (C) Landowska's musical performances were not devoid of emotion.

    (D) Landowska's repertoire emphasized works of long-lasting interest and value.

    (E) Landowska advocated the study of Classical style or form.

Explanation

The second paragraph of the passage suggests that the primary difference between the Classical and the Romantic styles of playing is that the former puts emphasis on technical mastery and faithfulness to the original score, while the latter focuses on the emotional aspects of a performance. Therefore, **Choice C** is correct.

Questions 24 and 25 are based on this passage.

Scientists formerly believed that the rocky planets—Earth, Mercury, Venus, and Mars—were created by the rapid gravitational collapse of a dust cloud, a deflation giving rise to a dense orb. That view was challenged in the 1960s, when studies of
Line Moon craters revealed that these craters were caused by the impact of objects that
5 were in great abundance about 4.5 billion years ago but whose number appeared to have quickly decreased shortly thereafter. This observation rejuvenated Otto Schmidt's 1944 theory of accretion. According to this theory, cosmic dust gradually lumped into ever-larger conglomerates: particulates, gravel, small and then larger balls, planetesimals (tiny planets), and, ultimately, planets. As the planetesimals
10 became larger, their numbers decreased. Consequently, the number of collisions between planetesimals decreased.

Description

The passage describes two theories of planetary formation in the solar system: the rapid collapse theory and the accretion theory. The passage mentions that the former theory was dominant before the 1960s and discusses how data obtained in the 1960s reignited scientific interest in the latter theory.

For the following question, consider each of the choices separately and select <u>all</u> that apply.

24. The passage provides evidence that Schmidt would be likely to DISAGREE with the theory presented in the first sentence over

    [A] the length of time it took for the rocky planets to form

    [B] the most likely causes of the Moon's impact craters

    [C] the importance of cosmic dust as a seminal material in planetary formation

Explanation

Choice A is correct. The question asks what Schmidt would disagree with in the rapid-collapse theory.

   Choice A is correct: According to Schmidt's own theory, "cosmic dust gradually lumped into ever-larger conglomerates"; this means that planetary formation was a prolonged process, while in the rapid-collapse theory, it happened quickly.

   Choice B is incorrect: Both theories agree that Moon craters were caused by the impact of cosmic bodies that crashed into the Moon's surface.

   Choice C is incorrect: Both theories agree that cosmic dust was the material from which the planets ultimately formed.

25. Which of the following best describes the "observation" (line 6) referred to in the passage?

    (A) The rocky planets were created by the rapid gravitational collapse of a dust cloud.

    (B) Certain features on the Moon's surface are impact craters caused by collisions with objects such as planetesimals.

    (C) The rocky planets were formed by a slow accretion of cosmic dust into increasingly larger bodies.

    (D) The number of objects colliding with the Moon appears to have been high for a while and then rapidly diminished.

    (E) There are far fewer planetesimals in existence today than there were about 4.5 billion years ago.

Explanation

The "observation" mentioned in the passage is the finding that Moon's craters "were caused by the impact of objects that were in great abundance about 4.5 billion years ago but whose number appeared to have quickly decreased shortly thereafter." The answer choice that is closest in meaning to this description is **Choice D**.

PRACTICE SET 2

For each question, indicate the best answer, using the directions given.

> **For each of Questions 1 to 7, select <u>one</u> entry for each blank from the corresponding column of choices. Fill all blanks in the way that best completes the text.**

1. By recognizing commonalities among all the major political parties and by promoting a collaborative decision-making process, the prime minister has made good on his promise to cultivate a leadership style that emphasizes _____.

Ⓐ	growth
Ⓑ	politics
Ⓒ	ideology
Ⓓ	cooperation
Ⓔ	differentiation

2. In his unexpurgated autobiography, Mark Twain commented freely on the flaws and foibles of his country, making some observations so _____ that his heirs and editors feared they would damage Twain's reputation if not withheld.

Ⓐ	buoyant
Ⓑ	acerbic
Ⓒ	premonitory
Ⓓ	laudatory
Ⓔ	temperate

3. That the artist chose to remain in his hometown does not mean that he remained (i) _____; on the contrary, he (ii) _____ the international artistic movements of his day.

Blank (i)		Blank (ii)	
Ⓐ	provincial	Ⓓ	knew nothing about
Ⓑ	capricious	Ⓔ	made light of
Ⓒ	obstinate	Ⓕ	kept abreast of

4. An innovation of the eighteenth-century cookbook writer Mary Cole was that in her work she (i) _____ the earlier books from which her recipes were drawn. Even in those numerous instances in which she had collated into a single version, which she could have called her own, the recipes of several earlier writers, she (ii) _____ them.

Blank (i)		Blank (ii)	
Ⓐ	preserved	Ⓓ	took pains to cite
Ⓑ	enhanced	Ⓔ	sought to imitate
Ⓒ	acknowledged	Ⓕ	could not surpass

5. The lizards snapped up insects that are so (i) _____ that other potential predators avoid them. Among the lizards' prey were some beetles that they initially (ii) _____ because the insects were spraying their hot, irritant defense chemical at the time. Yet even these produced no apparent ill effects, since the lizards, having eaten, proceeded on their way (iii) _____ enough.

Blank (i)	Blank (ii)	Blank (iii)
Ⓐ rare	Ⓓ sought	Ⓖ erratically
Ⓑ nutritious	Ⓔ rejected	Ⓗ laboriously
Ⓒ noxious	Ⓕ resembled	Ⓘ nonchalantly

6. When the normally (i) _____ film director was interviewed, it was only the topic of her next movie that (ii) _____ her flow of words. Her (iii) _____ on that subject suggested that it was an unwelcome one.

Blank (i)	Blank (ii)	Blank (iii)
Ⓐ assiduous	Ⓓ diverted	Ⓖ taciturnity
Ⓑ loquacious	Ⓔ stanched	Ⓗ alacrity
Ⓒ diffident	Ⓕ accentuated	Ⓘ rhapsody

7. Bureaucrats tend to (i) _____. So it is surprising that the European Commission is proposing to hand back some of its antitrust powers to national governments. Such a willingness to (ii) _____ power is quite (iii) _____. Perhaps the commission, so often a byword for meddling, bungling, and even corruption, is starting to put its house in order following the forced resignation of the previous lot of commissioners last year.

Blank (i)	Blank (ii)	Blank (iii)
Ⓐ value complex procedures	Ⓓ devolve	Ⓖ troubling
Ⓑ guard their authority jealously	Ⓔ misuse	Ⓗ encouraging
Ⓒ shirk many of their responsibilities	Ⓕ appropriate	Ⓘ predictable

For each of Questions 8 to 13, select **one** answer choice unless otherwise directed.

Question 8 is based on this passage.

Despite a dramatic increase in the number of people riding bicycles for recreation in Parkville, a recent report by the Parkville Department of Transportation shows that the number of accidents involving bicycles has decreased for the third consecutive year.

8. Which of the following, if true during the last three years, best reconciles the apparent discrepancy in the facts?

  (A) The Parkville Department of Recreation confiscated abandoned bicycles and sold them at auction to any interested Parkville residents.

  (B) Increased automobile and bus traffic in Parkville had been the leading cause of the most recent increase in automobile accidents.

  (C) Because of the local increase in the number of people bicycling for recreation, many out-of-town bicyclists ride in the Parkville area.

  (D) The Parkville Police Department enforced traffic rules for bicycle riders much more vigorously and began requiring recreational riders to pass a bicycle safety course.

  (E) The Parkville Department of Transportation canceled a program that required all bicycles to be inspected and registered each year.

Questions 9 to 11 are based on this passage.

What makes a worker ant perform one particular task rather than another? From the 1970s to the mid-1980s, researchers emphasized internal factors within individual ants, such as polymorphism, the presence in the nest of workers of different shapes and sizes, each suited to a particular task. Other elements then considered to have
Line
5 primary influence upon an ant's career were its age—it might change tasks as it got older—and its genetics. However, subsequent ant researchers have focused on external prompts for behavior. In advocating this approach, Deborah Gordon cites experiments in which intervention in a colony's makeup perturbed worker activity. By removing workers or otherwise altering the nest conditions, researchers were able to change the
10 tasks performed by individual workers.

For the following question, consider each of the choices separately and select all that apply.

9. According to the passage, which of the following factors were considered from the 1970s to the mid-1980s to influence the division of labor among a colony's worker ants?

  [A] Ants' inherited traits
  [B] The age of the ants
  [C] The ants' experiences outside the nest

For the following question, consider each of the choices separately and select <u>all</u> that apply.

10. It can be inferred from the passage that Gordon and earlier researchers would agree with which of the following statements about worker ants?

   [A] Disruption of the nest can affect workers' roles.

   [B] Genetics predominates over other factors in determining a worker ant's role.

   [C] An individual worker's tasks can change during its lifetime.

For the following question, consider each of the choices separately and select <u>all</u> that apply.

11. The last sentence has which of the following functions in the passage?

   [A] It explains how the experiments performed by Gordon differed from those performed by earlier researchers.

   [B] It justifies the methodology of the experiments cited by Gordon.

   [C] It gives details showing how the experiments cited by Gordon support her position.

Questions 12 and 13 are based on this passage.

This passage is adapted from material published in 2001.

In 1998 scientists using the neutrino detector in Kamioka, Japan, were able to observe several thousand neutrinos—elusive, tiny subatomic particles moving at nearly the speed of light and passing through almost everything in their path. The Kamioka find-
Line
5 ings have potentially far-reaching ramifications. They strongly suggest that the neutrino has mass, albeit an infinitesimal amount. Even a tiny mass means that neutrinos would outweigh all the universe's visible matter, because of their vast numbers. The findings also suggest that a given neutrino does not have one stable mass or one stable identity; instead it oscillates from one identity or "flavor" (physicists' term describing how neutrinos interact with other particles) to another. This oscillation may explain
10 why, although the Sun is a large source of neutrinos, detectors capture far fewer solar neutrinos than the best theory of solar physics predicts: the neutrinos may be changing to flavors undetectable by detectors. Finally, while the standard particle-physics model—which describes all matter in terms of twelve fundamental particles and four fundamental forces—does not allow for neutrinos with mass, there are theories that
15 do. Further experiments to confirm that neutrinos have mass could help physicists determine which, if any, of these theories is correct.

12. The primary purpose of the passage is to

   (A) evaluate the merits of a particular theory in light of new evidence

   (B) discuss scientists' inability to account for certain unexpected discoveries

   (C) point out certain shortcomings in a long-standing theory

   (D) compare several alternative explanations for a particular phenomenon

   (E) consider some implications of certain scientific findings

13. According to the passage, one significant implication of the discovery that neutrinos have mass is that such a discovery would

(A) cast doubt on the solar origins of many of the neutrinos that reach Earth

(B) help to establish the validity of the standard particle-physics model

(C) indicate that most of the visible matter of the universe is composed of neutrinos

(D) entail that the total weight of all the visible matter in the universe is less than that of all the neutrinos in the universe

(E) mean that the speed with which neutrinos normally move can be slowed by certain types of matter

---

For each of Questions 14 to 18, select the <u>two</u> answer choices that, when used to complete the sentence, fit the meaning of the sentence as a whole <u>and</u> produce completed sentences that are alike in meaning.

---

14. In film studies—a visually oriented discipline that is _____ backlit close-ups, eyeline matches, and voyeuristic gazes—scholars have often been tone-deaf to the sounds of music.

A fixated on

B obsessed with

C unconcerned with

D amused by

E bothered by

F indifferent to

15. Consumers may think that genetic engineering of foods is something new, but humans have been modifying plants for ages; the _____ is not that new genes are introduced but that genes can now be moved from one species to another.

A novelty

B quandary

C advantage

D innovation

E discrepancy

F predicament

16. Although the compound is abundant in the environment at large, its presence in the air is not _____; only in the form of underwater sediment does it cause damage.

A trivial

B detectable

C deleterious

D substantive

E detrimental

F inconsequential

17. Deacon attempts what seems impossible: a book rich in scientific insights, in a demanding discipline, that nevertheless is accessible to _____.

- A skeptics
- B experts
- C nonspecialists
- D zealots
- E authorities
- F laypersons

18. Despite relying on the well-to-do for commissions, the portrait painter was no _____: he depicted the character of those he painted as he perceived it.

- A hypocrite
- B egotist
- C sycophant
- D adulator
- E braggart
- F coward

For each of Questions 19 to 25, select <u>one</u> answer choice unless otherwise directed.

Question 19 is based on this passage.

Mayor: Four years ago, when we reorganized the city police department in order to save money, critics claimed that the reorganization would make the police less responsive to citizens and would thus lead to more crime. The police have compiled theft statistics from the years following the reorganization that show that the critics were wrong. There was an overall decrease in reports of thefts of all kinds, including small thefts.

Line
5

19. Which of the following, if true, most seriously challenges the mayor's argument?

- (A) When city police are perceived as unresponsive, victims of theft are less likely to report thefts to the police.
- (B) The mayor's critics generally agree that police statistics concerning crime reports provide the most reliable available data on crime rates.
- (C) In other cities where police departments have been similarly reorganized, the numbers of reported thefts have generally risen following reorganization.
- (D) The mayor's reorganization of the police department failed to save as much money as it was intended to save.
- (E) During the four years immediately preceding the reorganization, reports of all types of theft had been rising steadily in comparison to reports of other crimes.

Questions 20 to 23 are based on this passage.

During the 1920s, most advocates of scientific management, Frederick Taylor's method for maximizing workers' productivity by rigorously routinizing their jobs, opposed the five-day workweek. Although scientific managers conceded that reducing hours might
Line provide an incentive to workers, in practice they more often used pay differentials to
5 encourage higher productivity. Those reformers who wished to embrace both scientific management and reduced hours had to make a largely negative case, portraying the latter as an antidote to the rigors of the former.

In contrast to the scientific managers, Henry Ford claimed that shorter hours led to greater productivity and profits. However, few employers matched either Ford's vision
10 or his specific interest in mass marketing a product—automobiles—that required leisure for its use, and few unions succeeded in securing shorter hours through bargaining. At its 1928 convention, the American Federation of Labor (AFL) boasted of approximately 165,000 members working five-day, 40-hour weeks. But although this represented an increase of about 75,000 since 1926, about 70 percent of the total came
15 from five extremely well-organized building trades' unions.

20. The passage is primarily concerned with discussing which of the following?
    (A) The relative merits of two points of view regarding a controversy
    (B) The potential benefits to workers in the 1920s of a change in employers' policies
    (C) The reasons for a labor-management disagreement during the 1920s
    (D) The status of a contested labor issue during the 1920s
    (E) The role of labor unions in bringing about a reform

21. It can be inferred that the author of the passage mentions "automobiles" (line 10) primarily to suggest that
    (A) Ford's business produced greater profits than did businesses requiring a workweek longer than five days
    (B) Ford, unlike most other employers, encouraged his employees to use the products they produced
    (C) Ford may have advocated shorter hours because of the particular nature of his business
    (D) unions were more likely to negotiate for shorter hours in some businesses than in others
    (E) automobile workers' unions were more effective than other unions in securing a five-day workweek

22. It can be inferred that the author of the passage would probably agree with which of the following claims about the boast referred to in lines 12–13?

Ⓐ It is based on a mistaken estimation of the number of AFL workers who were allowed to work a five-day, 40-hour week in 1928.

Ⓑ It could create a mistaken impression regarding the number of unions obtaining a five-day, 40-hour week during the 1920s.

Ⓒ It exaggerates the extent of the increase between 1926 and 1928 in AFL members working a five-day, 40-hour week.

Ⓓ It overestimates the bargaining prowess of the AFL building trades' unions during the 1920s.

Ⓔ It is based on an overestimation of the number of union members in the AFL in 1928.

23. According to the passage, the "reformers" (line 5) claimed that

Ⓐ neither scientific management nor reduced hours would result in an improvement in the working conditions of most workers

Ⓑ the impact that the routinization of work had on workers could be mitigated by a reduction in the length of their workweek

Ⓒ there was an inherent tension between the principles of scientific management and a commitment to reduced workweeks

Ⓓ scientific managers were more likely than other managers to use pay differentials to encourage higher productivity

Ⓔ reducing the length of the workweek would increase productivity more effectively than would increases in pay

Questions 24 and 25 are based on this passage.

In November 1753, the British author Sarah Fielding accepted half the payment for her novel *The Cry* and asked that the other half, when due, go to her "or to whomsoever I shall appoint," perhaps indicating that the remaining share was intended for someone
Line else. Indeed, many think that the novel was a collaborative venture between Fielding
5 and Jane Collier. This particular collaboration was likely enough, as the two were close friends with common interests. They wrote jointly authored letters, were both published authors with a lively interest in each other's work, and were enthusiastic supporters of didacticism and innovation in fiction—central concerns of *The Cry*. However, contemporaries ascribed the work solely to Fielding, and there is nothing in the novel
10 that is incompatible with Fielding's other writings.

For the following question, consider each of the choices separately and select all that apply.

24. The passage presents which of the following as evidence in favor of Fielding and Collier's having collaborated in writing *The Cry*?

Ⓐ Their friendship

Ⓑ Their joint authorship of correspondence

Ⓒ Their approach to fiction

25. It can be inferred that the author of the passage would agree with which of the following claims about *The Cry*?

Ⓐ It develops themes commonly found in published works.

Ⓑ It reflects an interest in the purposes to which fiction may be put.

Ⓒ It contains elements that are incompatible with any of Collier's solo writings.

Ⓓ It shows that the extent of Collier and Fielding's shared interests was not as wide as is generally thought.

Ⓔ Parts of it were written jointly by Fielding and Collier.

<u>ANSWER KEY</u>

PRACTICE SET 2

1. **Choice D**: cooperation
2. **Choice B**: acerbic
3. **Choice A**: provincial; **Choice F**: kept abreast of
4. **Choice C**: acknowledged; **Choice D**: took pains to cite
5. **Choice C**: noxious; **Choice E**: rejected; **Choice I**: nonchalantly
6. **Choice B**: loquacious; **Choice E**: stanched; **Choice G**: taciturnity
7. **Choice B**: guard their authority jealously; **Choice D**: devolve; **Choice H**: encouraging
8. **Choice D**: The Parkville Police Department enforced traffic rules for bicycle riders much more vigorously and began requiring recreational riders to pass a bicycle safety course.
9. **Choice A**: Ants' inherited traits
   Choice B: The age of the ants
10. **Choice C**: An individual worker's tasks can change during its lifetime.
11. **Choice C**: It gives details showing how the experiments cited by Gordon support her position.
12. **Choice E**: consider some implications of certain scientific findings
13. **Choice D**: entail that the total weight of all the visible matter in the universe is less than that of all the neutrinos in the universe
14. **Choice A**: fixated on AND **Choice B**: obsessed with
15. **Choice A**: novelty AND **Choice D**: innovation
16. **Choice C**: deleterious AND **Choice E**: detrimental
17. **Choice C**: nonspecialists AND **Choice F**: laypersons
18. **Choice C**: sycophant AND **Choice D**: adulator
19. **Choice A**: When city police are perceived as unresponsive, victims of theft are less likely to report thefts to the police.
20. **Choice D**: The status of a contested labor issue during the 1920s
21. **Choice C**: Ford may have advocated shorter hours because of the particular nature of his business
22. **Choice B**: It could create a mistaken impression regarding the number of unions obtaining a five-day, 40-hour week during the 1920s.
23. **Choice B**: the impact that the routinization of work had on workers could be mitigated by a reduction in the length of their workweek
24. **Choice A**: Their friendship
    AND
    Choice B: Their joint authorship of correspondence
    AND
    Choice C: Their approach to fiction
25. **Choice B**: It reflects an interest in the purposes to which fiction may be put.

Answers and Explanations

PRACTICE SET 2

For each question, indicate the best answer, using the directions given.

> **For each of Questions 1 to 7, select <u>one</u> entry for each blank from the corresponding column of choices. Fill all blanks in the way that best completes the text.**

1. By recognizing commonalities among all the major political parties and by promoting a collaborative decision-making process, the prime minister has made good on his promise to cultivate a leadership style that emphasizes _____.

Ⓐ	growth
Ⓑ	politics
Ⓒ	ideology
Ⓓ	cooperation
Ⓔ	differentiation

Explanation

The second half of the sentence states that the prime minister has kept his promise to cultivate a certain leadership style; the "by" that begins the first part of the sentence indicates that the actions it describes are cited as examples of this style of leadership. The blank, then, must be filled with a word that describes the prime minister's focus on recognizing commonalities and promoting collaboration. "Cooperation" does this. None of the other choices touches upon the prime minister's efforts to work with others in the political process; indeed, "ideology" and "differentiation" might well imply the opposite.

Thus the correct answer is **cooperation** (Choice D).

2. In his unexpurgated autobiography, Mark Twain commented freely on the flaws and foibles of his country, making some observations so _____ that his heirs and editors feared they would damage Twain's reputation if not withheld.

Ⓐ	buoyant
Ⓑ	acerbic
Ⓒ	premonitory
Ⓓ	laudatory
Ⓔ	temperate

Explanation

The blank must be filled with a word that characterizes Mark Twain's comments on the "flaws and foibles" of his country; since pointing out flaws implies that the comments are critical, "laudatory," meaning flattering, is not the correct choice. "Buoyant," meaning lighthearted, would also be an unlikely adjective to apply to criticism, and both it and "temperate" suggest an inoffensiveness that would not explain the heirs' and editors' fears that publishing the comments would damage Twain's reputation. "Premonitory" suggests that Twain's observations were predictive or that their purpose was to warn, something not supported by any other information in the sentence. "Acerbic," however, implies a bitterness of tone that could very plausibly accompany criticism, and it also suggests why Twain's heirs and editors were worried about the remarks' effect on the writer's reputation.

Thus the correct answer is **acerbic** (Choice B).

3. That the artist chose to remain in his hometown does not mean that he remained (i) _____; on the contrary, he (ii) _____ the international artistic movements of his day.

Blank (i)	Blank (ii)
Ⓐ provincial	Ⓓ knew nothing about
Ⓑ capricious	Ⓔ made light of
Ⓒ obstinate	Ⓕ kept abreast of

Explanation

The first part of the sentence suggests that the answer to Blank (i) names a quality that someone who chose to remain in his hometown might tend to have; in addition, the second part of the sentence suggests that this quality has to do with that person's attitude toward the wider world. The answer choice for Blank (i) that best fits these conditions is "provincial," so it is correct. Someone who is the opposite of provincial is interested in what is happening outside of his or her narrow domain, so the correct answer choice for Blank (ii) is "kept abreast of."

"Obstinate" may seem a plausible choice for Blank (i), as those who fit the "provincial" stereotype often not only are uninterested in other people's opinions but also actively resist any pressure to change. However, "obstinate" by itself does not imply any particular attitude toward the world beyond one's immediate environment, as one can be interested in other people's opinions while at the same time clinging firmly to one's own.

Thus the correct answer is **provincial** (Choice A) and **kept abreast of** (Choice F).

4. An innovation of the eighteenth-century cookbook writer Mary Cole was that in her work she (i) _____ the earlier books from which her recipes were drawn. Even in those numerous instances in which she had collated into a single version, which she could have called her own, the recipes of several earlier writers, she (ii) _____ them.

Blank (i)	Blank (ii)
Ⓐ preserved	Ⓓ took pains to cite
Ⓑ enhanced	Ⓔ sought to imitate
Ⓒ acknowledged	Ⓕ could not surpass

Explanation

The second sentence suggests that Cole did not call certain recipes her own even though doing so would have been justified. Blank (ii) must describe Cole's actual practice, which contrasts with calling the recipes her own. Among the answer choices only "took pains to cite" provides a direct contrast, so it is correct. Because the second sentence is presented as a special or extreme case of the first, the answer to Blank (i) must be similar in meaning to Blank (ii). "Acknowledged" is the only choice that fits this criterion, so it is the correct answer to Blank (i).

Thus the correct answer is **acknowledged** (Choice C) and **took pains to cite** (Choice D).

5. The lizards snapped up insects that are so (i) _____ that other potential predators avoid them. Among the lizards' prey were some beetles that they initially (ii) _____ because the insects were spraying their hot, irritant defense chemical at the time. Yet even these produced no apparent ill effects, since the lizards, having eaten, proceeded on their way (iii) _____ enough.

Blank (i)	Blank (ii)	Blank (iii)
Ⓐ rare	Ⓓ sought	Ⓖ erratically
Ⓑ nutritious	Ⓔ rejected	Ⓗ laboriously
Ⓒ noxious	Ⓕ resembled	Ⓘ nonchalantly

Explanation

Blank (i) calls for a description of insects that predators would generally avoid. "Noxious," meaning harmful, is the correct answer; there is no reason to suspect that predators would avoid nutritious or rare prey. Blank (ii) characterizes the lizards' initial response to beetles they eventually ate, and since it is followed by a clause beginning with "because," the lizards' response must be explained by the beetles' irritant-spraying behavior. "Rejected" fits these criteria; animals routinely avoid unpleasant stimuli. "Sought" is incorrect because it is unlikely that lizards would seek out prey with such defensive behavior, and "resembled" is incorrect because nothing else in the passage suggests that the described behavior is shared by the lizards. Finally, the author states that eating the beetles apparently did not harm the lizards; the "since" of the last sentence introduces the evidence on which this observation is based. Thus Blank (iii) must be filled by a word that suggests the lizards were unharmed. "Erratic" or "laborious" postmeal locomotion might indicate otherwise; therefore the correct answer for Blank (iii) is "nonchalantly."

Thus the correct answer is **noxious** (Choice C), **rejected** (Choice E), and **nonchalantly** (Choice I).

6. When the normally (i) _____ film director was interviewed, it was only the topic of her next movie that (ii) _____ her flow of words. Her (iii) _____ on that subject suggested that it was an unwelcome one.

Blank (i)	Blank (ii)	Blank (iii)
(A) assiduous	(D) diverted	(G) taciturnity
(B) loquacious	(E) stanched	(H) alacrity
(C) diffident	(F) accentuated	(I) rhapsody

Explanation

The reader is told that the director's reaction to being asked about her next movie indicates that it is an unwelcome subject. Of the choices for Blank (iii), both "alacrity" and "rhapsody" would indicate excitement or eagerness to talk about this topic, making them implausible choices. "Taciturnity," on the other hand, indicates an unwillingness or reserve about speaking; it is therefore the correct choice. This particular reaction is contrasted to the director's normal conversational style, so the answer to Blank (i) must indicate a ready willingness to converse. "Loquacious," meaning talkative, is the choice that fits; neither "diffident," which means reserved, nor "assiduous," which means diligent, conveys the necessary contrast to taciturnity. Finally, Blank (ii) suggests that the topic of the director's next movie provoked a verbal reaction different from her usual one. Since the director is normally a talkative person, the unwelcome topic likely checked her conversation; therefore, "stanched" is the correct answer. "Accentuated" indicates the opposite, and while "diverted" might seem plausible, it suggests a potential change of topic unsupported by the rest of the passage.

Thus the correct answer is **loquacious** (Choice B), **stanched** (Choice E), and **taciturnity** (Choice G).

7. Bureaucrats tend to (i) _____. So it is surprising that the European Commission is proposing to hand back some of its antitrust powers to national governments. Such a willingness to (ii) _____ power is quite (iii) _____. Perhaps the commission, so often a byword for meddling, bungling, and even corruption, is starting to put its house in order following the forced resignation of the previous lot of commissioners last year.

Blank (i)	Blank (ii)	Blank (iii)
(A) value complex procedures	(D) devolve	(G) troubling
(B) guard their authority jealously	(E) misuse	(H) encouraging
(C) shirk many of their responsibilities	(F) appropriate	(I) predictable

Explanation

The second sentence states that the European Commission's current actions are surprising, so they must run counter to the general tendency of bureaucrats described in Blank (i). Since the commission is considering giving up powers it currently possesses, "guard their authority jealously" expresses the opposite of this action, so it is the correct choice. The other two options could potentially describe the process of delegating powers back to national governments; therefore the commission's actions would not be described as surprising in the context of either of those bureaucratic tendencies. Blank (ii) calls for a word that paraphrases the commission's proposal; since "devolve" is a synonym for delegate, it is the correct choice. "Appropriate" expresses the opposite, while "misuse" suggests a negative judgment about the commission's actions belied by the author's hope that they mark a positive turn. Blank (iii) calls for an adjective describing the commission's actions. Since the author is hopeful that this latest proposal marks a new direction for a commission whose history is described in negative terms, the correct choice for Blank (iii) is "encouraging." "Predictable" does not fit because the proposal is described as potentially marking a break in the commission's former bad practices, and "troubling" does not work because that change is described as a positive rather than a negative one.

Thus the correct answer is **guard their authority jealously** (Choice B), **devolve** (Choice D), and **encouraging** (Choice H).

For each of Questions 8 to 13, select **one** answer choice unless otherwise directed.

Question 8 is based on this passage.

Despite a dramatic increase in the number of people riding bicycles for recreation in Parkville, a recent report by the Parkville Department of Transportation shows that the number of accidents involving bicycles has decreased for the third consecutive year.

8. Which of the following, if true during the last three years, best reconciles the apparent discrepancy in the facts?

    (A) The Parkville Department of Recreation confiscated abandoned bicycles and sold them at auction to any interested Parkville residents.

    (B) Increased automobile and bus traffic in Parkville had been the leading cause of the most recent increase in automobile accidents.

    (C) Because of the local increase in the number of people bicycling for recreation, many out-of-town bicyclists ride in the Parkville area.

    (D) The Parkville Police Department enforced traffic rules for bicycle riders much more vigorously and began requiring recreational riders to pass a bicycle safety course.

    (E) The Parkville Department of Transportation canceled a program that required all bicycles to be inspected and registered each year.

Explanation

The correct answer is **Choice D**. Enforcing traffic rules and educating bicyclists about safety will obviously tend to reduce the number of bicycle accidents. Actions mentioned in the other answer choices will not have this effect. Choices A and C would explain the increase in the number of bicyclists in Parkville but not the decrease in bicycle accidents. The number of automobile accidents (Choice B) is not correlated with the number of bicycle accidents. Finally, cancellation of a bicycle inspection program (Choice E), if anything, would tend to *increase* the number of bicycle accidents.

Questions 9 to 11 are based on this passage.

What makes a worker ant perform one particular task rather than another? From the 1970s to the mid-1980s, researchers emphasized internal factors within individual ants, such as polymorphism, the presence in the nest of workers of different shapes and sizes, each suited to a particular task. Other elements then considered to have
Line
5   primary influence upon an ant's career were its age—it might change tasks as it got older—and its genetics. However, subsequent ant researchers have focused on external prompts for behavior. In advocating this approach, Deborah Gordon cites experiments in which intervention in a colony's makeup perturbed worker activity. By removing workers or otherwise altering the nest conditions, researchers were able to change the
10 tasks performed by individual workers.

Description

The passage discusses research aimed at discovering factors that determine the division of labor among ants and talks about a shift in focus from internal to external factors that occurred during the 1980s.

For the following question, consider each of the choices separately and select all that apply.

9. According to the passage, which of the following factors were considered from the 1970s to the mid-1980s to influence the division of labor among a colony's worker ants?

   [A] Ants' inherited traits
   [B] The age of the ants
   [C] The ants' experiences outside the nest

Explanation

Choices A and B are correct. The question asks about the factors considered to affect ant roles in the earlier period under discussion. Describing the period from the 1970s to the mid-1980s, the passage states that "Other elements then considered to have primary influence upon an ant's career were its age . . . and its genetics."

Choice C is incorrect: the passage never discusses ants' experiences outside the nest.

For the following question, consider each of the choices separately and select all that apply.

10. It can be inferred from the passage that Gordon and earlier researchers would agree with which of the following statements about worker ants?

    [A] Disruption of the nest can affect workers' roles.
    [B] Genetics predominates over other factors in determining a worker ant's role.
    [C] An individual worker's tasks can change during its lifetime.

Explanation

Choice C is correct. The question asks about points that Gordon and earlier researchers would agree on.

Choice A is incorrect: Nest disruption is an external factor favored by later researchers such as Gordon, but there is no suggestion that earlier researchers considered it a factor.

Choice B is incorrect: Earlier researchers might have thought that genetics was a predominant factor, but the later work showed that other factors could override genetics.

Choice C is correct: Both earlier and later researchers knew that an individual worker ant can change its role. According to the passage, the earlier researchers thought that an ant "might change tasks as it got older," and later researchers "were able to change the tasks performed by individual workers."

For the following question, consider each of the choices separately and select all that apply.

11. The last sentence has which of the following functions in the passage?

    [A] It explains how the experiments performed by Gordon differed from those performed by earlier researchers.
    [B] It justifies the methodology of the experiments cited by Gordon.
    [C] It gives details showing how the experiments cited by Gordon support her position.

Explanation

Choice C is correct. The question asks about the role of the last sentence.

Choice A is incorrect: the passage never mentions any experiments performed by earlier researchers.

Choice B is incorrect: the last sentence simply describes the experiments and their results but does not make any attempt to justify their methodology.

Choice C is correct: the experiments described in the last sentence show that ants' roles in the nest can be affected by external conditions, and Gordon is described in the passage as "advocating this approach."

Questions 12 and 13 are based on this passage.

This passage is excerpted from material published in 2001.

In 1998 scientists using the neutrino detector in Kamioka, Japan, were able to observe several thousand neutrinos—elusive, tiny subatomic particles moving at nearly the speed of light and passing through almost everything in their path. The Kamioka find-

Line
5
ings have potentially far-reaching ramifications. They strongly suggest that the neutrino has mass, albeit an infinitesimal amount. Even a tiny mass means that neutrinos would outweigh all the universe's visible matter, because of their vast numbers. The findings also suggest that a given neutrino does not have one stable mass or one stable identity; instead it oscillates from one identity or "flavor" (physicists' term describing how neutrinos interact with other particles) to another. This oscillation may explain

10
why, although the Sun is a large source of neutrinos, detectors capture far fewer solar neutrinos than the best theory of solar physics predicts: the neutrinos may be changing to flavors undetectable by detectors. Finally, while the standard particle-physics model—which describes all matter in terms of twelve fundamental particles and four fundamental forces—does not allow for neutrinos with mass, there are theories that

15
do. Further experiments to confirm that neutrinos have mass could help physicists determine which, if any, of these theories is correct.

Description

The passage discusses the observations of neutrinos made by physicists in Japan. It mentions two properties of neutrinos suggested by the observations—the nonzero mass and the ability to change flavor—and discusses the ramifications of these results.

12. The primary purpose of the passage is to
   - (A) evaluate the merits of a particular theory in light of new evidence
   - (B) discuss scientists' inability to account for certain unexpected discoveries
   - (C) point out certain shortcomings in a long-standing theory
   - (D) compare several alternative explanations for a particular phenomenon
   - (E) consider some implications of certain scientific findings

Explanation

The passage discusses the "potentially far-reaching ramifications" of two findings made during an observation of neutrinos: that neutrinos have nonzero mass and that they are capable of changing their flavor. Therefore the correct answer is **Choice E**.

13. According to the passage, one significant implication of the discovery that neutrinos have mass is that such a discovery would

    Ⓐ cast doubt on the solar origins of many of the neutrinos that reach Earth

    Ⓑ help to establish the validity of the standard particle-physics model

    Ⓒ indicate that most of the visible matter of the universe is composed of neutrinos

    Ⓓ entail that the total weight of all the visible matter in the universe is less than that of all the neutrinos in the universe

    Ⓔ mean that the speed with which neutrinos normally move can be slowed by certain types of matter

Explanation

The passage states that "Even a tiny mass [of a neutrino] means that neutrinos would outweigh all the universe's visible matter, because of their vast numbers." Therefore the correct answer is **Choice D**.

For each of Questions 14 to 18, select the <u>two</u> answer choices that, when used to complete the sentence, fit the meaning of the sentence as a whole <u>and</u> produce completed sentences that are alike in meaning.

---

14. In film studies—a visually oriented discipline that is _____ backlit close-ups, eyeline matches, and voyeuristic gazes—scholars have often been tone-deaf to the sounds of music.

    A fixated on

    B obsessed with

    C unconcerned with

    D amused by

    E bothered by

    F indifferent to

Explanation

The sentence suggests a difference between a scholarly discipline's attentions to the visual versus the aural, with the latter being relatively ignored in favor of the former. The blank must therefore designate this attention, which "unconcerned with" and "indifferent to" do not. "Amused by" conveys a lesser degree of attention and a more positive affect than both "fixated on" and "obsessed with" and lacks another word that would produce a sentence with the same meaning.

    Thus the correct answer is **fixated on** (Choice A) and **obsessed with** (Choice B).

15. Consumers may think that genetic engineering of foods is something new, but humans have been modifying plants for ages; the _____ is not that new genes are introduced but that genes can now be moved from one species to another.

    A novelty
    B quandary
    C advantage
    D innovation
    E discrepancy
    F predicament

Explanation

The last part of the sentence makes a distinction between the fact of genetic modification and the particulars of how this modification is done. This distinction is made in order to support the sentence's implication that consumers who believe that genetic engineering itself is new are mistaken. Therefore, the distinction must relate to what about genetic engineering is in fact new, so the blank must be completed with words that are synonymous with "newness." Both "novelty" and "innovation" fit this description, and the pairing produces sentences alike in meaning, so it is the correct answer. Of the other responses, while "quandary" and "predicament" are synonymous, nothing in the rest of the sentence mentions the problematic aspects of genetic engineering; therefore they do not fit the meaning of the sentence as well as the correct pairing. "Advantage" has no synonym among the choices, nor does the passage otherwise mention genetic engineering's benefits. "Discrepancy" likewise has no synonyms among the choices; it also does not describe the subject of the distinction made in the latter half of the sentence.

Thus the correct answer is **novelty** (Choice A) and **innovation** (Choice D).

16. Although the compound is abundant in the environment at large, its presence in the air is not _____; only in the form of underwater sediment does it cause damage.

    A trivial
    B detectable
    C deleterious
    D substantive
    E detrimental
    F inconsequential

Explanation

The "only" that follows the blank indicates that the effect of the compound in water is an exception to its general state in the air. Since the compound is dangerous underwater, it follows that it is generally harmless in the air. The blank is preceded by "not," so in order for the phrase to mean "harmless," it must be filled by words that are synonymous with "harmful." "Deleterious" and "detrimental" mean just that, and as synonyms they produce sentences alike in meaning, so they are the correct response. Of the other choices, "trivial" and "inconsequential" are synonyms, but they, like the other two choices, do not produce the necessary contrast with the last part of the sentence.

Thus the correct answer is **deleterious** (Choice C) and **detrimental** (Choice E).

17. Deacon attempts what seems impossible: a book rich in scientific insights, in a demanding discipline, that nevertheless is accessible to _____.

    A skeptics
    B experts
    C nonspecialists
    D zealots
    E authorities
    F laypersons

Explanation

The "nevertheless" that precedes the blank indicates that the book's accessibility contrasts in some way to its scientific insights and demanding subject matter. Among the choices for the blanks, there are two pairings that would yield similar meanings: "experts/authorities" and "nonspecialists/laypersons." Considering these two pairings, it would not be surprising if a book rich in scientific insights were accessible to experts, whereas writing such a book accessible to those not in the field would be a feat. "Nonspecialists/laypersons," then, provides the necessary contrast to the book's other qualities, so it is the correct response. The other two choices, "skeptics" and "zealots," can be eliminated straightaway because neither has a synonym among the other responses; in addition, neither helps form the contrast that the use of "nevertheless" requires.

Thus the correct answer is **nonspecialists** (Choice C) and **laypersons** (Choice F).

18. Despite relying on the well-to-do for commissions, the portrait painter was no _____: he depicted the character of those he painted as he perceived it.

    A hypocrite
    B egotist
    C sycophant
    D adulator
    E braggart
    F coward

Explanation

The sentence indicates that despite being paid by wealthy patrons to paint their portraits, the painter depicted his subjects as he saw them. This fact indicates that the painter was not a "sycophant" or "adulator" in that he did not seek to flatter his patrons. Although both "hypocrite" and "coward" make some sense when inserted in the blank, neither produces a sentence similar in meaning to that produced by any other option. "Braggart" and "egotist" are similar in meaning, but neither fits the sentence's focus on the painter's honest depiction of his subjects.

Thus the correct answer is **sycophant** (Choice C) and **adulator** (Choice D).

For each of Questions 19 to 25, select <u>one</u> answer choice unless otherwise directed.

Question 19 is based on this passage.

Mayor: Four years ago, when we reorganized the city police department in order to save money, critics claimed that the reorganization would make the police less responsive to citizens and would thus lead to more crime. The police have compiled theft statistics from the years following the reorganization that show that the critics were wrong. There was an overall decrease in reports of thefts of all kinds, including small thefts.

Line
5

19. Which of the following, if true, most seriously challenges the mayor's argument?

   (A) When city police are perceived as unresponsive, victims of theft are less likely to report thefts to the police.

   (B) The mayor's critics generally agree that police statistics concerning crime reports provide the most reliable available data on crime rates.

   (C) In other cities where police departments have been similarly reorganized, the numbers of reported thefts have generally risen following reorganization.

   (D) The mayor's reorganization of the police department failed to save as much money as it was intended to save.

   (E) During the four years immediately preceding the reorganization, reports of all types of theft had been rising steadily in comparison to reports of other crimes.

Explanation

The argument—that the reorganization did not lead to more crime—hinges upon statistics compiled from reports of crime, and therefore assumes that such reports are indicative of the actual incidence of crime. Something that weakens this connection between reports and incidence of theft, then, would challenge the mayor's argument. **Choice A** does exactly that, so it is the correct answer. Choices B and E would strengthen rather than challenge the mayor's argument, so they are incorrect. Choice C might give one reason to question the mayor's conclusion, but it does not speak to his argument, which does not involve other cities, so it is not the correct choice. Choice D is incorrect because the mayor's argument makes no claims regarding the economics of the reorganization, only its effectiveness at crime reduction.

Questions 20 to 23 are based on this passage.

During the 1920s, most advocates of scientific management, Frederick Taylor's method for maximizing workers' productivity by rigorously routinizing their jobs, opposed the five-day workweek. Although scientific managers conceded that reducing hours might provide an incentive to workers, in practice they more often used pay differentials to encourage higher productivity. Those reformers who wished to embrace both scientific management and reduced hours had to make a largely negative case, portraying the latter as an antidote to the rigors of the former.

In contrast to the scientific managers, Henry Ford claimed that shorter hours led to greater productivity and profits. However, few employers matched either Ford's vision or his specific interest in mass marketing a product—automobiles—that required leisure for its use, and few unions succeeded in securing shorter hours through bargaining. At its 1928 convention, the American Federation of Labor (AFL) boasted of approximately 165,000 members working five-day, 40-hour weeks. But although this represented an increase of about 75,000 since 1926, about 70 percent of the total came from five extremely well-organized building trades' unions.

Description

The passage describes the opposition of most advocates of scientific management to reducing work hours during the 1920s and then describes the positions taken by a few reformers and by Henry Ford to justify workweek reduction. It notes that most employers, however, did not agree with Ford and points to some supporting labor data.

20. The passage is primarily concerned with discussing which of the following?

(A) The relative merits of two points of view regarding a controversy

(B) The potential benefits to workers in the 1920s of a change in employers' policies

(C) The reasons for a labor-management disagreement during the 1920s

(D) The status of a contested labor issue during the 1920s

(E) The role of labor unions in bringing about a reform

Explanation

The passage is primarily concerned with discussing the opposition to, and the advocacy and adoption of, 40-hour workweeks during the 1920s; therefore **Choice D** is the correct answer. Because the passage lays out different viewpoints but does not consider their relative merits, Choice A is not correct. The passage does not discuss the benefit to workers of a 40-hour workweek or the opinion or role of labor unions on the issue, so Choices B, C, and E are incorrect.

21. It can be inferred that the author of the passage mentions "automobiles" (line 10) primarily to suggest that

    (A) Ford's business produced greater profits than did businesses requiring a workweek longer than five days

    (B) Ford, unlike most other employers, encouraged his employees to use the products they produced

    (C) Ford may have advocated shorter hours because of the particular nature of his business

    (D) unions were more likely to negotiate for shorter hours in some businesses than in others

    (E) automobile workers' unions were more effective than other unions in securing a five-day workweek

Explanation

Choice C is the correct answer. The mention of "automobiles" is directly followed by the observation that it is a product whose use requires leisure. Thus it can be inferred that one factor leading Ford to advocate shorter hours is that workers with newfound leisure time would become consumers of his product. There is no indication that Ford was unlike other employers in encouraging employees to consume their own products, so Choice B is incorrect. Choice A is incorrect because the passage does not say that Ford's business was highly profitable. Choices D and E are incorrect because the mention of automobiles is not connected to the likelihood or success of different types of unions in securing shorter hours.

22. It can be inferred that the author of the passage would probably agree with which of the following claims about the boast referred to in lines 12–13?

    (A) It is based on a mistaken estimation of the number of AFL workers who were allowed to work a five-day, 40-hour week in 1928.

    (B) It could create a mistaken impression regarding the number of unions obtaining a five-day, 40-hour week during the 1920s.

    (C) It exaggerates the extent of the increase between 1926 and 1928 in AFL members working a five-day, 40-hour week.

    (D) It overestimates the bargaining prowess of the AFL building trades' unions during the 1920s.

    (E) It is based on an overestimation of the number of union members in the AFL in 1928.

Explanation

The sentence mentioning this boast is followed by an explanation that although the number of workers with 40-hour weeks increased significantly, most of this gain could be attributed to just a few unions. Since the author is seemingly correcting a misimpression—that this increase involved many unions—**Choice B** is the correct answer. Because the passage does not suggest that the statistics themselves are questionable, Choices A and C are incorrect. Since the passage makes no mention of the total number of AFL members, Choice E cannot be correct. Choice D is incorrect because the boast makes no reference to the building trades' unions.

23. According to the passage, the "reformers" (line 5) claimed that

　Ⓐ neither scientific management nor reduced hours would result in an improvement in the working conditions of most workers

　Ⓑ the impact that the routinization of work had on workers could be mitigated by a reduction in the length of their workweek

　Ⓒ there was an inherent tension between the principles of scientific management and a commitment to reduced workweeks

　Ⓓ scientific managers were more likely than other managers to use pay differentials to encourage higher productivity

　Ⓔ reducing the length of the workweek would increase productivity more effectively than would increases in pay

Explanation

The sentence in question states that the reformers had to portray reduced hours as "an antidote" to the rigors of scientific management. Since an antidote can negate or reverse ill effects, **Choice B**, which states that the effects of scientific management (previously described as "rigorously routinizing" jobs) can be mitigated by workweek reduction, is the correct choice. Choice A is incorrect because there is no evidence that the reformers made negative claims about the effect of changes on working conditions; similarly, since no mention is made of the reformers' attitudes towards increases in pay, Choice E cannot be correct. The passage states something similar to Choice D, but this is not put into the mouths of the reformers, so that choice is incorrect. Choice C might seem appealing, since the debate on productivity is couched as one between scientific management and workweek reduction. But the reformers are claiming that the two can be combined to increase production. Therefore Choice C is incorrect.

Questions 24 and 25 are based on this passage.

In November 1753, the British author Sarah Fielding accepted half the payment for her novel *The Cry* and asked that the other half, when due, go to her "or to whomsoever I shall appoint," perhaps indicating that the remaining share was intended for someone

Line
　　else. Indeed, many think that the novel was a collaborative venture between Fielding

5　　and Jane Collier. This particular collaboration was likely enough, as the two were close friends with common interests. They wrote jointly authored letters, were both published authors with a lively interest in each other's work, and were enthusiastic supporters of didacticism and innovation in fiction—central concerns of *The Cry*. However, contemporaries ascribed the work solely to Fielding, and there is nothing in the novel

10　　that is incompatible with Fielding's other writings.

Description

The passage discusses the question of the provenance of the eighteenth-century novel *The Cry* and suggests that the novel could have been a collaboration between two authors, but that at the time of its publication it was believed to be the work of only one writer, Sarah Fielding.

For the following question, consider each of the choices separately and select all that apply.

24. The passage presents which of the following as evidence in favor of Fielding and Collier's having collaborated in writing *The Cry*?

    [A] Their friendship

    [B] Their joint authorship of correspondence

    [C] Their approach to fiction

Explanation

All three choices are correct. The question asks what is offered as evidence of the joint authorship of *The Cry*.

    Choice A is correct: the passage states that Fielding and Collier "were close friends."

    Choice B is correct: the passage states that Fielding and Collier "wrote jointly authored letters."

    Choice C is correct: the passage states that Fielding and Collier were both "enthusiastic supporters of didacticism and innovation in fiction."

25. It can be inferred that the author of the passage would agree with which of the following claims about *The Cry*?

    (A) It develops themes commonly found in published works.

    (B) It reflects an interest in the purposes to which fiction may be put.

    (C) It contains elements that are incompatible with any of Collier's solo writings.

    (D) It shows that the extent of Collier and Fielding's shared interests was not as wide as is generally thought.

    (E) Parts of it were written jointly by Fielding and Collier.

Explanation

The passage states that *The Cry*'s "central concerns" are "didacticism and innovation in fiction," so **Choice B** is correct. The passage does not discuss how popular the novel's themes are (Choice A), whether the writing is compatible with Collier's (Choice C), or what the novel shows about the extent of Collier and Fielding's joint interests (Choice D). Finally, Choice E is incorrect, as the author of the passage never takes a stand on whether the novel was written by Fielding alone or in collaboration with Collier.

PRACTICE SET 3

For each question, indicate the best answer, using the directions given.

> **For each of Questions 1 to 7, select <u>one</u> entry for each blank from the corresponding column of choices. Fill all blanks in the way that best completes the text.**

1. While not _____ the arguments in favor of the proposal for new highway construction, the governor nevertheless decided to veto the proposal.

Ⓐ	optimistic about
Ⓑ	convinced by
Ⓒ	happy with
Ⓓ	sanguine about
Ⓔ	unsympathetic to

2. The children's _____ natures were in sharp contrast to the even-tempered dispositions of their parents.

Ⓐ	mercurial
Ⓑ	blithe
Ⓒ	phlegmatic
Ⓓ	apathetic
Ⓔ	cunning

3. The first major exhibits of modern art left the public (i) _____, its (ii) _____ intensified by the response of art critics, who stooped to vituperation to express their disgust with the new art.

Blank (i)	Blank (ii)
Ⓐ aghast	Ⓓ shock
Ⓑ bemused	Ⓔ apathy
Ⓒ unsurprised	Ⓕ empathy

4. While many outside the company attributed the company's success to its president's (i) _____, insiders realized that this success owed more to the president's inflexibility than to any (ii) _____ that the president might be supposed to have displayed.

Blank (i)	Blank (ii)
Ⓐ perseverance	Ⓓ obduracy
Ⓑ popularity	Ⓔ caprice
Ⓒ prescience	Ⓕ foresight

5. With the rate of technological (i) _____ accelerating—many people now consider a personal computer (ii) _____ after three years—the question of how to properly dispose of old equipment is no small matter.

Blank (i)	Blank (ii)
Ⓐ affordability	Ⓓ outdated
Ⓑ complexity	Ⓔ familiar
Ⓒ obsolescence	Ⓕ inestimable

6. In the nineteenth century the (i) _____ advanced mechanical printing techniques made it possible for newspaper owners to print newspapers cheaply and in mass quantities, but unlike many other mechanized industries, where machines (ii) _____ workers, the new printing machines required trained compositors to run them, thereby (iii) _____ the demand for skilled printing labor.

Blank (i)	Blank (ii)	Blank (iii)
Ⓐ wide application of	Ⓓ marginalized	Ⓖ ignoring
Ⓑ extensive resistance to	Ⓔ intrigued	Ⓗ anticipating
Ⓒ great expense of	Ⓕ isolated	Ⓘ increasing

7. It may be that a kind of pendulum is built into United States politics: if a particular interest group scores a major victory, its supporters (i) _____ and its adversaries (ii) _____ their efforts, so that the victory is soon (iii) _____.

Blank (i)	Blank (ii)	Blank (iii)
Ⓐ consider new possibilities	Ⓓ abandon	Ⓖ reversed
Ⓑ grow complacent	Ⓔ redouble	Ⓗ augmented
Ⓒ become even more focused	Ⓕ defend	Ⓘ institutionalized

For each of **Questions 8 to 14**, select **one** answer choice unless otherwise directed.

Questions 8 to 10 are based on this passage.

The binary planet hypothesis—that Earth and the Moon formed simultaneously by the accretion of smaller objects—does not explain why the Moon's iron core is so small relative to the Moon's total volume, compared with Earth's core relative to Earth's total volume. According to the giant-impact hypothesis, the Moon was created during a collision between Earth and a large object about the size of Mars. Computer simulations of this impact show that both of the objects would melt in the impact and the dense core of the impactor would fall as molten rock into the liquefied iron core of Earth. The ejected matter—mantle rock that had surrounded the cores of both objects—would be almost devoid of iron. This matter would become the Moon.

Line

5

For the following question, consider each of the choices separately and select all that apply.

8. According to the passage, the binary planet hypothesis holds that
   - A Earth and the Moon were formed at the same time
   - B smaller objects joined together to form Earth and the Moon
   - C the Moon's core is the same absolute size as Earth's core

9. The giant-impact hypothesis as described in the passage answers all of the following questions EXCEPT:
   - Ⓐ What happened to the rock that surrounded the impactor's core after the impactor hit Earth?
   - Ⓑ What happened to the impactor's core after the impactor hit Earth?
   - Ⓒ Where did the impactor that collided with Earth originate?
   - Ⓓ Why is the Moon's iron core small relative to that of Earth?
   - Ⓔ What was the size of the impactor relative to that of Mars?

10. Which of the following best describes the organization of the passage?
   - Ⓐ The development of one theory into another is outlined.
   - Ⓑ Two explanations are provided, both of which are revealed as inadequate.
   - Ⓒ A theory is presented, and then evidence that undermines that theory is discussed.
   - Ⓓ Similarities and differences between two theories are described.
   - Ⓔ A flawed hypothesis is introduced, and then an alternative hypothesis is presented.

Most recent work on the history of leisure in Europe has been based on the central hypothesis of a fundamental discontinuity between preindustrial and industrial societies. According to this view, the modern idea of leisure did not exist in medieval and early modern Europe: the modern distinction between the categories of work and leisure was a product of industrial capitalism. Preindustrial societies had festivals (together with informal and irregular breaks from work), while industrial societies have leisure in the form of weekends and vacations. The emergence of leisure is therefore part of the process of modernization. If this theory is correct, there is what Michel Foucault called a conceptual rupture between the two periods, and so the very idea of a history of leisure before the Industrial Revolution is an anachronism.

To reject the idea that leisure has had a continuous history from the Middle Ages to the present is not to deny that late medieval and early modern Europeans engaged in many pursuits that are now commonly considered leisure or sporting activities—jousting, hunting, tennis, card playing, travel, and so on—or that Europe in this period was dominated by a privileged class that engaged in these pursuits. What is involved in the discontinuity hypothesis is the recognition that the people of the Middle Ages and early modern Europe did not regard as belonging to a common category activities (hunting and gambling, for example) that are usually classified together today under the heading of leisure. Consider fencing: today it may be considered a "sport," but for the gentleman of the Renaissance it was an art or science. Conversely, activities that today may be considered serious, notably warfare, were often described as pastimes.

Serious pitfalls therefore confront historians of leisure who assume continuity and who work with the modern concepts of leisure and sport, projecting them back onto the past without asking about the meanings contemporaries gave to their activities. However, the discontinuity hypothesis can pose problems of its own. Historians holding this view attempt to avoid anachronism by means of a simple dichotomy, cutting European history into two eras, preindustrial and industrial, setting up the binary opposition between a "festival culture" and a "leisure culture." The dichotomy remains of use insofar as it reminds us that the rise of industrial capitalism was not purely a phenomenon of economic history, but had social and cultural preconditions and consequences. The dichotomy, however, leads to distortions when it reduces a great variety of medieval and early modern European ideas, assumptions, and practices to the simple formula implied by the phrase "festival culture."

11. The primary purpose of the passage is to
   (A) refute the idea that the history of leisure is discontinuous
   (B) show why one of two approaches is more useful in studying the history of leisure
   (C) suggest the need for a new, more inclusive concept to replace the concept of leisure
   (D) trace the development of a theory about the history of leisure
   (E) point out the basis for, and the limits of, an approach to the history of leisure

12. The author of the passage asserts that the "dichotomy" (line 26) can lead to which of the following?

   (A) Reliance on only one of several equally valid theoretical approaches

   (B) The imposition of modern conceptions and meanings on past societies

   (C) Failure to take into account the complexity of certain features of European culture

   (D) Failure to utilize new conceptual categories in the study of the history of leisure

   (E) Failure to take account of the distinction between preindustrial and industrial societies

13. According to the passage, the "simple dichotomy" (line 26) is useful primarily because it serves as

   (A) a way of calling historians' attention to certain facts about the Industrial Revolution

   (B) an antidote to the oversimplification encouraged by such terms as "festival culture"

   (C) a device for distinguishing between the work and the leisure activities of preindustrial Europeans

   (D) a way of understanding the privileged class of medieval Europe by viewing its activities in modern terms

   (E) a tool for separating social history, including the history of leisure, from economic history

14. Which of the following best describes the organization of the passage as a whole?

   (A) Two hypotheses are discussed, and evidence in support of one is presented.

   (B) A hypothesis is presented and discussed, and a limitation to the hypothesis is identified.

   (C) A hypothesis is proposed, its supposed advantages are shown to be real, and its supposed disadvantages are shown to be illusory.

   (D) A problem is identified, two hypotheses are advanced to resolve it, and both are rejected.

   (E) A problem is identified, two resolutions are proposed, and a solution combining elements of both is recommended.

For each of Questions 15 to 19, select the **two** answer choices that, when used to complete the sentence, fit the meaning of the sentence as a whole **and** produce completed sentences that are alike in meaning.

15. If big sums are to be spent on cleaning up environmental disasters, it is better to spend them on unglamorous but _____ problems such as unsanitary water in Third World countries.

    A futile
    B ephemeral
    C pressing
    D controversial
    E transitory
    F critical

16. The process of establishing a literary canon is seen by some as, in part, an attempt by certain scholars to make their own labors central and to relegate the work of others to _____ status.

    A orthodox
    B marginal
    C mainstream
    D definitive
    E conditional
    F peripheral

17. The mayor is more ideologically consistent than is widely believed: her long-term commitment to tax reform, for example, is not indicative of _____.

    A perspicacity
    B capriciousness
    C callousness
    D fickleness
    E clearheadedness
    F insensitivity

18. At first glance Watkins Park, with its meandering stream and its thicket of greenery, seems _____; however, upon closer inspection one is quickly reminded that the park is in the middle of a major city.

    A bucolic
    B remarkable
    C urban
    D noteworthy
    E pastoral
    F spurious

19. Although relying on much of the recent scholarship on the bison, Lott's book is a distinctly _____ and even idiosyncratic contribution to the field.

  A derivative
  B original
  C innovative
  D imitative
  E insightful
  F surprising

For each of Questions 20 to 25, select <u>one</u> answer choice unless otherwise directed.

Question 20 is based on this passage.

James W. Coleman's book on John Edgar Wideman's literary career addresses the needs of a general, if well-read, public rather than the esoteric vanities of scholarly specialists, whom he neither ignores nor flatters. To assume the former audience was

Line   familiar with every work Wideman ever penned would have been pretentious. Instead,
  5   Coleman furnishes more than ample descriptive criticism and background information, avoiding the cryptic allusiveness that is favored by some academic critics but that discourages the undergraduate audience he likely envisioned. Unfortunately, this accent on bringing serious Wideman criticism to a broader audience often frustrates the reader who wishes that announced themes, techniques, and stylistic devices would
  10   not whisk by as quickly as world capitals on a seven-day package tour of the globe.

20. The reference to "a seven-day package tour of the globe" (line 10) is most likely meant to suggest a treatment that is

  Ⓐ inclusive
  Ⓑ cursory
  Ⓒ focused
  Ⓓ broad based
  Ⓔ substantial

Question 21 is based on this passage.

The painter Peter Brandon never dated his works, and their chronology is only now beginning to take shape in the critical literature. A recent dating of a Brandon self-portrait to 1930 is surely wrong. Brandon was 63 years old in 1930, yet the painting shows a young, dark-haired man—obviously Brandon, but clearly not a man of 63.

21. Which of the following, if justifiably assumed, allows the conclusion to be properly drawn?

   Ⓐ There is no securely dated self-portrait of Brandon that he painted when he was significantly younger than 63.

   Ⓑ In refraining from dating his works, Brandon intended to steer critical discussion of them away from considerations of chronology.

   Ⓒ Until recently, there was very little critical literature on the works of Brandon.

   Ⓓ Brandon at age 63 would not have portrayed himself in a painting as he had looked when he was a young man.

   Ⓔ Brandon painted several self-portraits that showed him as a man past the age of 60.

Questions 22 to 24 are based on this passage.

Experts have differed about where the genus *Varanus* (monitor lizards) originated. Because most existing species live in Australia, early researchers concluded that *Varanus* originated in Australia and subsequently island hopped westward along the Indo-Australian archipelago. Herpetologist Robert Mertens later argued that *Varanus*
Line
5 probably originated in the archipelago. Chromosomal analysis has since supported Mertens' contention, and in addition, geologic evidence points to a collision between the archipelago and the Australian landmass after *Varanus* evolved—a fact that could account for the genus' present distribution.

    A related puzzle for scientists is the present distribution of *Varanus'* largest surviv-
10 ing species, the Komodo dragon. These carnivores live only on four small islands in the archipelago where, scientists note, the prey base is too small to support mammalian carnivores. But the Komodo dragon has recently been shown to manage body temperature much more efficiently than do mammalian carnivores, enabling it to survive on about a tenth of the food energy required by a mammalian carnivore
15 of comparable size.

22. It can be inferred from the passage that the geographical distribution of the Komodo dragon is

   Ⓐ currently less restricted than it was at the time researchers first began investigating the origins of the genus *Varanus*

   Ⓑ currently more restricted than it was at the time researchers first began investigating the origins of the genus *Varanus*

   Ⓒ less restricted than is the distribution of the genus *Varanus* as a whole

   Ⓓ more restricted than is the distribution of the genus *Varanus* as a whole

   Ⓔ viewed as evidence in favor of the hypothesis that the genus *Varanus* originated in the Indo-Australian archipelago

23. Which of the following elements in the debate over the origin of *Varanus* is NOT provided in the passage?

   Ⓐ The evidence that led Mertens to argue that *Varanus* originated in the Indo-Australian archipelago

   Ⓑ The evidence that led early researchers to argue that *Varanus* originated in Australia

   Ⓒ A possible explanation of how *Varanus* might have spread to the Indo-Australian archipelago if it had originated in Australia

   Ⓓ A possible explanation of how *Varanus* might have spread to Australia if it had originated in the Indo-Australian archipelago

   Ⓔ An indication of the general present-day distribution of *Varanus* species between Australia and the Indo-Australian archipelago

24. It can be inferred that which of the following is true of the "geologic evidence" (line 6)?

   Ⓐ It was first noted by Mertens as evidence in favor of his theory about the origins of *Varanus*.

   Ⓑ It cannot rule out either one of the theories about the origins of *Varanus* discussed in the passage.

   Ⓒ It accounts for the present distribution of the Komodo dragon.

   Ⓓ It has led to renewed interest in the debate over the origins of *Varanus*.

   Ⓔ It confirms the conclusions reached by early researchers concerning the origins of *Varanus*.

Question 25 is based on this passage.

Geographers and historians have traditionally held the view that Antarctica was first sighted around 1820, but some sixteenth-century European maps show a body that resembles the polar landmass, even though explorers of the period never saw it. Some
Line   scholars, therefore, argue that the continent must have been discovered and mapped
5   by the ancients, whose maps are known to have served as models for the European cartographers.

25. Which of the following, if true, is most damaging to the inference drawn by the scholars?

   Ⓐ The question of who first sighted Antarctica in modern times is still much debated, and no one has been able to present conclusive evidence.

   Ⓑ Between 3,000 and 9,000 years ago, the world was warmer than it is now, and the polar landmass was presumably smaller.

   Ⓒ There are only a few sixteenth-century global maps that show a continental landmass at the South Pole.

   Ⓓ Most attributions of surprising accomplishments to ancient civilizations or even extraterrestrials are eventually discredited or rejected as preposterous.

   Ⓔ Ancient philosophers believed that there had to be a large landmass at the South Pole to balance the northern continents and make the world symmetrical.

ANSWER KEY

PRACTICE SET 3

1. **Choice E**: unsympathetic to
2. **Choice A**: mercurial
3. **Choice A**: aghast; **Choice D**: shock
4. **Choice C**: prescience; **Choice F**: foresight
5. **Choice C**: obsolescence; **Choice D**: outdated
6. **Choice A**: wide application of; **Choice D**: marginalized; **Choice I**: increasing
7. **Choice B**: grow complacent; **Choice E**: redouble; **Choice G**: reversed
8. **Choice A**: Earth and the Moon were formed at the same time
   AND
   Choice B: smaller objects joined together to form Earth and the Moon
9. **Choice C**: Where did the impactor that collided with Earth originate?
10. **Choice E**: A flawed hypothesis is introduced, and then an alternative hypothesis is presented.
11. **Choice E**: point out the basis for, and the limits of, an approach to the history of leisure
12. **Choice C**: Failure to take into account the complexity of certain features of European culture
13. **Choice A**: a way of calling historians' attention to certain facts about the Industrial Revolution
14. **Choice B**: A hypothesis is presented and discussed, and a limitation to the hypothesis is identified.
15. **Choice C**: pressing AND **Choice F**: critical
16. **Choice B**: marginal AND **Choice F**: peripheral
17. **Choice B**: capriciousness AND **Choice D**: fickleness
18. **Choice A**: bucolic AND **Choice E**: pastoral
19. **Choice B**: original AND **Choice C**: innovative
20. **Choice B**: cursory
21. **Choice D**: Brandon at age 63 would not have portrayed himself in a painting as he had looked when he was a young man.
22. **Choice D**: more restricted than is the distribution of the genus *Varanus* as a whole
23. **Choice A**: The evidence that led Mertens to argue that *Varanus* originated in the Indo-Australian archipelago
24. **Choice B**: It cannot rule out either one of the theories about the origins of *Varanus* discussed in the passage.
25. **Choice E**: Ancient philosophers believed that there had to be a large landmass at the South Pole to balance the northern continents and make the world symmetrical.

Answers and Explanations

PRACTICE SET 3

For each question, indicate the best answer, using the directions given.

> For each of Questions 1 to 7, select **one** entry for each blank from the corresponding column of choices. Fill all blanks in the way that best completes the text.

1. While not _____ the arguments in favor of the proposal for new highway construction, the governor nevertheless decided to veto the proposal.

Ⓐ	optimistic about
Ⓑ	convinced by
Ⓒ	happy with
Ⓓ	sanguine about
Ⓔ	unsympathetic to

Explanation

"Nevertheless" indicates that the governor's action—vetoing the proposal—was done despite some inclination to act otherwise. The first part of the sentence, then, must show that the governor had some reason to support the proposal. Thus the correct response, when preceded by "not," should describe an attitude toward the arguments in favor of the proposal that would lead the governor to support it. Four of the choices, "optimistic about," "convinced by," "happy with," and "sanguine about," indicate positive attitudes. When they are negated by the "not" that precedes the blank, then, they all indicate reasons that the governor would not support the proposal, so they are the opposite of what is called for. However, if the governor was not "unsympathetic to" the arguments for the proposal, he would have had a reason to support the measure he ultimately vetoed.

Thus the correct answer is **unsympathetic to** (Choice E).

2. The children's _____ natures were in sharp contrast to the even-tempered dispositions of their parents.

Ⓐ	mercurial
Ⓑ	blithe
Ⓒ	phlegmatic
Ⓓ	apathetic
Ⓔ	cunning

Explanation

The children's natures are the opposite to those of their parents; since the parents are even tempered, the word that fills the blank must mean the opposite of even tempered. "Mercurial," meaning quickly changing, exactly fits, so it is the correct choice. Although the other answer choices encompass a range of temperaments ("blithe" means happy, "phlegmatic" means unemotional, "apathetic" means uncaring), none suggest a tendency to change from one state to another, so none of them contrast as well with "even-tempered."

Thus the correct answer is **mercurial** (Choice A).

3. The first major exhibits of modern art left the public (i) _____, its (ii) _____ intensified by the response of art critics, who stooped to vituperation to express their disgust with the new art.

Blank (i)	Blank (ii)
Ⓐ aghast	Ⓓ shock
Ⓑ bemused	Ⓔ apathy
Ⓒ unsurprised	Ⓕ empathy

Explanation

The sentence implies that the public and the art critics had similar negative reactions to the modern art exhibits; the words "vituperation" and "disgust" further suggest that this reaction was very intense. Thus answers to both Blank (i) and Blank (ii) must be synonymous with "strong negative reaction." The only combination of the answer choices that matches this
meaning is "aghast" and "shock," so this answer is correct.

Thus the correct answer is **aghast** (Choice A) and **shock** (Choice D).

4. While many outside the company attributed the company's success to its president's (i) _____, insiders realized that this success owed more to the president's inflexibility than to any (ii) _____ that the president might be supposed to have displayed.

Blank (i)	Blank (ii)
Ⓐ perseverance	Ⓓ obduracy
Ⓑ popularity	Ⓔ caprice
Ⓒ prescience	Ⓕ foresight

Explanation

The second part of the sentence suggests that there is a contrast between a negative quality of the president ("inflexibility") that was the actual primary cause of the company's success and a positive quality named by Blank (ii) that the outsiders took to be the cause. Among the answer choices for Blank (ii), only "foresight" denotes a positive quality, so it is the correct answer. The sentence as a whole implies that the answer to Blank (i) must be similar in meaning to the answer for Blank (ii); the only answer choice that is synonymous with "foresight" is "prescience," so it is the correct answer for Blank (i).

Thus the correct answer is **prescience** (Choice C) and **foresight** (Choice F).

5. With the rate of technological (i) _____ accelerating—many people now consider a personal computer (ii) _____ after three years—the question of how to properly dispose of old equipment is no small matter.

Blank (i)	Blank (ii)
(A) affordability	(D) outdated
(B) complexity	(E) familiar
(C) obsolescence	(F) inestimable

Explanation

Since the last part of the sentence mentions the problem of disposing of old equipment, it is likely that the three-year-old personal computer described by Blank (ii) will be characterized by a word that suggests why it is being disposed of. Neither "familiar" nor "inestimable" suggests something that needs to be cast off, while "outdated" does; therefore, it is the correct response. Since the outdated three-year-old computer is presented as an example of the trend in technology mentioned in the first part of the sentence, Blank (i) must be completed with a word that characterizes this outdatedness. "Obsolescence" does exactly that, so it is the correct response. Neither "affordability" nor "complexity" is exemplified by computers that become quickly outdated, so they are incorrect.

Thus the correct answer is **obsolescence** (Choice C) and **outdated** (Choice D).

6. In the nineteenth century the (i) _____ advanced mechanical printing techniques made it possible for newspaper owners to print newspapers cheaply and in mass quantities, but unlike many other mechanized industries, where machines (ii) _____ workers, the new printing machines required trained compositors to run them, thereby (iii) _____ the demand for skilled printing labor.

Blank (i)	Blank (ii)	Blank (iii)
(A) wide application of	(D) marginalized	(G) ignoring
(B) extensive resistance to	(E) intrigued	(H) anticipating
(C) great expense of	(F) isolated	(I) increasing

Explanation

The author states that in the nineteenth century great quantities of newspapers could be printed cheaply, and Blank (i) calls for something related to advanced mechanical printing techniques that allowed this to happen. Of the choices, "great expense of" contradicts the assertion that newspaper printing became cheap, while "extensive resistance to" advanced technology would likely result in no notable changes in the industry. Thus "wide application of" is the correct answer. Blank (iii) must describe the effect of new printing machines on the skilled labor market. Since the author states that these machines required trained workers, jobs would have been created that did not previously exist. Thus the correct answer is "increasing." As for the other choices, there is no evidence that the demand for skilled printing labor was ignored and no mention of future demand for skilled labor that might have been anticipated. Blank (ii) requires a word that characterizes the effect of machines on workers in other mechanized industries, which the author contrasts to the newspaper industry's need for trained operators. The implication is that the mechanization of other industries did not require trained workers but rather that machines simply replaced human labor. This suggests that the answer to Blank (ii) is "marginalized." Since the passage contains no references to workers' interest in the machines or to their working conditions, neither "intrigued" nor "isolated" makes sense.

Thus the correct answer is **wide application of** (Choice A), **marginalized** (Choice D), and **increasing** (Choice I).

7. It may be that a kind of pendulum is built into United States politics: if a particular interest group scores a major victory, its supporters (i) _____ and its adversaries (ii) _____ their efforts, so that the victory is soon (iii) _____.

Blank (i)	Blank (ii)	Blank (iii)
(A) consider new possibilities	(D) abandon	(G) reversed
(B) grow complacent	(E) redouble	(H) augmented
(C) become even more focused	(F) defend	(I) institutionalized

Explanation

The colon indicates that the second half of the sentence will explain the first. What is being explained is an analogy between United States politics and a pendulum, so it follows that the second half of the sentence shows how momentum in politics swings back and forth. Blank (iii) must be filled with a word that describes this seesawing effect; "reversed" does so. "Augmented" instead suggests momentum that builds upon itself, while "institutionalized" would characterize change that once made is difficult to undo, so neither of those choices fit. Blanks (i) and (ii) then must be filled with a pair of choices whose contrast explains why reversals in political momentum happen. "Grow complacent" and "redouble" do this, suggesting that the motivation of partisans on both sides of an issue is affected in opposite ways by a victory for either side. For Blank (i), "become even more focused" suggests that other victories for the winning side would follow the initial one, while "consider new possibilities" implies an expansion rather than a reversal of a political agenda. For Blank (ii), neither "abandon" nor "defend" suggests the political will that could lead to the reversal of a defeat.

Thus the correct answer is **grow complacent** (Choice B), **redouble** (Choice E), and **reversed** (Choice G).

For each of Questions 8 to 14, select one answer choice unless otherwise directed.

Questions 8 to 10 are based on this passage.

The binary planet hypothesis—that Earth and the Moon formed simultaneously by the accretion of smaller objects—does not explain why the Moon's iron core is so small relative to the Moon's total volume, compared with Earth's core relative to Earth's total volume. According to the giant-impact hypothesis, the Moon was created during a collision between Earth and a large object about the size of Mars. Computer simulations of this impact show that both of the objects would melt in the impact and the dense core of the impactor would fall as molten rock into the liquefied iron core of Earth. The ejected matter—mantle rock that had surrounded the cores of both objects—would be almost devoid of iron. This matter would become the Moon.

Line
5

Description

The passage discusses two hypotheses about the formation of Earth's moon and explains why one of them appears to be more plausible than the other.

For the following question, consider each of the choices separately and select all that apply.

8. According to the passage, the binary planet hypothesis holds that
   A Earth and the Moon were formed at the same time
   B smaller objects joined together to form Earth and the Moon
   C the Moon's core is the same absolute size as Earth's core

Explanation

Choices A and B are correct. The question asks what the binary planet hypothesis holds.

  Choice A is correct: According to the first sentence of the passage, the binary planet hypothesis holds that "Earth and the Moon formed simultaneously," that is, at the same time.

  Choice B is correct: According to the first sentence of the passage, the binary planet hypothesis holds that Earth and the Moon formed "by the accretion of smaller objects," that is, by smaller objects joining together.

  Choice C is incorrect: The passage does not mention the absolute sizes of Earth's core and the Moon's core; it only compares their sizes relative to the volumes of the two objects.

9. The giant-impact hypothesis as described in the passage answers all of the following questions EXCEPT:
   (A) What happened to the rock that surrounded the impactor's core after the impactor hit Earth?
   (B) What happened to the impactor's core after the impactor hit Earth?
   (C) Where did the impactor that collided with Earth originate?
   (D) Why is the Moon's iron core small relative to that of Earth?
   (E) What was the size of the impactor relative to that of Mars?

Explanation

The questions in Choices A, B, D, and E are all answered by the giant-impact hypothesis: for Choice A, the rock that surrounded the impactor's core "would become the Moon"; for Choice B, the impactor's core "would fall as molten rock into the liquefied iron core of the Earth"; for Choice D, the Moon's iron core is small relative to the Earth's core because the matter that formed the Moon was "almost devoid of iron"; and for Choice E, the passage states that the impactor was "a large object about the size of Mars." But nothing in the passage refers to the origin of the impactor, so **Choice C** is the correct answer.

10. Which of the following best describes the organization of the passage?

   Ⓐ The development of one theory into another is outlined.

   Ⓑ Two explanations are provided, both of which are revealed as inadequate.

   Ⓒ A theory is presented, and then evidence that undermines that theory is discussed.

   Ⓓ Similarities and differences between two theories are described.

   Ⓔ A flawed hypothesis is introduced, and then an alternative hypothesis is presented.

Explanation

The passage begins by presenting the binary planet hypothesis about the formation of Earth and the Moon and claiming that the hypothesis fails to explain the disparity in the sizes of Earth's iron core and the Moon's iron core relative to their volumes. The passage then introduces an alternative—the giant-impact hypothesis—and argues that this alternative explains the disparity better. Thus, **Choice E** is correct. The second theory is not presented as having been developed out of the first, so Choice A is incorrect; only the first theory is revealed as inadequate, so Choice B is incorrect; and the two theories are not compared extensively, so Choice D is incorrect. Although "a theory [the binary planet hypothesis] is presented, and then evidence that undermines that theory [the disparity related to iron cores] is discussed," that description fails to capture the organization of the passage as a whole, so Choice C is incorrect.

Most recent work on the history of leisure in Europe has been based on the central hypothesis of a fundamental discontinuity between preindustrial and industrial societies. According to this view, the modern idea of leisure did not exist in medieval and
Line early modern Europe: the modern distinction between the categories of work and
5 leisure was a product of industrial capitalism. Preindustrial societies had festivals (together with informal and irregular breaks from work), while industrial societies have leisure in the form of weekends and vacations. The emergence of leisure is therefore part of the process of modernization. If this theory is correct, there is what Michel Foucault called a conceptual rupture between the two periods, and so the very idea of
10 a history of leisure before the Industrial Revolution is an anachronism.

To reject the idea that leisure has had a continuous history from the Middle Ages to the present is not to deny that late medieval and early modern Europeans engaged in many pursuits that are now commonly considered leisure or sporting activities—jousting, hunting, tennis, card playing, travel, and so on—or that Europe in this period
15 was dominated by a privileged class that engaged in these pursuits. What is involved in the discontinuity hypothesis is the recognition that the people of the Middle Ages and early modern Europe did not regard as belonging to a common category activities (hunting and gambling, for example) that are usually classified together today under the heading of leisure. Consider fencing: today it may be considered a "sport," but for
20 the gentleman of the Renaissance it was an art or science. Conversely, activities that today may be considered serious, notably warfare, were often described as pastimes.

Serious pitfalls therefore confront historians of leisure who assume continuity and who work with the modern concepts of leisure and sport, projecting them back onto the past without asking about the meanings contemporaries gave to their activities.
25 However, the discontinuity hypothesis can pose problems of its own. Historians holding this view attempt to avoid anachronism by means of a simple dichotomy, cutting European history into two eras, preindustrial and industrial, setting up the binary opposition between a "festival culture" and a "leisure culture." The dichotomy remains of use insofar as it reminds us that the rise of industrial capitalism was not purely a
30 phenomenon of economic history, but had social and cultural preconditions and consequences. The dichotomy, however, leads to distortions when it reduces a great variety of medieval and early modern European ideas, assumptions, and practices to the simple formula implied by the phrase "festival culture."

Description

The passage deals with the historical study of leisure in Europe and discusses the view that the concept of leisure underwent a fundamental change at the time of the Industrial Revolution (the "discontinuity" hypothesis). The second paragraph explains how the hypothesis can accommodate certain historical data, and the third paragraph discusses the usefulness of the hypothesis while at the same time outlining some potential drawbacks.

11. The primary purpose of the passage is to
    - (A) refute the idea that the history of leisure is discontinuous
    - (B) show why one of two approaches is more useful in studying the history of leisure
    - (C) suggest the need for a new, more inclusive concept to replace the concept of leisure
    - (D) trace the development of a theory about the history of leisure
    - (E) point out the basis for, and the limits of, an approach to the history of leisure

Explanation

The first paragraph of the passage tells us that the difference between preindustrial and industrial society in Europe was so great that "the modern distinction between the categories of work and leisure" (lines 4–5) cannot be meaningfully applied to the former, implying that there exists a discontinuity between the two periods. The second paragraph argues that the discontinuity approach can accommodate historical data. Finally, the third paragraph admits that, while useful in some respects, this approach "can pose problems of its own" (line 25) and briefly describes these problems. All this points to **Choice E** as correct.

12. The author of the passage asserts that the "dichotomy" (line 26) can lead to which of the following?
    - (A) Reliance on only one of several equally valid theoretical approaches
    - (B) The imposition of modern conceptions and meanings on past societies
    - (C) Failure to take into account the complexity of certain features of European culture
    - (D) Failure to utilize new conceptual categories in the study of the history of leisure
    - (E) Failure to take account of the distinction between preindustrial and industrial societies

Explanation

The word "dichotomy" appears only in the last paragraph of the passage. One of the key claims there is that the dichotomy "reduces a great variety . . . to the simple formula" (lines 31–33). Therefore **Choice C** is correct.

13. According to the passage, the "simple dichotomy" (line 26) is useful primarily because it serves as
    - (A) a way of calling historians' attention to certain facts about the Industrial Revolution
    - (B) an antidote to the oversimplification encouraged by such terms as "festival culture"
    - (C) a device for distinguishing between the work and the leisure activities of preindustrial Europeans
    - (D) a way of understanding the privileged class of medieval Europe by viewing its activities in modern terms
    - (E) a tool for separating social history, including the history of leisure, from economic history

Explanation

"Simple dichotomy" is mentioned in line 26. The passage states that this dichotomy "remains of use insofar as it reminds us that the rise of industrial capitalism" (lines 28–29) was not just an economic phenomenon, but also a social and a cultural phenomenon. This points to **Choice A** as correct.

14. Which of the following best describes the organization of the passage as a whole?

   Ⓐ Two hypotheses are discussed, and evidence in support of one is presented.

   Ⓑ A hypothesis is presented and discussed, and a limitation to the hypothesis is identified.

   Ⓒ A hypothesis is proposed, its supposed advantages are shown to be real, and its supposed disadvantages are shown to be illusory.

   Ⓓ A problem is identified, two hypotheses are advanced to resolve it, and both are rejected.

   Ⓔ A problem is identified, two resolutions are proposed, and a solution combining elements of both is recommended.

Explanation

The main purpose of the passage is to discuss the idea of "the central hypothesis of a fundamental discontinuity between preindustrial and industrial societies" (lines 1–3) in terms of the development of the concept of leisure. Most of the passage is focused on demonstrating the usefulness of this hypothesis; however, the second part of the third paragraph mentions some "distortions" (line 31) that may result if the hypothesis is accepted. Therefore **Choice B** is correct. Choices A, D, and E are incorrect, as only one hypothesis/solution is discussed in the passage. Choice C is incorrect, as the passage does not mention that the "distortions" (line 31) caused by accepting the hypothesis are illusory.

> **For each of Questions 15 to 19, select the <u>two</u> answer choices that, when used to complete the sentence, fit the meaning of the sentence as a whole <u>and</u> produce completed sentences that are alike in meaning.**

15. If big sums are to be spent on cleaning up environmental disasters, it is better to spend them on unglamorous but _____ problems such as unsanitary water in Third World countries.

   Ⓐ futile

   Ⓑ ephemeral

   Ⓒ pressing

   Ⓓ controversial

   Ⓔ transitory

   Ⓕ critical

Explanation

The blank calls for words that characterize the types of environmental problems worth spending large sums on. Among the choices are two sets of near synonyms: "ephemeral/transitory" and "pressing/critical." Of these two pairings, only the latter makes sense in the context of the rest of the sentence—it would be unlikely for anyone to advocate spending large sums on problems that will be quickly gone without any intervention, as "ephemeral" and "transitory" imply, nor would unsanitary water likely be characterized as a merely temporary dilemma. Of the other two options, neither "futile" nor "controversial" has a synonym among the answer choices, so they can be ruled out on that account; in addition, neither would be used to justify the expenditure of large sums of money.

Thus the correct answer is **pressing** (Choice C) and **critical** (Choice F).

16. The process of establishing a literary canon is seen by some as, in part, an attempt by certain scholars to make their own labors central and to relegate the work of others to _____ status.

   [A] orthodox
   [B] marginal
   [C] mainstream
   [D] definitive
   [E] conditional
   [F] peripheral

Explanation

The attempt by certain scholars to make their own work central is contrasted to the way they treat the work of others. The blank, then, must be completed with a pairing whose meaning is the opposite of central. Of the choices, "orthodox," "mainstream," and "definitive" are all too close in meaning to "central" to provide the necessary contrast; therefore they are incorrect. "Conditional" suggests a status that is yet to be determined, a nuance unsupported by anything else in the sentence; therefore it is also incorrect. The two remaining answers, "marginal" and "peripheral," are synonyms with meanings that contrast nicely with "central."

Thus the correct answer is **marginal** (Choice B) and **peripheral** (Choice F).

17. The mayor is more ideologically consistent than is widely believed: her long-term commitment to tax reform, for example, is not indicative of _____.

   [A] perspicacity
   [B] capriciousness
   [C] callousness
   [D] fickleness
   [E] clearheadedness
   [F] insensitivity

Explanation

The first part of the sentence suggests that the mayor is widely believed to be the opposite of ideologically consistent, while the portion of the sentence following the colon provides support for the assertion that her reputation for wavering is undeserved. The blank, then, must be completed with words that mean the opposite of ideological consistency. "Capriciousness" and " fickleness" are both opposites of consistency, so they are the correct answers. Of the other possible responses, one other pairing—"insensitivity" and "callousness"—are synonyms that would yield sentences alike in meaning, while the other two choices are also close in meaning. But neither of these pairs provides the necessary contrast to consistency that the sentence's structure calls for.

Thus the correct answer is **capriciousness** (Choice B) and **fickleness** (Choice D).

18. At first glance Watkins Park, with its meandering stream and its thicket of greenery, seems _____ ; however, upon closer inspection one is quickly reminded that the park is in the middle of a major city.

- [A] bucolic
- [B] remarkable
- [C] urban
- [D] noteworthy
- [E] pastoral
- [F] spurious

Explanation

The sentence characterizes certain physical features of the park and contrasts them with the park's location within a major city. The blank must describe those features so as to provide that contrast, which "urban" and "spurious" do not. While "remarkable" and "noteworthy" produce sentences with the same meaning, they also do not provide the required contrast between the park's features and its location.

Thus the correct answer is **bucolic** (Choice A) and **pastoral** (Choice E).

19. Although relying on much of the recent scholarship on the bison, Lott's book is a distinctly _____ and even idiosyncratic contribution to the field.

- [A] derivative
- [B] original
- [C] innovative
- [D] imitative
- [E] insightful
- [F] surprising

Explanation

The "although" that begins the sentence indicates that the words that fill the blank will contrast with the author's reliance on recent scholarship. Of the choices, "derivative" and "imitative" both describe works that lean too heavily on the work of others; since these would not form a contrast with the first part of the sentence, they do not fit the blank. "Original" and "innovative" do describe qualities that are the opposite of reliant on the work of others, and they also yield sentences that are alike in meaning, so they are the correct answers. Of the other two responses, while both "insightful" and "surprising" contrast in some ways with the first part of the sentence, neither has a synonym among the other choices.

Thus the correct answer is **original** (Choice B) and **innovative** (Choice C).

For each of Questions 20 to 25, select <u>one</u> answer choice unless otherwise directed.

Question 20 is based on this passage.

James W. Coleman's book on John Edgar Wideman's literary career addresses the needs of a general, if well-read, public rather than the esoteric vanities of scholarly specialists, whom he neither ignores nor flatters. To assume the former audience was
Line familiar with every work Wideman ever penned would have been pretentious. Instead,
5 Coleman furnishes more than ample descriptive criticism and background information, avoiding the cryptic allusiveness that is favored by some academic critics but that discourages the undergraduate audience he likely envisioned. Unfortunately, this accent on bringing serious Wideman criticism to a broader audience often frustrates the reader who wishes that announced themes, techniques, and stylistic devices would
10 not whisk by as quickly as world capitals on a seven-day package tour of the globe.

Description

The passage discusses Coleman's approach to writing John Edgar Wideman's literary biography and claims that it was intended for the general public rather than for the academic community. The passage also describes the book's weak and strong points from the point of view of its intended audience.

20. The reference to "a seven-day package tour of the globe" (line 10) is most likely meant to suggest a treatment that is

Ⓐ inclusive
Ⓑ cursory
Ⓒ focused
Ⓓ broad based
Ⓔ substantial

Explanation

Choice B is correct. The phrase occurs in the last sentence of the passage; this sentence claims that Coleman's narrative progresses too fast, and the analogy with the "seven-day package tour of the globe" is meant to emphasize the fact that Coleman does not spend enough time on describing important aspects of Wideman's work. Therefore the correct answer choice is "cursory."

Question 21 is based on this passage.

The painter Peter Brandon never dated his works, and their chronology is only now beginning to take shape in the critical literature. A recent dating of a Brandon self-portrait to 1930 is surely wrong. Brandon was 63 years old in 1930, yet the painting shows a young, dark-haired man—obviously Brandon, but clearly not a man of 63.

21. Which of the following, if justifiably assumed, allows the conclusion to be properly drawn?

    (A) There is no securely dated self-portrait of Brandon that he painted when he was significantly younger than 63.

    (B) In refraining from dating his works, Brandon intended to steer critical discussion of them away from considerations of chronology.

    (C) Until recently, there was very little critical literature on the works of Brandon.

    (D) Brandon at age 63 would not have portrayed himself in a painting as he had looked when he was a young man.

    (E) Brandon painted several self-portraits that showed him as a man past the age of 60.

Explanation

The passage concludes that the self-portrait must be improperly dated and cites as proof the discrepancy between Brandon's actual age (63) in 1930 and his youthful appearance in the painting. The assumption is that a self-portrait depicts the artist's current appearance; therefore, **Choice D** is the correct answer. Since the argument does not depend on the existence or absence of other self-portraits, Choices A and E are incorrect. The argument also does not depend upon Brandon's motivations for not dating his works or upon the lack of critical literature about his work, so Choices B and C are incorrect.

Questions 22 to 24 are based on this passage.

Experts have differed about where the genus *Varanus* (monitor lizards) originated. Because most existing species live in Australia, early researchers concluded that *Varanus* originated in Australia and subsequently island hopped westward along the Indo-Australian archipelago. Herpetologist Robert Mertens later argued that *Varanus*
Line
5 probably originated in the archipelago. Chromosomal analysis has since supported Mertens' contention, and in addition, geologic evidence points to a collision between the archipelago and the Australian landmass after *Varanus* evolved—a fact that could account for the genus' present distribution.

A related puzzle for scientists is the present distribution of *Varanus*' largest surviv-
10 ing species, the Komodo dragon. These carnivores live only on four small islands in the archipelago where, scientists note, the prey base is too small to support mammalian carnivores. But the Komodo dragon has recently been shown to manage body temperature much more efficiently than do mammalian carnivores, enabling it to survive on about a tenth of the food energy required by a mammalian carnivore
15 of comparable size.

Description

The passage begins by identifying a question that has long puzzled scientists. The first paragraph is devoted to considering two possible answers to the question. The second paragraph introduces a question that is related to the question discussed in the first paragraph. It then provides a possible answer to it.

22. It can be inferred from the passage that the geographical distribution of the Komodo dragon is

   (A) currently less restricted than it was at the time researchers first began investigating the origins of the genus *Varanus*

   (B) currently more restricted than it was at the time researchers first began investigating the origins of the genus *Varanus*

   (C) less restricted than is the distribution of the genus *Varanus* as a whole

   (D) more restricted than is the distribution of the genus *Varanus* as a whole

   (E) viewed as evidence in favor of the hypothesis that the genus *Varanus* originated in the Indo-Australian archipelago

Explanation

Choice D is correct. Because the Komodo dragon, a species of *Varanus*, is restricted to "four small islands in the archipelago" but "most existing species" of the genus *Varanus* as a whole live in Australia, the geographical distribution of the genus includes species in both places. The distribution of the Komodo dragon is restricted to only one of these places and is thus more restricted than the genus as a whole, not less restricted. Thus, Choice C is incorrect. Choices A and B are incorrect because the passage does not describe the specific change in the geographic distribution of the Komodo dragon, but rather just describes its present distribution. Choice E is incorrect because the passage does not present its discussion of the Komodo dragon as evidence for either hypothesis of the origin of *Varanus* but rather as a "related puzzle."

23. Which of the following elements in the debate over the origin of *Varanus* is NOT provided in the passage?

Ⓐ The evidence that led Mertens to argue that *Varanus* originated in the Indo-Australian archipelago

Ⓑ The evidence that led early researchers to argue that *Varanus* originated in Australia

Ⓒ A possible explanation of how *Varanus* might have spread to the Indo-Australian archipelago if it had originated in Australia

Ⓓ A possible explanation of how *Varanus* might have spread to Australia if it had originated in the Indo-Australian archipelago

Ⓔ An indication of the general present-day distribution of *Varanus* species between Australia and the Indo-Australian archipelago

Explanation

Choice A is correct. The passage provides support for Mertens' argument by providing later chromosomal evidence as well as geologic evidence but it does not provide nor describe the evidence with which Mertens originally argued. Choices B and E are incorrect because the passage states that early researchers argued for a specific origin for *Varanus* "because most existing species live in Australia," which indicates the present-day distribution of species. Choices C and D are incorrect because the passage provides geologic evidence to suggest a possible explanation for how *Varanus* may have spread to either Australia or the archipelago regardless of its origin.

24. It can be inferred that which of the following is true of the "geologic evidence" (line 6)?

Ⓐ It was first noted by Mertens as evidence in favor of his theory about the origins of *Varanus*.

Ⓑ It cannot rule out either one of the theories about the origins of *Varanus* discussed in the passage.

Ⓒ It accounts for the present distribution of the Komodo dragon.

Ⓓ It has led to renewed interest in the debate over the origins of *Varanus*.

Ⓔ It confirms the conclusions reached by early researchers concerning the origins of *Varanus*.

Explanation

Choice B is correct. The passage presents the "geologic evidence" so as to provide a possible explanation for the prevalence of the various species of *Varanus* in Australia if indeed Mertens' theory is correct. But the evidence itself does not rule out the possibility that the earlier theory is correct and that Mertens is not, so the "geologic evidence" cannot rule out either theory. Choice A is incorrect because there is no specific indication that Mertens first provided this evidence, and the chronology of the presentation suggests that he did not. Choice C is incorrect as the Komodo dragon lives only in the archipelago, and Choice D is incorrect as there is no mention in the passage of a specifically renewed interest in the debate. Choice E is incorrect since the "geologic evidence" does not rule out nor confirm either Mertens' conclusions or those of earlier researchers.

Question 25 is based on this passage.

Geographers and historians have traditionally held the view that Antarctica was first sighted around 1820, but some sixteenth-century European maps show a body that resembles the polar landmass, even though explorers of the period never saw it. Some scholars, therefore, argue that the continent must have been discovered and mapped by the ancients, whose maps are known to have served as models for the European cartographers.

Line

5

25. Which of the following, if true, is most damaging to the inference drawn by the scholars?

Ⓐ The question of who first sighted Antarctica in modern times is still much debated, and no one has been able to present conclusive evidence.

Ⓑ Between 3,000 and 9,000 years ago, the world was warmer than it is now, and the polar landmass was presumably smaller.

Ⓒ There are only a few sixteenth-century global maps that show a continental landmass at the South Pole.

Ⓓ Most attributions of surprising accomplishments to ancient civilizations or even extraterrestrials are eventually discredited or rejected as preposterous.

Ⓔ Ancient philosophers believed that there had to be a large landmass at the South Pole to balance the northern continents and make the world symmetrical.

Explanation

The inference that Antarctica was discovered by the ancients would be weakened if there were an alternative explanation of why the ancients might have drawn a landmass in that area on their maps. **Choice E** provides just such an explanation, so it is the correct answer. Choice A is incorrect because the identity of the modern discoverer of the Antarctica has no bearing on why the continent was included on sixteenth-century maps. Since the ancients referred to in the passage likely postdate the warm period mentioned in Choice B, that option is also incorrect. The passage never mentions how many sixteenth-century maps show a southern polar landmass, and the argument does not depend upon any particular quantity, so Choice C is incorrect. Choice D comments upon the conclusion but does not pertain to the argument itself, so it is also incorrect.

7 Overview of the *GRE*® Analytical Writing Measure

The Analytical Writing measure assesses the ability to articulate and support complex ideas, examine claims and accompanying evidence, sustain a focused and coherent discussion, and control the elements of standard written English. The measure requires you to provide focused responses based on the tasks presented, so you can accurately demonstrate your skill in directly responding to a task. You will be presented with two separately timed analytical writing tasks:

- a 30-minute "Analyze an Issue" task
- a 30-minute "Analyze an Argument" task

The Issue task presents an opinion on an issue of broad interest followed by specific instructions on how to respond to that issue. You are required to evaluate the issue, considering its complexities, and develop an argument with reasons and examples to support your views.

The Argument task presents a different challenge from that of the Issue task: it requires you to evaluate a given argument according to specific instructions. You will need to consider the logical soundness of the argument rather than to agree or disagree with the position it presents.

The two tasks are complementary in that one requires you to construct your own argument by taking a position and providing evidence supporting your views on the issue, whereas the other requires you to evaluate someone else's argument by assessing its claims and evaluating the evidence it provides.

The Analytical Writing Measure of the Computer-delivered GRE revised General Test

Structure of the Analytical Writing Measure

Measure	Number of Questions	Allotted Time
Analytical Writing (One section with two separately timed tasks)	One "Analyze an Issue" task and one "Analyze an Argument" task	30 minutes per task

The Analytical Writing section will always come first in the test. Within the section, the timing for each task is shown when the task is presented.

The Analytical Writing measure of the computer-delivered revised General Test uses an elementary word processor developed by ETS so that individuals familiar with a specific commercial word processing software do not have an advantage or disadvantage. This software contains the following functionality: insert text, delete text, cut and paste, and undo the previous action. Tools such as a spelling checker and grammar checker are not available in the ETS software, in large part to maintain fairness with those examinees who must handwrite their essays at paper-based administrations.

Scratch Paper

You will receive a supply of scratch paper before you begin the test. You can replenish your supply of scratch paper as necessary throughout the test by asking the test administrator.

Test-taking Strategies

It is important to budget your time. Within the 30-minute time limit for each task, you will need to allow sufficient time to think about the topic, plan a response, and compose your essay. Although GRE readers understand the time constraints under which you write and will consider your response a first draft, you will still want to produce the best possible example of your writing.

Save a few minutes at the end of each timed task to check for obvious errors. Although an occasional typographical, spelling, or grammatical error will not affect your score, severe or persistent errors will detract from the overall effectiveness of your writing and lower your score.

How the Analytical Writing Measure Is Scored

For the Analytical Writing section, each essay receives a score from at least one trained reader, using a six-point holistic scale. In holistic scoring, readers are trained to assign scores on the basis of the overall quality of an essay in response to the assigned task. The essay score is then reviewed by *e-rater*®, a computerized program developed by ETS, which is used to monitor the human reader. If the *e-rater* evaluation and the human score agree, the human score is used as the final score. If they disagree by a certain amount, a second human score is obtained, and the final score is the average of the two human scores.

The final scores on the two essays are then averaged and rounded to the nearest half-point interval on the 0–6 score scale. A single score is reported for the Analytical Writing measure. The primary emphasis in scoring the Analytical Writing section is on your critical thinking and analytical writing skills rather than on grammar and mechanics. Scoring guides for the Issue and Argument prompts are included in this publication, and on the GRE website at **www.ets.org/gre/scores/how**.

Independent Intellectual Activity

Your essay responses on the Analytical Writing section will be reviewed by ETS essay-similarity-detection software and by experienced essay readers during the scoring process. In light of the high value placed on independent intellectual activity within graduate schools and universities, your essay response should represent your original work. ETS reserves the right to cancel test scores of any test taker when an essay response includes any of the following:

- text that is unusually similar to that found in one or more other GRE essay responses;
- quoting or paraphrasing, without attribution, language that appears in any published or unpublished sources, including sources from the Internet and/or sources provided by any third party;
- unacknowledged use of work that has been produced through collaboration with others without citation of the contribution of others;
- essays submitted as work of the test taker that appear to have been borrowed in whole or in part from elsewhere or prepared by another person.

When one or more of the above circumstances occurs, ETS may conclude, in its professional judgment, that the essay response does not reflect the independent writing skills that this test seeks to measure. When ETS reaches that conclusion, it cancels the Analytical Writing scores, and because Analytical Writing scores are an integral part of GRE revised General Test scores, those scores are canceled as well.

The Analytical Writing Measure of the Paper-delivered GRE revised General Test

Structure of the Analytical Writing Measure

Measure	Number of Questions	Allotted Time
Analytical Writing (Two sections)	Section One: "Analyze an Issue" task Section Two: "Analyze an Argument" task	30 minutes per section

The Analytical Writing sections will always be first. The directions at the beginning of each section specify the total number of questions in the section and the time allowed for the section.

In the paper-delivered revised General Test, the topics in the Analytical Writing measure will be presented in the test book, and you will handwrite your essay responses in the test book in the space provided.

Test-taking Strategies

It is important to budget your time. Within the 30-minute time limit for each section, you will need to allow sufficient time to think about the topic, plan a response, and compose your essay. Although GRE readers understand the time constraints under which you write and will consider your response a first draft, you will still want to produce the best possible example of your writing.

Save a few minutes at the end of each timed section to check for obvious errors. Although an occasional spelling or grammatical error will not affect your score, severe and persistent errors will detract from the overall effectiveness of your writing and lower your score.

During the actual administration of the revised General Test, you may work only on the particular writing section the test center supervisor designates and only for the time allowed. You may *not* go back to an earlier section of the test after the supervisor announces, "Please stop work" for that section. The supervisor is authorized to dismiss you from the center for doing so.

How the Analytical Writing Measure Is Scored

For the Analytical Writing section, each essay receives a score from two trained readers, using a six-point holistic scale. In holistic scoring, readers are trained to assign scores on the basis of the overall quality of an essay in response to the assigned task. If the two assigned scores differ by more than one point on the scale, the discrepancy is adjudicated by a third GRE reader. Otherwise, the two scores on each essay are averaged.

The final scores on the two essays are then averaged and rounded to the nearest half-point interval on the 0–6 score scale. A single score is reported for the Analytical Writing measure. The primary emphasis in scoring the Analytical Writing section is on your critical thinking and analytical writing skills rather than on grammar and mechanics. Scoring guides for the Issue and Argument prompts are included in this publication, and they are available on the GRE website at **www.ets.org/gre/scores/how**.

Independent Intellectual Activity

Your essay responses on the Analytical Writing section will be reviewed by ETS essay-similarity-detection software and by experienced essay readers during the scoring process. In light of the high value placed on independent intellectual activity within graduate schools and universities, your essay response should represent your original work. ETS reserves the right to cancel test scores of any test taker when an essay response includes any of the following:

- text that is unusually similar to that found in one or more other GRE essay responses;
- quoting or paraphrasing, without attribution, language that appears in any published or unpublished sources, including sources from the Internet and/or sources provided by any third party
- unacknowledged use of work that has been produced through collaboration with others without citation of the contribution of others;
- essays submitted as work of the test taker that appear to have been borrowed in whole or in part from elsewhere or prepared by another person.

When one or more of the above circumstances occurs, ETS may conclude, in its professional judgment, that the essay response does not reflect the independent writing skills that this test seeks to measure. When ETS reaches that conclusion, it cancels the Analytical Writing scores, and because Analytical Writing scores are an integral part of GRE revised General Test scores, those scores are canceled as well.

Score Reporting

An Analytical Writing score is reported on a 0-6 score scale, in half-point increments. If you do not provide a response for either of the tasks in the measure, you will receive a No Score (NS) for that measure.

Descriptions of the analytical writing abilities characteristic of particular score levels are available in this publication on page 213, and on the GRE website at **www.ets.org/gre/awscoredescriptions**.

Preparing for the Analytical Writing Measure

Everyone—even the most practiced and confident of writers—should spend some time preparing for the Analytical Writing measure before arriving at the test center. It is important to review the skills measured and how the section is scored. It is also useful to review the scoring guides and score level descriptions, sample topics, scored sample essay responses, and reader commentary for each task.

The tasks in the Analytical Writing measure relate to a broad range of subjects—from the fine arts and humanities to the social and physical sciences—but no task requires specific content knowledge. In fact, each task has been field-tested to ensure that it possesses several important characteristics, including the following:

- *GRE*® test takers, regardless of their field of study or special interests, understood the task and could easily respond to it.
- The task elicited the kinds of complex thinking and persuasive writing that university faculty consider important for success at the graduate level.
- The responses were varied in content and in the way the writers developed their ideas.

To help you prepare for the Analytical Writing measure, the GRE Program has published the entire pool of tasks from which your test tasks will be selected. You might find it helpful to review the Issue and Argument pools. You can view the published pools at **www.ets.org/gre/awtopics**.

Analyze an Issue Task

Understanding the Issue Task

The Analyze an Issue task assesses your ability to think critically about a topic of general interest according to specific instructions and to clearly express your thoughts about it in writing. Each issue topic makes a claim that test takers can discuss from various perspectives and apply to many different situations or conditions. The issue statement is followed by specific instructions. Your task is to present a compelling case for your own position on the issue according to the specific instructions. Before beginning your written response, be sure to read the issue and instructions carefully and think about the issue from several points of view, considering the complexity of ideas associated with those views. Then, make notes about the position you want to develop and list the main reasons and examples that you could use to support that position.

It is important that you address the central issue according to the specific instructions. Each task is accompanied by one of the following sets of instructions.

- Write a response in which you discuss the extent to which you agree or disagree with the statement and explain your reasoning for the position you take. In developing and supporting your position, you should consider ways in which the statement might or might not hold true and explain how these considerations shape your position.
- Write a response in which you discuss the extent to which you agree or disagree with the recommendation and explain your reasoning for the position you take. In developing and supporting your position, describe specific circumstances in which adopting the recommendation would or would not be advantageous and explain how these examples shape your position.
- Write a response in which you discuss the extent to which you agree or disagree with the claim. In developing and supporting your position, be sure to address the most compelling reasons and/or examples that could be used to challenge your position.
- Write a response in which you discuss which view more closely aligns with your own position and explain your reasoning for the position you take. In developing and supporting your position, you should address both of the views presented.
- Write a response in which you discuss the extent to which you agree or disagree with the claim and the reason on which that claim is based.
- Write a response in which you discuss your views on the policy and explain your reasoning for the position you take. In developing and supporting your position, you should consider the possible consequences of implementing the policy and explain how these consequences shape your position.

The GRE readers scoring your response are not looking for a "right" answer—in fact, there is no correct position to take. Instead, the readers are evaluating the skill with which you address the specific instructions and articulate and develop an argument to support your evaluation of the issue.

Understanding the Context for Writing: Purpose and Audience

The Issue task is an exercise in critical thinking and persuasive writing. The purpose of this task is to determine how well you can develop a compelling argument supporting your own evaluation of an issue and communicate that argument in writing to an academic audience. Your audience consists of GRE readers who are carefully trained to apply the scoring criteria identified in the scoring guide for the Analyze an Issue task (see pages 209–210).

To get a clearer idea of how GRE readers apply the Issue scoring criteria to actual responses, you should review scored sample Issue essay responses and reader commentary. The sample responses, particularly at the 5 and 6 score levels, will show you a variety of successful strategies for organizing, developing, and communicating a persuasive argument. The reader commentary discusses specific aspects of evaluation and writing, such as the use of examples, development and support, organization, language fluency, and word choice. For each response, the reader commentary points out aspects that are particularly persuasive as well as any that detract from the overall effectiveness of the essay.

Preparing for the Issue Task

Because the Issue task is meant to assess the persuasive writing skills that you have developed throughout your education, it has been designed neither to require any particular course of study nor to advantage students with a particular type of training.

Many college textbooks on composition offer advice on persuasive writing and argumentation that you might find useful, but even this advice might be more technical and specialized than you need for the Issue task. You will not be expected to know specific critical thinking or writing terms or strategies; instead, you should be able to respond to the specific instructions and use reasons, evidence, and examples to support your position on an issue. Suppose, for instance, that an Issue topic asks you to consider a policy that would require government financial support for art museums and the implications of implementing the policy. If your position is that government should fund art museums, you might support your position by discussing the reasons art is important and explain that government funding would make access to museums available to everyone. On the other hand, if your position is that government should not support museums, you might point out that, given limited governmental funds, art museums are not as deserving of governmental funding as are other, more socially important, institutions, which would suffer if the policy were implemented. Or, if you are in favor of government funding for art museums only under certain conditions, you might focus on the artistic criteria, cultural concerns, or political conditions that you think should determine how—or whether—art museums receive government funds. It is not your position that matters so much as the critical thinking skills you display in developing your position.

An excellent way to prepare for the Issue task is to practice writing on some of the published topics. There is no "best" approach: some people prefer to start practicing without regard to the 30-minute time limit; others prefer to take a "timed test" first and practice within the time limit. No matter which approach you take when you practice the Issue task, you should review the task directions, then

- carefully read the claim and the specific instructions and make sure you understand them; if they seem unclear, discuss them with a friend or teacher
- think about the claim and instructions in relation to your own ideas and experiences, to events you have read about or observed, and to people you have known; this is the knowledge base from which you will develop compelling reasons and examples in your argument that reinforce, negate, or qualify the claim in some way
- decide what position on the issue you want to take and defend
- decide what compelling evidence (reasons and examples) you can use to support your position

Remember that this is a task in critical thinking and persuasive writing. The most successful responses will explore the complexity of the claim and instructions. As you prepare for the Issue task, you might find it helpful to ask yourself the following questions:

- What precisely is the central issue?
- What precisely are the instructions asking me to do?
- Do I agree with all or with any part of the claim? Why or why not?
- Does the claim make certain assumptions? If so, are they reasonable?
- Is the claim valid only under certain conditions? If so, what are they?
- Do I need to explain how I interpret certain terms or concepts used in the claim?
- If I take a certain position on the issue, what reasons support my position?
- What examples—either real or hypothetical—could I use to illustrate those reasons and advance my point of view? Which examples are most compelling?

Once you have decided on a position to defend, consider the perspective of others who might not agree with your position. Ask yourself:

- What reasons might someone use to refute or undermine my position?
- How should I acknowledge or defend against those views in my essay?

To plan your response, you might want to summarize your position and make brief notes about how you will support the position you're going to take. When you've done this, look over your notes and decide how you will organize your response. Then write a response developing your position on the issue. Even if you don't write a full response, you should find it helpful to practice with a few of the Issue topics and to sketch out your possible responses. After you have practiced with some of the topics, try writing responses to some of the topics within the 30-minute time limit so that you have a good idea of how to use your time in the actual test.

It would probably be helpful to get some feedback on your response from an instructor who teaches critical thinking or writing or to trade papers on the same topic with other students and discuss one another's responses in relation to the scoring guide. Try to determine how each paper meets or misses the criteria for each score point in the guide. Comparing your own response to the scoring guide will help you see how and where you might need to improve.

The Form of Your Response

You are free to organize and develop your response in any way that you think will effectively communicate your ideas about the issue and the instructions. Your response may, but need not, incorporate particular writing strategies learned in English composition or writing-intensive college courses. GRE readers will not be looking for a particular developmental strategy or mode of writing; in fact, when GRE readers are trained, they review hundreds of Issue responses that, although highly diverse in content and form, display similar levels of critical thinking and persuasive writing. Readers will see, for example, some Issue responses at the 6 score level that begin by briefly summarizing the writer's position on the issue and then explicitly announcing the main points to be argued. They will see others that lead into the writer's position by making a prediction, asking a series of questions, describing a scenario, or defining critical terms in the quotation. The readers know that a writer can earn a high score by giving multiple examples or by presenting a single, extended example. Look at the sample Issue responses, particularly at the 5 and 6 score levels, to see how other writers have successfully developed and organized their arguments.

You should use as many or as few paragraphs as you consider appropriate for your argument—for example, you will probably need to create a new paragraph whenever your discussion shifts to a new cluster of ideas. What matters is not the number of examples, the number of paragraphs, or the form your argument takes but, rather, the cogency of your ideas about the issue and the clarity and skill with which you communicate those ideas to academic readers.

Sample Issue Task

> As people rely more and more on technology to solve problems, the ability of humans to think for themselves will surely deteriorate.
>
> Discuss the extent to which you agree or disagree with the statement and explain your reasoning for the position you take. In developing and supporting your position, you should consider ways in which the statement might or might not hold true and explain how these considerations shape your position.

Strategies for This Topic

In this task, you are asked to discuss the extent to which you agree or disagree with the statement. Thus, responses may range from strong agreement or strong disagreement, to qualified agreement or qualified disagreement. You are also instructed to explain your reasoning and consider ways in which the statement might or might not hold true. A successful response need not comment on all or any one of the points listed below and may well discuss other reasons or examples not mentioned here in support of its position.

Although this topic is accessible to respondents of all levels of ability, for any response to receive a top score, it is particularly important that you remain focused on the task and provide clearly relevant examples and/or reasons to support the point of view you are expressing. Lower level responses may be long and full of examples of modern technology, but those examples may not be clearly related to a particular position. For example, a respondent who strongly disagrees with the statement may choose to use computer technology as proof that thinking ability is not deteriorating. The mere existence of computer technology, however, does not adequately prove this point (perhaps the ease of computer use inhibits our thinking ability). To receive a higher-level score, the respondent should explain in what ways computer technology may call for or require thinking ability.

This topic could elicit a wide variety of approaches, especially considering the different possible interpretations of the phrase "the ability of humans to think for themselves." Although most respondents may take it to mean problem solving, others, with equal effectiveness, could interpret it as emotional and social intelligence (i.e., the ability to communicate/connect with others). With any approach, it is possible to discuss examples such as calculators, word processing tools such as spell and grammar check, tax return software, Internet research, and a variety of other common household and business technologies.

You may agree with the prompt and argue that:

- reliance on technology leads to dependency; we come to rely on problem-solving technologies to such a degree that when they fail, we are in worse shape than if we did not have them in the first place
- everyday technologies such as calculators and cash registers have decreased our ability to perform simple calculations, a "use it or lose it" approach to thinking ability

Or you may take issue with the prompt and argue that technology facilitates and improves our thinking skills, arguing that:

- developing, implementing, and using technology requires problem solving
- technology frees us from mundane problem solving (e.g., calculations) and allows us to engage in more complex thinking
- technology provides access to information otherwise unavailable
- technology connects people at a distance and allows them to share ideas

- technology is dependent on the human ability to think and make choices (every implementation of and advance in technology is driven by human intelligence and decision making)

On the other hand, you could decide to explore the middle ground in the debate and point out that while technology may diminish some mental skill sets, it enables other (perhaps more important) types of thinking to thrive. Such a response might distinguish between complex problem solving and simple "data maintenance" (i.e., performing calculations and organizing information). Other approaches could include taking a historical, philosophical, or sociological stance, or, with equal effectiveness, using personal examples to illustrate a position. One could argue that the value or detriment of relying on technology is determined by the individual (or society) using it or that only those who develop technology (i.e., technical specialists) are maintaining their problem-solving skills, while the rest of us are losing them.

Again, it is important for you to avoid overly general examples, or lists of examples without expansion. It is also essential to do more than paraphrase the prompt. Please keep in mind that what counts is the ability to clearly express a particular point of view in relation to the issue and specific task instructions and to support that position with relevant reasons and/or examples.

Essay Responses and Reader Commentary

Score 6 Response*

> The statement linking technology negatively with free thinking plays on recent human experience over the past century. Surely there has been no time in history where the lived lives of people have changed more dramatically. A quick reflection on a typical day reveals how technology has revolutionized the world. Most people commute to work in an automobile that runs on an internal combustion engine. During the workday, chances are high that the employee will interact with a computer that processes information on silicon bridges that are .09 microns wide. Upon leaving home, family members will be reached through wireless networks that utilize satellites orbiting the earth. Each of these common occurences would have been inconceivable at the turn of the 19th century.
>
> The statement attempts to bridge these dramatic changes to a reduction in the ability for humans to think for themselves. The assumption is that an increased reliance on technology negates the need for people to think creatively to solve previous quandaries. Looking back at the introduction, one could argue that without a car, computer, or mobile phone, the hypothetical worker would need to find alternate methods of transport, information processing, and communication. Technology short circuits this thinking by making the problems obsolete.
>
> However, this reliance on technology does not necessarily preclude the creativity that marks the human species. The prior examples reveal that technology allows for convenience. The car, computer, and phone all release additional time for people to live more efficiently. This efficiency does not preclude the need for humans to think for themselves. In fact, technology frees humanity to not only tackle new problems, but may itself create new issues that did not exist without technology. For example, the proliferation of automobiles has introduced a need for fuel conservation on a global scale. With increasing energy demands from emerging markets, global warming becomes a concern inconceivable to the horse-and-buggy generation. Likewise dependence on oil has created nation-states that are not dependent on taxation, allowing ruling parties to oppress minority groups such as women. Solutions to these complex problems require the unfettered imaginations of maverick scientists and politicians.

*All responses in this publication are reproduced exactly as written, including GRE errors, misspellings, etc., if any.

In contrast to the statement, we can even see how technology frees the human imagination. Consider how the digital revolution and the advent of the internet has allowed for an unprecedented exchange of ideas. WebMD, a popular internet portal for medical information, permits patients to self research symptoms for a more informed doctor visit. This exercise opens pathways of thinking that were previously closed off to the medical layman. With increased interdisciplinary interactions, inspiration can arrive from the most surprising corners. Jeffrey Sachs, one of the architects of the UN Millenium Development Goals, based his ideas on emergency care triage techniques. The unlikely marriage of economics and medicine has healed tense, hyperinflation environments from South America to Eastern Europe.

This last example provides the most hope in how technology actually provides hope to the future of humanity. By increasing our reliance on technology, impossible goals can now be achieved. Consider how the late 20th century witnessed the complete elimination of smallpox. This disease had ravaged the human race since prehistorical days, and yet with the technology of vaccines, free thinking humans dared to imagine a world free of smallpox. Using technology, battle plans were drawn out, and smallpox was systematically targeted and eradicated.

Technology will always mark the human experience, from the discovery of fire to the implementation of nanotechnology. Given the history of the human race, there will be no limit to the number of problems, both new and old, for us to tackle. There is no need to retreat to a Luddite attitude to new things, but rather embrace a hopeful posture to the possibilities that technology provides for new avenues of human imagination.

Reader Commentary

The author of this essay stakes out a clear and insightful position on the issue and follows the specific instructions by discussing ways in which the statement might or might not hold true, using specific reasons and examples to support that position. The essay cogently argues that technology does not decrease our ability to think for ourselves. It merely provides "additional time for people to live more efficiently." In fact, the problems that have developed alongside the growth of technology (pollution, political unrest in oil-producing nations) actually call for more creative thinking, not less. In further examples, the essay shows how technology allows for the linking of ideas that may never have been connected in the past (like medicine and economic models), pushing people to think in new ways. Examples are persuasive and fully developed; reasoning is logically sound and well supported.

Ideas in the essay are connected logically, with effective transitions used both between paragraphs ("However," or "In contrast to the statement") and within paragraphs. Sentence structure is varied and complex, and the essay clearly demonstrates facility with the "conventions of standard written English (i.e., grammar, usage, and mechanics)" (see Issue Scoring Guide, pages 209–210), with only minor errors appearing. Thus, this essay meets all the requirements for receiving a top score, a 6.

Score 5 Response

Surely many of us have expressed the following sentiment, or some variation on it, during our daily commutes to work: "People are getting so stupid these days!" Surrounded as we are by striding and strident automatons with cell phones glued to their ears, PDA's gripped in their palms, and omniscient, omnipresent CNN gleaming in their eyeballs, it's tempting to believe that technology has isolated and infantilized us, essentially transforming us into dependent, conformist morons best equipped to sideswip one another in our SUV's.

Furthermore, hanging around with the younger, pre-commute generation, whom tech-savviness seems to have rendered lethal, is even less reassuring. With "Teen People" style trends shooting through the air from tiger-striped PDA to zebra-striped PDA, and with the latest starlet gossip zipping from juicy Blackberry to teeny, turbocharged cell phone, technology seems to support young people's worst tendencies to follow the crowd. Indeed, they have seemingly evolved into intergalactic conformity police. After all, today's tech-aided teens are, courtesy of authentic, hands-on video games, literally trained to kill; courtesy of chat and instant text messaging, they have their own language; they even have tiny cameras to efficiently photodocument your fashion blunders! Is this adolescence, or paparazzi terrorist training camp?

With all this evidence, it's easy to believe that tech trends and the incorporation of technological wizardry into our everyday lives have served mostly to enforce conformity, promote dependence, heighten comsumerism and materialism, and generally create a culture that values self-absorption and personal entitlement over cooperation and collaboration. However, I argue that we are merely in the inchoate stages of learning to live with technology while still loving one another. After all, even given the examples provided earlier in this essay, it seems clear that technology hasn't impaired our thinking and problem-solving capacities. Certainly it has incapacitated our behavior and manners; certainly our values have taken a severe blow. However, we are inarguably more efficient in our badness these days. We're effective worker bees of ineffectiveness!

If technology has so increased our senses of self-efficacy that we can become veritable agents of the awful, virtual CEO's of selfishness, certainly it can be beneficial. Harnessed correctly, technology can improve our ability to think and act for ourselves. The first challenge is to figure out how to provide technology users with some direlyneeded direction.

Reader Commentary

The language of this essay clearly illustrates both its strengths and weaknesses. The flowery and sometimes uncannily keen descriptions are often used to powerful effect, but at other times the writing is awkward and the comparisons somewhat strained. See, for example, the ungainly sequence of independent clauses in the second to last sentence of paragraph 2 ("After all, today's tech-aided teens . . .").

There is consistent evidence of facility with syntax and complex vocabulary ("Surrounded as we are by striding and strident automatons with cell phones glued to their ears, PDA's gripped in their palms, and omniscient, omnipresent CNN gleaming in their eyeballs, it's tempting to believe . . ."). Such lucid prose, however, is often countered with an over-reliance upon abstractions and tangential reasoning (what does the fact that video games "literally train [teens] to kill" have to do with the use or deterioration of thinking abilities, for example?).

Because this essay takes a complex approach to the issue (arguing, in effect, that technology neither enhances nor reduces our ability to think for ourselves, but can be used to do one or the other depending on the user) and because the author makes use of "appropriate vocabulary and sentence variety" (see Issue Scoring Guide, pages 209–210), a score of 5 is appropriate.

Score 4 Response

In all actuality, I think it is more probable that our bodies will surely deteriorate long before our minds do in any significant amount. Who can't say that technology has made us lazier, but that's the key word, lazy, not stupid. The ever increasing amount of technology that we incorporate into our daily lives makes people think and learn every day, possibly more than ever before. Our abilities to think, learn, philosophize, etc. may even reach limits never dreamed of before by average people. Using technology to solve problems will continue to help us realize our potential as a human race.

If you think about it, using technology to solve more complicating problems gives humans a chance to expand their thinking and learning, opening up whole new worlds for many people. Many of these people are glad for the chance to expand their horizons by learning more, going to new places, and trying new things. If it wasn't for the invention of new technological devices, I wouldn't be sitting at this computer trying to philosophize about technology. It would be extremely hard for children in much poorer countries to learn and think for themselves with out the invention of the internet. Think what an impact the printing press, a technologically superior mackine at the time, had on the ability of the human race to learn and think.

Right now we are seeing a golden age of technology, using it all the time during our every day lives. When we get up there's instant coffee and the microwave and all these great things that help us get ready for our day. But we aren't allowing our minds to deteriorate by using them, we are only making things easier for ourselves and saving time for other important things in our days. Going off to school or work in our cars instead of a horse and buggy. Think of the brain power and genius that was used to come up with that single invention that has changed the way we move across this globe.

Using technology to solve our continually more complicated problems as a human race is definately a good thing. Our ability to think for ourselves isn't deteriorating, it's continuing to grow, moving on to higher though functions and more ingenious ideas. The ability to use what technology we have is an example

Reader Commentary

This essay meets all the criteria of a 4-level essay. The writer develops a clear position ("Using technology to solve problems will continue to help us realize our potential as a human race"). The position is then developed with relevant reasons ("using technology to solve more complicat[ed] problems gives humans a chance to expand their thinking and learning . . ." and "we are seeing a golden age of technology"). Point 1, "Using technology," is supported with the simple, but relevant notions that technology allows us access to information and abilities to which we would not normally have access. Similarly, point 2, "the golden age," is supported by the basic description of our technologically saturated social condition. Though the development and organization of the essay does suffer from an occasional misstep (see paragraph 3's abrupt progression from coffeepots to the benefits of technology to cars), the essay as a whole flows smoothly and logically from one idea to the next.

It is useful to compare this essay to the 3-level essay presented next. Though they both utilize some very superficial discussion and often fail to probe deeply into the issue, this writer does, however, take the analysis a step further. In paragraph 2, the distinction between this essay and the next one (the 3-level response) can most clearly be seen. To support the notion that advances in technology actually help increase thinking ability, the writer draws a clever parallel between the promise of modern, sophisticated technology (computer) and the equally substantial/pervasive technology of the past (printing press).

Like the analysis, the language in this essay clearly meets the requirements for a score of 4. The writer displays sufficient control of language and the conventions of standard written English. The preponderance of mistakes are of a cosmetic nature ("using technology to solve more complicating problems"). There is a sentence fragment ("Going off . . .") along with a comma splice ("Our ability . . . isn't deteriorating, it's continuing to grow . . .") in paragraph 4. These errors, though, are minor and do not interfere with the clarity of the ideas being presented.

Score 3 Response

There is no current proof that advancing technology will deteriorate the ability of humans to think. On the contrary, advancements in technology had advanced our vast knowledge in many fields, opening opportunities for further understanding and achievement. For example, the problem of dibilitating illnesses and diseases such as alzheimer's disease is slowing being solved by the technological advancements in stem cell research. The future ability of growing new brain cells and the possibility to reverse the onset of alzheimer's is now becoming a reality. This shows our initiative as humans to better our health demonstrates greater ability of humans to think.

One aspect where the ability of humans may initially be seen as an example of deteriorating minds is the use of internet and cell phones. In the past humans had to seek out information in many different enviroments and aspects of life. Now humans can sit in a chair and type anything into a computer and get an answer. Our reliance on this type of technology can be detrimental if not regulated and regularily substituted for other information sources such as human interactions and hands on learning. I think if humans understand that we should not have such a reliance on computer technology, that we as a species will advance further by utilizing the opportunity of computer technology as well as the other sources of information outside of a computer. Supplementing our knowledge with internet access is surely a way for technology to solve problems while continually advancing the human race.

Reader Commentary

This essay never moves beyond a superficial discussion of the issue. The writer attempts to develop two points: that advancements in technology have progressed our knowledge in many fields and that supplementing rather than relying on technology is "surely a way for technology to solve problems while continually advancing the human race." Each point, then, is developed with relevant but insufficient evidence. In discussing the ability of technology to advance knowledge in many fields (a broad subject rife with possible examples), the writer uses only one limited and very brief example from a specific field (medicine and stem-cell research).

Development of the second point is hindered by a lack of specificity and organization. The writer creates what might most be comparable to an outline. The writer cites a need for regulation/supplementation and warns of the detriment of over-reliance upon technology. However, the explanation of both the problem and the solution is vague and limited ("Our reliance . . . can be detrimental . . . If humans understand that we should not have such a reliance . . . we will advance further"). There is neither explanation of consequences nor clarification of what is meant by "supplementing." This second paragraph is a series of generalizations, which are loosely connected and lack a much needed grounding.

In the essay, there are some minor language errors and a few more serious flaws (e.g., "The future ability of growing new brain cells" or "One aspect where the ability of humans may initially be seen as an example of deteriorating minds . . ."). Despite the accumulation of such flaws, though, meaning is generally clear. This essay earns a score of 3, then, primarily for its limited development.

Score 2 Response

In recent centuries, humans have developed the technology very rapidly, and you may accept some merit of it, and you may see a distortion in society occured by it. To be lazy for human in some meaning is one of the fashion issues in thesedays. There are many symptoms and resons of it. However, I can not agree with the statement that the technology make humans to be reluctant to thinkng thoroughly.

Of course, you can see the phenomena of human laziness along with developed technology in some place. However, they would happen in specific condition, not general. What makes human to be laze of thinking is not merely technology, but the the tendency of human that they treat them as a magic stick and a black box. Not understanding the aims and theory of them couses the disapproval problems.

The most important thing to use the thechnology, regardless the new or old, is to comprehend the fundamental idea of them, and to adapt suit tech to tasks in need. Even if you recognize a method as a all-mighty and it is extremely over-spec to your needs, you can not see the result you want. In this procedure, humans have to consider as long as possible to acquire adequate functions. Therefore, humans can not escape from using their brain.

In addition, the technology as it is do not vain automatically, the is created by humans. Thus, the more developed tech and the more you want a convenient life, the more you think and emmit your creativity to breakthrough some banal method sarcastically.

Consequently, if you are not passive to the new tech, but offensive to it, you would not lose your ability to think deeply. Furthermore, you may improve the ability by adopting it.

Reader Commentary

The language of this essay is what most clearly links it to the score point of 2. Amidst sporadic moments of clarity, this essay is marred by serious errors in grammar, usage, and mechanics that often interfere with meaning. It is unclear what the writer means when he/she states, "To be lazy for human in some meaning is one of the fashion issues in thesedays," or ". . . to adapt suit tech to tasks in need." Despite such severe flaws, the writer has made an obvious attempt to respond to the prompt ("I can not agree with the statement that the technology make humans to be reluctant to thinking thoroughly") as well as an unclear attempt to support such an assertion ("Not understanding the aims and theory of them [technology] couses the disapproval problems" and "The most important thing to use the thechnology . . . is to comprehend the fundamental idea of them"). Holistically, the essay displays a seriously flawed but not fundamentally deficient attempt to develop and support its claims.

(Note: In this SPECIFIC case, the analysis is tied directly to the language. As the language falters, so too does the analysis.)

Score 1 Response

> Humans have invented machines but they have forgot it and have started everything technically so clearly their thinking process is deterioating.

Reader Commentary

The essay is clearly on topic, as evidenced by the writer's usage of the more significant terms from the prompt: "technically" (technologically), "humans", "thinking" (think) and deterioating" (deteriorate). Such usage is the only clear evidence of understanding. Meaning aside, the brevity of the essay (one sentence) clearly indicates the writer's inability to develop a response that addresses the specific instructions given ("Discuss the extent to which you agree or disagree with the statement above and explain your reasoning for the position you take").

The language, too, is clearly one-level, as the sentence fails to achieve coherence. The coherent phrases in this one-sentence response are those tied to the prompt: "Humans have invented machines" and "their thinking process is deterioating." Otherwise, the point being made is unclear.

Practice Analyze an Issue Tasks

Task 1

> Every individual in a society has a responsibility to obey just laws and to disobey and resist unjust laws.
>
> Write a response in which you discuss the extent to which you agree or disagree with the claim. In developing and supporting your position, be sure to address the most compelling reasons and/or examples that could be used to challenge your position.

Task 2

> Claim: The best test of an argument is its ability to convince someone with an opposing viewpoint.
>
> Reason: Only by being forced to defend an idea against the doubts and contrasting views of others does one really discover the value of that idea.
>
> Write a response in which you discuss the extent to which you agree or disagree with the claim and the reason on which that claim is based.

You may choose to write an essay response on one or both of the Analyze an Issue tasks above. After you have done so, review the scored sample essays and reader commentaries for these tasks on pages 214–227.

Analyze an Argument Task

Understanding the Argument Task

The Analyze an Argument task assesses your ability to understand, analyze, and evaluate arguments according to specific instructions and to clearly convey your evaluation in writing. The task consists of a brief passage in which the author makes a case for some course of action or interpretation of events by presenting claims backed by reasons and evidence. Your task is to discuss the logical soundness of the author's case according to the specific instructions by critically examining the line of reasoning. This task requires you to read the argument and instructions very carefully. You might want to read them more than once and possibly make brief notes about points you want to develop more fully in your response. In reading the argument, you should pay special attention to

- what is offered as evidence, support, or proof
- what is explicitly stated, claimed, or concluded
- what is assumed or supposed, perhaps without justification or proof
- what is not stated, but necessarily follows from what is stated

In addition, you should consider the structure of the argument—the way in which these elements are linked together to form a line of reasoning; that is, you should recognize the separate, sometimes implicit steps in the thinking process and consider whether the movement from each one to the next is logically sound. In tracing this line, look for transition words and phrases that suggest that the author is attempting to make a logical connection (e.g., however, thus, therefore, evidently, hence, in conclusion).

An important part of performing well on the Argument task is remembering what you are not being asked to do. You are not being asked to discuss whether the statements in the argument are true or accurate. You are not being asked to agree or disagree with the position stated. You are not being asked to express your own views on the subject being discussed (as you were in the Issue task). Instead, you are being asked to evaluate the logical soundness of an argument of another writer according to specific instructions and, in doing so, to demonstrate the critical thinking, perceptive reading, and analytical writing skills that university faculty consider important for success in graduate school.

It is important that you address the argument according to the specific instructions. Each task is accompanied by one of the following sets of instructions.

- Write a response in which you discuss what specific evidence is needed to evaluate the argument and explain how the evidence would weaken or strengthen the argument.
- Write a response in which you examine the stated and/or unstated assumptions of the argument. Be sure to explain how the argument depends on these assumptions and what the implications are for the argument if the assumptions prove unwarranted.
- Write a response in which you discuss what questions would need to be answered in order to decide whether the recommendation and the argument on which it is based are reasonable. Be sure to explain how the answers to these questions would help to evaluate the recommendation.
- Write a response in which you discuss what questions would need to be answered in order to decide whether the advice and the argument on which it is based are reasonable. Be sure to explain how the answers to these questions would help to evaluate the advice.

- Write a response in which you discuss what questions would need to be answered in order to decide whether the recommendation is likely to have the predicted result. Be sure to explain how the answers to these questions would help to evaluate the recommendation.
- Write a response in which you discuss what questions would need to be answered in order to decide whether the prediction and the argument on which it is based are reasonable. Be sure to explain how the answers to these questions would help to evaluate the prediction.
- Write a response in which you discuss one or more alternative explanations that could rival the proposed explanation and explain how your explanation(s) can plausibly account for the facts presented in the argument.
- Write a response in which you discuss what questions would need to be addressed in order to decide whether the conclusion and the argument on which it is based are reasonable. Be sure to explain how the answers to the questions would help to evaluate the conclusion.

"Analyze an Argument" is primarily a critical thinking task requiring a written response. Consequently, the analytical skills displayed in your evaluation carry great weight in determining your score; however, the clarity with which you convey ideas is also important to your overall score.

Understanding the Context for Writing: Purpose and Audience

The purpose of the task is to see how well equipped you are to insightfully evaluate an argument written by someone else and to effectively communicate your evaluation in writing to an academic audience. Your audience consists of GRE readers carefully trained to apply the scoring criteria identified in the scoring guide for the Analyze an Argument task (see pages 211–212).

To get a clearer idea of how GRE readers apply the Argument scoring criteria to actual essays, you should review scored sample Argument essay responses and reader commentary. The sample responses, particularly at the 5 and 6 score levels, will show you a variety of successful strategies for organizing and developing an insightful evaluation. The reader commentary discusses specific aspects of analytical writing, such as cogency of ideas, development and support, organization, syntactic variety, and facility with language. For each response, the reader commentary will point out aspects that are particularly effective and insightful as well as any that detract from the overall effectiveness of the responses.

Preparing for the Argument Task

Because the Argument task is meant to assess analytical writing and informal reasoning skills that you have developed throughout your education, it has been designed so as not to require any specific course of study or to advantage students with a particular type of training. Many college textbooks on rhetoric and composition have sections on informal logic and critical thinking that might prove helpful, but even these might be more detailed and technical than the task requires. You will not be expected to know methods of analysis or technical terms. For instance, in one topic an elementary school principal might conclude that the new playground equipment has improved student attendance because absentee rates have declined since it was installed. You will not need to see that the principal has committed the *post hoc, ergo propter hoc* fallacy; you will simply need to see that there are other possible explanations for the improved attendance, to offer some commonsense examples, and perhaps to suggest what would be necessary to verify the conclusion. For instance, absentee rates might have decreased because the climate was mild. This would have to be ruled out in order for the principal's conclusion to be valid.

Although you do not need to know special analytical techniques and terminology, you should be familiar with the directions for the Argument task and with certain key concepts, including the following:

- **alternative explanation:** a possible competing version of what might have caused the events in question; an alternative explanation undercuts or qualifies the original explanation because it too can account for the observed facts
- **analysis:** the process of breaking something (e.g., an argument) down into its component parts in order to understand how they work together to make up the whole
- **argument:** a claim or a set of claims with reasons and evidence offered as support; a line of reasoning meant to demonstrate the truth or falsehood of something
- **assumption:** a belief, often unstated or unexamined, that someone must hold in order to maintain a particular position; something that is taken for granted but that must be true in order for the *conclusion* to be true
- **conclusion:** the end point reached by a line of reasoning, valid if the reasoning is sound; the resulting assertion
- **counterexample:** an example, real or hypothetical, that refutes or disproves a statement in the *argument*
- **evaluation:** an assessment of the quality of evidence and reasons in an argument and of the overall merit of an *argument*

An excellent way to prepare for the Analyze an Argument task is to practice writing on some of the published Argument topics. There is no one way to practice that is best for everyone. Some prefer to start practicing without adhering to the 30-minute time limit. If you follow this approach, take all the time you need to evaluate the argument.

No matter which approach you take, you should

- carefully read the argument and the specific instructions—you might want to read them over more than once
- identify as many of the argument's claims, conclusions, and underlying assumptions as possible and evaluate their quality
- think of as many alternative explanations and counterexamples as you can
- think of what specific additional evidence might weaken or lend support to the claims
- ask yourself what changes in the argument would make the reasoning more sound

Write down each of these thoughts as a brief note. When you have gone as far as you can with your evaluation, look over the notes and put them in a good order for discussion (perhaps by numbering them). Then write an evaluation according to the specific instructions by fully developing each point that is relevant to those instructions. Even if you choose not to write a full essay response, you should find it very helpful to practice evaluating a few of the arguments and sketching out your responses. When you become quicker and more confident, you should practice writing some Argument responses within the 30-minute time limit so that you will have a good sense of how to pace yourself in the actual test. For example, you will not want to discuss one point so exhaustively or to provide so many equivalent examples that you run out of time to make your other main points.

You might want to get feedback on your response(s) from a writing instructor, a philosophy teacher, or someone who emphasizes critical thinking in his or her course. It can also be very informative to trade papers on the same topic with fellow students and discuss one another's responses in terms of the scoring guide. Focus not so much on giving the "right scores" as on seeing how the papers meet or miss the performance standards for each score point and what you therefore need to do in order to improve.

How to Interpret Numbers, Percentages, and Statistics in Argument Topics

Some arguments contain numbers, percentages, or statistics that are offered as evidence in support of the argument's conclusion. For example, an argument might claim that a certain community event is less popular this year than it was last year because only 100 people attended this year in comparison with 150 last year, a 33 percent decline in attendance. It is important to remember that you are not being asked to do a mathematical task with the numbers, percentages, or statistics. Instead you should evaluate these as evidence intended to support the conclusion. In the example above, the conclusion is that a community event has become less popular. You should ask yourself: does the difference between 100 people and 150 people support that conclusion? Note that, in this case, there are other possible explanations; for example, the weather might have been much worse this year, this year's event might have been held at an inconvenient time, the cost of the event might have gone up this year, or there might have been another popular event this year at the same time. Each of these could explain the difference in attendance, and thus would weaken the conclusion that the event was "less popular." Similarly, percentages might support or weaken a conclusion depending on what actual numbers the percentages represent. Consider the claim that the drama club at a school deserves more funding because its membership has increased by 100 percent. This 100 percent increase could be significant if there had been 100 members and now there are 200 members, whereas the increase would be much less significant if there had been 5 members and now there are 10. Remember that any numbers, percentages, or statistics in Argument tasks are used only as evidence in support of a conclusion, and you should always consider whether they actually support the conclusion.

The Form of Your Response

You are free to organize and develop your response in any way that you think will effectively communicate your evaluation of the argument. Your response may, but need not, incorporate particular writing strategies learned in English composition or writing-intensive college courses. GRE readers will not be looking for a particular developmental strategy or mode of writing. In fact, when GRE readers are trained, they review hundreds of Argument responses that, although highly diverse in content and form, display similar levels of critical thinking and analytical writing. Readers will see, for example, some essays at the 6 score level that begin by briefly summarizing the argument and then explicitly stating and developing the main points of the evaluation. The readers know that a writer can earn a high score by developing several points in an evaluation or by identifying a central feature in the argument and developing that evaluation extensively. You might want to look at the sample Argument responses, particularly at the 5 and 6 score levels, to see how other writers have successfully developed and organized their responses.

You should make choices about format and organization that you think support and enhance the overall effectiveness of your evaluation. This means using as many or as few paragraphs as you consider appropriate for your response—for example, creating a new paragraph when your discussion shifts to a new point of evaluation. You might want to organize your evaluation around the structure of the argument itself, discussing the argument line by line. Or you might want to first point out a central problem and then move on to discuss related weaknesses in the argument's line of reasoning. Similarly, you might want to use examples if they help illustrate an important point in your evaluation or move your discussion forward (remember, however, that, in terms of your ability to perform the Argument task effectively, it is your critical thinking and analytical writing, not your ability to come up with examples, that is being assessed). What matters is not the form the response takes, but how insightfully you evaluate the argument and how articulately you communicate your evaluation to academic readers within the context of the task.

Sample Argument Task

In surveys Mason City residents rank water sports (swimming, boating, and fishing) among their favorite recreational activities. The Mason River flowing through the city is rarely used for these pursuits, however, and the city park department devotes little of its budget to maintaining riverside recreational facilities. For years there have been complaints from residents about the quality of the river's water and the river's smell. In response, the state has recently announced plans to clean up Mason River. Use of the river for water sports is, therefore, sure to increase. The city government should for that reason devote more money in this year's budget to riverside recreational facilities.

Write a response in which you examine the stated and/or unstated assumptions of the argument. Be sure to explain how the argument depends on the assumptions and what the implications are if the assumptions prove unwarranted.

Strategies for This Topic

This argument cites a survey to support the prediction that the use of the Mason River is sure to increase and thus recommends that the city government should devote more money in this year's budget to the riverside recreational facilities.

In developing your evaluation, you are asked to examine the argument's stated and/or unstated assumptions and discuss what the implications are if the assumptions prove unwarranted. A successful response, then, must discuss both the argument's assumptions AND the implications of these assumptions for the argument. A response that does not address these aspects of the task will not receive a score of 4 or higher, regardless of the quality of its other features.

Though responses may well raise other points not mentioned here and need not mention all of these points, some assumptions of the argument, and some ways in which the argument depends on those assumptions, include:

- The assumption that people who rank water sports "among their favorite recreational activities" are actually likely to participate in them. (It is possible that they just like to watch them.) This assumption underlies the claim that use of the river for water sports is sure to increase after the state cleans up the Mason River and that the city should for that reason devote more money to riverside recreational facilities.

- The assumption that what residents say in surveys can be taken at face value. (It is possible that survey results exaggerate the interest in water sports.) This assumption underlies the claim that use of the river for water sports is sure to increase after the state cleans up the Mason River and that the city should for that reason devote more money to riverside recreational facilities.
- The assumption that Mason City residents would actually want to do water sports in the Mason River. (As recreational activities, it is possible that water sports are regarded as pursuits for vacations and weekends away from the city.) This assumption underlies the claim that use of the river for water sports is sure to increase after the state cleans up the Mason River and that the city should for that reason devote more money to riverside recreational facilities.
- The assumption that the park department devoting little of its budget to maintaining riverside recreational facilities means that these facilities are inadequately maintained. This assumption underlies the claim that the city should devote more money in this year's budget to riverside recreational facilities. If current facilities are adequately maintained, then increased funding might not be needed even if recreational use of the river does increase.
- The assumption that the riverside recreational facilities are facilities designed for people who participate in water sports and not some other recreational pursuit. This assumption underlies the claim that the city should devote more money in this year's budget to riverside recreational facilities.
- The assumption that the dirtiness of the river is the cause of its being little used and that cleaning up the river will be sufficient to increase recreational use of the river. (Residents might have complained about the water quality and smell even if they had no desire to boat, swim, or fish in the river.) This assumption underlies the claim that the state's plan to clean up the river will result in increased use of the river for water sports.
- The assumption that the complaints about the river are numerous and significant. This assumption motivates the state's plan to clean up the river and underlies the claim that use of the river for water sports is sure to increase. (Perhaps the complaints are coming from a very small minority, in which case cleaning the river might be a misuse of state funds.)
- The assumption that the state's cleanup will occur soon enough to require adjustments to this year's budget. This assumption underlies the claim that the city should devote more money in this year's budget to riverside recreational facilities.
- The assumption that the cleanup, when it happens, will benefit those parts of the river accessible from the city's facilities. This assumption underlies the claim that the city should devote more money to riverside recreational facilities.
- The assumption that the city government ought to devote more attention to maintaining a recreational facility if demand for that facility increases.
- The assumption that the city should finance the new project and not some other agency or group (public or private).

Should one or more of the above assumptions prove unwarranted, the implications for the argument are that:

- the logic of the argument falls apart/ is invalid/ is unsound.
- the state and city are spending their funds unnecessarily.

Essay Responses and Reader Commentary

Score 6 Response

While it may be true that the Mason City government ought to devote more money to riverside recreational facilities, this author's argument does not make a cogent case for increased resources based on river use. It is easy to understand why city residents would want a cleaner river, but this argument is rife with holes and assumptions, and thus, not strong enough to lead to increased funding.

Citing surveys of city residents, the author reports city resident's love of water sports. It is not clear, however, the scope and validity of that survey. For example, the survey could have asked residents if they prefer using the river for water sports or would like to see a hydroelectric dam built, which may have swayed residents toward river sports. The sample may not have been representative of city residents, asking only those residents who live upon the river. The survey may have been 10 pages long, with 2 questions dedicated to river sports. We just do not know. Unless the survey is fully representative, valid, and reliable, it can not be used to effectively back the author's argument.

Additionally, the author implies that residents do not use the river for swimming, boating, and fishing, despite their professed interest, because the water is polluted and smelly. While a polluted, smelly river would likely cut down on river sports, a concrete connection between the resident's lack of river use and the river's current state is not effectively made. Though there have been complaints, we do not know if there have been numerous complaints from a wide range of people, or perhaps from one or two individuals who made numerous complaints. To strengthen his/her argument, the author would benefit from implementing a normed survey asking a wide range of residents why they do not currently use the river.

Building upon the implication that residents do not use the river due to the quality of the river's water and the smell, the author suggests that a river clean up will result in increased river usage. If the river's water quality and smell result from problems which can be cleaned, this may be true. For example, if the decreased water quality and aroma is caused by pollution by factories along the river, this conceivably could be remedied. But if the quality and aroma results from the natural mineral deposits in the water or surrounding rock, this may not be true. There are some bodies of water which emit a strong smell of sulphur due to the geography of the area. This is not something likely to be afffected by a clean-up. Consequently, a river clean up may have no impact upon river usage. Regardless of whether the river's quality is able to be improved or not, the author does not effectively show a connection between water quality and river usage.

A clean, beautiful, safe river often adds to a city's property values, leads to increased tourism and revenue from those who come to take advantage of the river, and a better overall quality of life for residents. For these reasons, city government may decide to invest in improving riverside recreational facilities. However, this author's argument is not likely significantly persuade the city goverment to allocate increased funding.

Reader Commentary

This insightful response identifies important assumptions and thoroughly examines their implications. The proposal to spend more on riverside recreational facilities rests on a number of questionable assumptions, namely that:

- The survey provides a reliable basis for budget planning;
- The river's pollution and odor are the only reasons for its limited recreational use;
- Efforts to clean the water and remove the odor will be successful.

By showing that each assumption is highly suspect, this essay demonstrates the weakness of the entire argument. For example, paragraph 2 points out that the survey might not have used a representative sample, might have offered limited choices, and might have contained very few questions on water sports. Paragraph 3 examines the tenuous connection between complaints and limited use of the river for recreation. Complaints about water quality and odor may be coming from only a few people, and even if such complaints are numerous, other completely different factors may be much more significant in reducing river usage. Finally, paragraph 4 explains that certain geologic features may prevent effective river cleanup. Details such as these provide compelling support.

In addition, careful organization insures that each new point builds upon the previous ones. Note, for example, the clear transitions at the beginning of paragraphs 3 and 4, as well as the logical sequence of sentences within paragraphs (specifically paragraph 4).

Although this essay does contain minor errors, it still conveys ideas fluently. Note the effective word choices (e.g., "rife with . . . assumptions" and "may have swayed residents"). In addition, sentences are not merely varied; they also display skillful embedding of subordinate elements. Note, for example, the sustained parallelism in the first sentence of the concluding paragraph.

Since this response offers a cogent examination of the argument and also conveys meaning skillfully, it earns a score of 6.

Score 5 Response

The author of this proposal to increase the budget for Mason City riverside recreational facilities offers an interesting argument but to move forward on the proposal would definitely require more information and thought. While the correlations stated are logical and probable, there may be hidden factors that prevent the City from diverting resources to this project.

For example, consider the survey rankings among Mason City residents. The thought is that such high regard for water sports will translate into usage. But, survey responses can hardly be used as indicators of actual behavior. Many surveys conducted after the winter holidays reveal people who list exercise and weight loss as a top priority. Yet every profession does not equal a new gym membership. Even the wording of the survey results remain ambiguous and vague. While water sports may be among the residents' favorite activities, this allows for many other favorites. What remains unknown is the priorities of the general public. Do they favor these water sports above a softball field or soccer field? Are they willing to sacrifice the municipal golf course for better riverside facilities? Indeed the survey hardly provides enough information to discern future use of improved facilities.

Closely linked to the surveys is the bold assumption that a cleaner river will result in increased usage. While it is not illogical to expect some increase, at what level will people begin to use the river? The answer to this question requires a survey to find out the reasons our residents use or do not use the river. Is river water quality the primary limiting factor to usage or the lack of docks and piers? Are people more interested in water sports than the recreational activities that they are already engaged in? These questions will help the city government forecast how much river usage will increase and to assign a proportional increase to the budget.

Likewise, the author is optimistic regarding the state promise to clean the river. We need to hear the source of the voices and consider any ulterior motives. Is this a campaign year and the plans a campaign promise from the state representative? What is the timeline for the clean-up effort? Will the state fully fund this project? We can imagine the misuse of funds in renovating the riverside facilities only to watch the new buildings fall into dilapidation while the state drags the river clean-up.

Last, the author does not consider where these additional funds will be diverted from. The current budget situation must be assessed to determine if this increase can be afforded. In a sense, the City may not be willing to draw money away from other key projects from road improvements to schools and education. The author naively assumes that the money can simply appear without forethought on where it will come from.

Examining all the various angles and factors involved with improving riverside recreational facilities, the argument does not justify increasing the budget. While the proposal does highlight a possibility, more information is required to warrant any action.

Reader Commentary

Each paragraph in the body of this perceptive essay identifies and examines an unstated assumption that is crucial to the argument. The major assumptions discussed are:

- That a survey can accurately predict behavior,
- That cleaning the river will, in itself, increase recreational usage,
- That state plans to clean the river will actually be realized,
- That Mason City can afford to spend more on riverside recreational facilities.

Support within each paragraph is both thoughtful and thorough. Paragraph 2, for example, points out vagueness in the wording of the survey: Even if water sports rank among the favorite recreational activities of Mason City residents, other sports may still be much more popular. Thus, if the first assumption proves unwarranted, the argument to fund riverside facilities— rather than soccer fields or golf courses—becomes much weaker. Paragraph 4 considers several reasons why river cleanup plans may not be successful (the plans may be nothing more than campaign promises, or funding may not be adequate). Thus, the weakness of the third assumption undermines the argument that river recreation will increase and riverside improvements will be needed at all.

Instead of dismissing each assumption in isolation, this response places them in a logical order and considers their connections. Note the appropriate transitions between and within paragraphs, clarifying the links among the assumptions (e.g., "Closely linked to the surveys . . ." or "The answer to this question requires . . .").

Along with strong development, this response also displays facility with language.

Minor errors in punctuation are present, but word choices are apt and sentences suitably varied in pattern and length. The response uses a number of rhetorical questions, but the implied answers are always clear enough to support the points being made.

Thus, the response satisfies all requirements for a score of 5, but its development is not thorough or compelling enough for a 6.

Score 4 Response

The problem with the arguement is the assumption that if the Mason River were cleaned up, that people would use it for water sports and recreation. This is not necessarily true, as people may rank water sports among their favorite recreational activities, but that does not mean that those same people have the financial ability, time or equipment to pursue those interests.

However, even if the writer of the arguement is correct in assuming that the Mason River will be used more by the city's residents, the arguement does not say why the recreational facilities need more money. If recreational facilities already exist along the Mason River, why should the city allot more money to fund them? If the recreational facilities already in existence will be used more in the coming years, then they will be making more money for themselves, eliminating the need for the city government to devote more money to them.

According to the arguement, the reason people are not using the Mason River for water sports is because of the smell and the quality of water, not because the recreational facilities are unacceptable.

If the city government alloted more money to the recreational facilities, then the budget is being cut from some other important city project. Also, if the assumptions proved unwarranted, and more people did not use the river for recreation, then much money has been wasted, not only the money for the recreational facilities, but also the money that was used to clean up the river to attract more people in the first place.

Reader Commentary

This competent response identifies some important unstated assumptions:

- That cleaning up the Mason River will lead to increased recreational use,
- That existing facilities along the river need more funding.

Paragraph 1 offers reasons why the first assumption is questionable (e.g., residents may not have the necessary time or money for water sports). Similarly, paragraphs 2 and 3 explain that riverside recreational facilities may already be adequate and may, in fact, produce additional income if usage increases. Thus, the response is adequately developed and satisfactorily organized to show how the argument depends on questionable assumptions.

This essay does not, however, rise to a score of 5 because it fails to consider several other unstated assumptions (e.g., that the survey is reliable or that the efforts to clean the river will be successful). Furthermore, the final paragraph makes some extraneous, unsupported assertions of its own. Mason City may actually have a budget surplus so that cuts to other projects will not be necessary, and cleaning the river may provide other real benefits even if it is not used more for water sports.

This response is generally free of errors in grammar and usage and displays sufficient control of language to support a score of 4.

Score 3 Response

Surveys are created to speak for the people; however, surveys do not always speak for the whole community. A survey completed by Mason City residents concluded that the residents enjoy water sports as a form of recreation. If that is so evident, why has the river not been used? The blame can not be soley be placed on the city park department. The city park department can only do as much as they observe. The real issue is not the residents use of the river, but their desire for a more pleasant smell and a more pleasant sight. If the city government cleans the river, it might take years for the smell to go away. If the budget is changed to accomodate the clean up of the Mason River, other problems will arise. The residents will then begin to complain about other issues in their city that will be ignored because of the great emphasis being placed on Mason River. If more money is taken out of the budget to clean the river an assumption can be made. This assumption is that the budget for another part of city maintenance or building will be tapped into to. In addition, to the budget being used to clean up Mason River, it will also be allocated in increasing riverside recreational facilites. The government is trying to appease its residents, and one can warrant that the role of the government is to please the people. There are many assumptions being made; however, the government can not make the assumption that people want the river to be cleaned so that they can use it for recreational water activities. The government has to realize the long term effects that their decision will have on the monetary value of their budget.

Reader Commentary

Even though much of this essay is tangential, it offers some relevant examination of the argument's assumptions. The early sentences mention a questionable assumption (that the survey results are reliable) but do not explain how the survey might have been flawed. Then the response drifts to irrelevant matters—a defense of the city park department, a prediction of budget problems, and the problem of pleasing city residents. Some statements even introduce unwarranted assumptions that are not part of the original argument (e.g., "The residents will then begin to complain about other issues," and "This assumption is that the budget for another part of city maintenance or building will be tapped into."). Near the end, the response does correctly note that city government should not assume that residents want to use the river for recreation. Hence, the proposal to increase funding for riverside recreational facilities may not be justified.

In summary, the language in this response is reasonably clear, but its examination of unstated assumptions remains limited, and therefore the essay earns a score of 3.

Score 2 Response

This statement looks like logical, but there are some wrong sentences in it which is not logical.

First, this statement mentions raking water sports as their favorite recreational activities at the first sentence. However, it seems to have a ralation between the first sentence and the setence which mentions that increase the quality of the river's water and the river's smell. This is a wrong cause and result to solve the problem.

Second, as a reponse to the complaints from residents, the state plan to clean up the river. As a result, the state expects that water sports will increase. When you look at two sentences, the result is not appropriate for the cause.

Third, the last statement is the conclusion. However, even though residents rank water sports, the city government might devote the budget to another issue. This statement is also a wrong cause and result.

In summary, the statement is not logical because there are some errors in it. The supporting setences are not strong enough to support this issue.

Reader Commentary

Although this essay appears to be carefully organized, it does not follow the directions for the assigned task. In his/her vague references to causal fallacies, the writer attempts logical analysis but never refers explicitly or implicitly to any unusual assumptions.

Furthermore, several errors in grammar and sentence structure interfere with meaning (e.g., "This statement looks like logical, but there are some wrong sentences in it which is not logical.").

Because this response "does not follow the directions for the assigned task" (see the Argument Scoring Guide, pages 211–212) and contains errors in sentence structure and logical development, it earns a score of 2.

Score 1 Response

> The statement assumes that everyone in Mason City enjoys some sort of recreational activity, which may not be necessarily true. They statement also assumes that if the state cleans up the river, the use of the river for water sports will definitely increase.

Reader Commentary

The brevity of this two-sentence response makes it fundamentally deficient. Sentence one states an assumption that is actually not present in the argument, and sentence two correctly states an assumption but provides no discussion of its implications. Although the response may begin to address the assigned task, it offers no development. As such, it clearly "provides little evidence of the ability to develop an organized response (i.e., is disorganized and/or extremely brief)" (see Argument Scoring Guide, pages 211–212) and should earn a score of 1.

Practice Analyze an Argument Tasks

Task 1

> The following appeared in a health magazine published in Corpora.
>
> "Medical experts say that only one-quarter of Corpora's citizens meet the current standards for adequate physical fitness, even though twenty years ago, one-half of all of Corpora's citizens met the standards as then defined. But these experts are mistaken when they suggest that spending too much time using computers has caused a decline in fitness. Since overall fitness levels are highest in regions of Corpora where levels of computer ownership are also highest, it is clear that using computers has not made citizens less physically fit. Instead, as shown by this year's unusually low expenditures on fitness-related products and services, the recent decline in the economy is most likely the cause, and fitness levels will improve when the economy does."
>
> Write a response in which you examine the stated and/or unstated assumptions of the argument. Be sure to explain how the argument depends on these assumptions and what the implications are for the argument if the assumptions prove unwarranted.

Task 2

> Collectors prize the ancient life-size clay statues of human figures made on Kali Island but have long wondered how Kalinese artists were able to depict bodies with such realistic precision. Since archaeologists have recently discovered molds of human heads and hands on Kali, we can now conclude that the ancient Kalinese artists used molds of actual bodies, not sculpting tools and techniques, to create these statues. This discovery explains why Kalinese miniature statues were abstract and entirely different in style: molds could be used only for life-size sculptures. It also explains why few ancient Kalinese sculpting tools have been found. In light of this discovery, collectors predict that the life-size sculptures will decrease in value while the miniatures increase in value.
>
> Write a response in which you discuss what questions would need to be answered in order to decide whether the prediction and the argument on which it is based are reasonable. Be sure to explain how the answers to these questions would help to evaluate the prediction.

You may choose to write an essay response on one or both of the Analyze an Argument tasks above. After you have done so, review the scored sample essays and reader commentaries for these tasks on pages 228–241.

GRE Scoring Guide: Analyze an Issue Task

Score 6

In addressing the specific task directions, a 6 response presents a cogent, well-articulated analysis of the issue and conveys meaning skillfully.

A typical response in this category
- articulates a clear and insightful position on the issue in accordance with the assigned task
- develops the position fully with compelling reasons and/or persuasive examples
- sustains a well-focused, well-organized analysis, connecting ideas logically
- conveys ideas fluently and precisely, using effective vocabulary and sentence variety
- demonstrates superior facility with the conventions of standard written English (i.e., grammar, usage, and mechanics) but may have minor errors

Score 5

In addressing the specific task directions, a 5 response presents a generally thoughtful, well-developed analysis of the issue and conveys meaning clearly.

A typical response in this category
- presents a clear and well-considered position on the issue in accordance with the assigned task
- develops the position with logically sound reasons and/or well-chosen examples
- is focused and generally well organized, connecting ideas appropriately
- conveys ideas clearly and well, using appropriate vocabulary and sentence variety
- demonstrates facility with the conventions of standard written English but may have minor errors

Score 4

In addressing the specific task directions, a 4 response presents a competent analysis of the issue and conveys meaning with acceptable clarity.

A typical response in this category
- presents a clear position on the issue in accordance with the assigned task
- develops the position with relevant reasons and/or examples
- is adequately focused and organized
- demonstrates sufficient control of language to express ideas with acceptable clarity
- generally demonstrates control of the conventions of standard written English but may have some errors

GRE Scoring Guide: Analyze an Issue Task (continued)

Score 3

A 3 response demonstrates some competence in addressing the specific task directions, in analyzing the issue, and in conveying meaning but is obviously flawed.

A typical response in this category exhibits ONE OR MORE of the following characteristics:

- is vague or limited in addressing the specific task directions and/or in presenting or developing a position on the issue
- is weak in the use of relevant reasons or examples or relies largely on unsupported claims
- is limited in focus and/or organization
- has problems in language and sentence structure that result in a lack of clarity
- contains occasional major errors or frequent minor errors in grammar, usage, or mechanics that can interfere with meaning

Score 2

A 2 response largely disregards the specific task directions and/or demonstrates serious weaknesses in analytical writing.

A typical response in this category exhibits ONE OR MORE of the following characteristics:

- is unclear or seriously limited in addressing the specific task directions and/or in presenting or developing a position on the issue
- provides few, if any, relevant reasons or examples in support of its claims
- is poorly focused and/or poorly organized
- has serious problems in language and sentence structure that frequently interfere with meaning
- contains serious errors in grammar, usage, or mechanics that frequently obscure meaning

Score 1

A 1 response demonstrates fundamental deficiencies in analytical writing.

A typical response in this category exhibits ONE OR MORE of the following characteristics:

- provides little or no evidence of understanding the issue
- provides little evidence of the ability to develop an organized response (e.g., is disorganized and/or extremely brief)
- has severe problems in language and sentence structure that persistently interfere with meaning
- contains pervasive errors in grammar, usage, or mechanics that result in incoherence

Score 0

Off topic (i.e., provides no evidence of an attempt to respond to the assigned topic), is in a foreign language, merely copies the topic, consists of only keystroke characters, or is illegible or nonverbal.

GRE Scoring Guide: Analyze an Argument Task

Score 6

In addressing the specific task directions, a 6 response presents a cogent, well-articulated examination of the argument and conveys meaning skillfully.

A typical response in this category
- clearly identifies aspects of the argument relevant to the assigned task and examines them insightfully
- develops ideas cogently, organizes them logically, and connects them with clear transitions
- provides compelling and thorough support for its main points
- conveys ideas fluently and precisely, using effective vocabulary and sentence variety
- demonstrates superior facility with the conventions of standard written English (i.e., grammar, usage, and mechanics) but may have minor errors

Score 5

In addressing the specific task directions, a 5 response presents a generally thoughtful, well-developed examination of the argument and conveys meaning clearly.

A typical response in this category
- clearly identifies aspects of the argument relevant to the assigned task and examines them in a generally perceptive way
- develops ideas clearly, organizes them logically, and connects them with appropriate transitions
- offers generally thoughtful and thorough support for its main points
- conveys ideas clearly and well, using appropriate vocabulary and sentence variety
- demonstrates facility with the conventions of standard written English but may have minor errors

Score 4

In addressing the specific task directions, a 4 response presents a competent examination of the argument and conveys meaning with acceptable clarity.

A typical response in this category
- identifies and examines aspects of the argument relevant to the assigned task but may also discuss some extraneous points
- develops and organizes ideas satisfactorily but may not connect them with transitions
- supports its main points adequately but may be uneven in its support
- demonstrates sufficient control of language to convey ideas with acceptable clarity
- generally demonstrates control of the conventions of standard written English but may have some errors

GRE Scoring Guide: Analyze an Argument Task (continued)

Score 3

A 3 response demonstrates some competence in addressing the specific task directions, in examining the argument, and in conveying meaning but is obviously flawed.

A typical response in this category exhibits ONE OR MORE of the following characteristics:
- does not identify or examine most of the aspects of the argument relevant to the assigned task, although some relevant examination of the argument is present
- mainly discusses tangential or irrelevant matters, or reasons poorly
- is limited in the logical development and organization of ideas
- offers support of little relevance and value for its main points
- has problems in language and sentence structure that result in a lack of clarity
- contains occasional major errors or frequent minor errors in grammar, usage, or mechanics that can interfere with meaning

Score 2

A 2 response largely disregards the specific task directions and/or demonstrates serious weaknesses in analytical writing.

A typical response in this category exhibits ONE OR MORE of the following characteristics:
- does not present an examination based on logical analysis, but may instead present the writer's own views on the subject
- does not follow the directions for the assigned task
- does not develop ideas, or is poorly organized and illogical
- provides little, if any, relevant or reasonable support for its main points
- has serious problems in language and sentence structure that frequently interfere with meaning
- contains serious errors in grammar, usage, or mechanics that frequently obscure meaning

Score 1

A 1 response demonstrates fundamental deficiencies in analytical writing.

A typical response in this category exhibits ONE OR MORE of the following characteristics:
- provides little or no evidence of understanding the argument
- provides little evidence of the ability to develop an organized response (e.g., is disorganized and/or extremely brief)
- has severe problems in language and sentence structure that persistently interfere with meaning
- contains pervasive errors in grammar, usage, or mechanics that result in incoherence

Score 0

Off topic (i.e., provides no evidence of an attempt to respond to the assigned topic), is in a foreign language, merely copies the topic, consists of only keystroke characters, or is illegible, or nonverbal.

Score Level Descriptions

Although the GRE Analytical Writing measure contains two discrete analytical writing tasks, a single combined score is reported because it is more reliable than is a score for either task alone. The reported score, the average of the scores for the two tasks, ranges from 0 to 6, in half-point increments.

The statements below describe, for each score level, the overall quality of critical thinking and analytical writing demonstrated across both the Issue and Argument tasks. The Analytical Writing section is designed to assess both critical thinking skills and writing ability. Thus, many aspects of analytical writing, including reasoning skills, organization, and degree of control of the conventions of standard written English are taken into consideration in the determination of a final score. For a full description of how these criteria are used to assess essay responses, please refer to the scoring guides for the Issue and Argument tasks, which are available on the GRE website at **www.ets.org/gre/revised/scoreguides**.

Scores 6 and 5.5: Sustains insightful, in-depth analysis of complex ideas; develops and supports main points with logically compelling reasons and/or highly persuasive examples; is well focused and well organized; skillfully uses sentence variety and precise vocabulary to convey meaning effectively; demonstrates superior facility with sentence structure and language usage but may have minor errors that do not interfere with meaning.

Scores 5 and 4.5: Provides generally thoughtful analysis of complex ideas; develops and supports main points with logically sound reasons and/or well-chosen examples; is generally focused and well organized; uses sentence variety and vocabulary to convey meaning clearly; demonstrates good control of sentence structure and language usage but may have minor errors that do not interfere with meaning.

Scores 4 and 3.5: Provides competent analysis of ideas; develops and supports main points with relevant reasons and/or examples; is adequately organized; conveys meaning with reasonable clarity; demonstrates satisfactory control of sentence structure and language usage but may have some errors that affect clarity.

Scores 3 and 2.5: Displays some competence in analytical writing, although the writing is flawed in at least one of the following ways: limited analysis or development; weak organization; weak control of sentence structure or language usage, with errors that often result in vagueness or lack of clarity.

Scores 2 and 1.5: Displays serious weaknesses in analytical writing. The writing is seriously flawed in at least one of the following ways: serious lack of analysis or development; lack of organization; serious and frequent problems in sentence structure or language usage, with errors that obscure meaning.

Scores 1 and 0.5: Displays fundamental deficiencies in analytical writing. The writing is fundamentally flawed in at least one of the following ways: content that is extremely confusing or mostly irrelevant to the assigned tasks; little or no development; severe and pervasive errors that result in incoherence.

Score 0: The examinee's analytical writing skills cannot be evaluated because the responses do not address any part of the assigned tasks, are merely attempts to copy the assignments, are in a foreign language, or display only indecipherable text.

Score NS: The examinee produced no text whatsoever.

Scored Sample Essays and Reader Commentary for the Practice Analyze an Issue Tasks on Page 195

Task 1

> Every individual in a society has a responsibility to obey just laws and to disobey and resist unjust laws.
>
> Write a response in which you discuss the extent to which you agree or disagree with the claim. In developing and supporting your position, be sure to address the most compelling reasons and/or examples that could be used to challenge your position.

Essay Responses and Reader Commentary

Score 6 Response

> Throughout history the conflict between one's own judgment and the judgment of the lawmakers has given rise to many conflicts, wars and revolutions. In that context, the claim that individuals should follow their own sense of righteousness by opposing laws that are in their opinion unfair and following laws that are fair is justified. Since individual judgment is subjective, however, I cannot completely agree with the claim.
>
> One of the negative consequences of blindly following a state's laws becomes clear when one considers authoritarian, ideologically extreme and fundamentalist countries. It is highly likely that power-hungry and oppressive governments like Nazi Germany and the Soviet Union are not founded on and buttressed by the most ethical laws. For example, when my grandfather was stationed with the German army in the Czech Republic in 1945, he was tasked with executing five Czech partisans. As a soldier, he should have followed orders and could have been sent to prison or executed himself if he disobeyed. He managed to convince his superior that his pistol was rusty and would not fire and thereby saved the lives of the partisans by disobeying a direct order. When a state's laws are in conflict with basic human codes of ethics, therefore, it becomes clear that one should disobey orders.
>
> Not all laws, however, violate human rights, so the decision to follow or oppose them is not black and white. In some cases a subjective sense of what is right might actually oppose a collective sense of what is right. For instance, I remember arguing with my parents while in 5th grade in school that, based on my antipathy towards school at the time, I had a right to freedom and should not be obliged to go to school. In fact, going to school is required by law in Germany, and I was arguing to break the law based on my own set of principles and rights. Since a sense of righteousness can be subjective, it is sometimes reasonable to accept laws that benefit the whole of society as well as the individual - even if the individual is not willing to accept that as a universal truth.
>
> I furthermore can't completely agree with the claim with respect to the statement that society should obey "just" laws. There are certainly circumstances in which a whole society's sense of right and wrong has been manipulated by years of propaganda. Consider the law passed in 1939 by Nazi Germany labeled the "Endloesung", i.e., the final solution. That law deprived Jewish people of any human rights and set the scene for the holocaust. Through years of brainwashing, a large proportion of German society

accepted that law and actually believed that Jews were an inferior race. Therefore, depending on the circumstances and the manipulative powers of a regime, even laws that appear just to some are utterly appalling to humanity as a whole. Hence, the subjective nature of right or wrong does not only vary from person to person but is also subject to manipulation and deceit. For this reason I cannot agree with the claim completely.

In conclusion, therefore, there are situations, such as when laws clearly oppose basic human rights, in which the claim is true and useful. However, an individual's interpretation of what is right is often subjective and vulnerable to biased influences by powerful regimes. Therefore the truth of the claim is limited.

Reader Commentary

This response presents a cogent, well-articulated analysis of the issue in accordance with the specific task directions. Each paragraph contributes significant analytical reasoning to support the nuanced position that while resistance to authority is obviously justified in the most clear-cut cases, a sense of justification can be too subjective to be reliable not only in a personal sense but also on a societal scale, as when entire populations become deluded. In presenting that analysis, the writer takes a position that one must disobey unjust laws (second paragraph) and obey those that are just (third paragraph). But, in accordance with the task direction to address any compelling reasons and/or examples that could be used to challenge one's position, the writer also recognizes a counterargument to his/her position in instances when people neither resist nor disobey unjust laws (fourth paragraph), particularly when they are "subject to manipulation and deceit." Furthermore, the examples and reasons are both compelling and persuasive as in the dramatic case of the Nazi soldier finding a way to disobey orders even though he "should" have followed them to save his own life. The response conveys ideas fluently and precisely via effective vocabulary and syntax, as in this example: "Therefore, depending on the circumstances and the manipulative powers of a regime, even laws that appear just to some are utterly appalling to humanity as a whole. Hence, the subjective nature of right or wrong does not only vary from person to person but is also subject to manipulation and deceit." For its well-articulated, cogent analysis of the issue, this response earns a score of 6.

Score 5 Response

Every individual in a society does have a responsibility to obey just laws and to potentially disobey and resist unjust laws to a certain extent. Laws are formed with the safety and well being of the society as a whole; therefore one would hope that most laws would be considered just. However, in extreme circumstances, disobeying a law that is seen as unjust, when seen as benefiting society as a whole, is acceptable. In these situations the "bar" for what stands as unjust needs to be set, and is nonnegotiable. Without a hard and fast line that is followed complete anarchy could ensue.

Every person has a responsibility to do what is just, whether it is in the eyes of the law or eyes of what is morally acceptable. To be a responsible and active member in a functioning society an individual needs to follow protocol. Laws that are set in place to control the safety of a community are crucial to the society's survival. Responsibility, although a daunting term, is appropriate in that in order for a law to be effective and functional individuals need to be held accountable for their actions. Just laws are not simply suggestions that should be followed; they are rules that need to be followed.

When it comes to unjust laws it is not such a black and white situation. If a law is unjust in every single situation, and at no point is morally acceptable, then it is an individual's responsibility to stand up against the law and demand change. However, there is no standard definition as to what is unjust. Each individual can read into this situation differently. For some, animal rights hold the most significance and any law that denies them complete rights is unjust. In that case most in society would not find it acceptable or morally right to fight laws that protect a human's security over an animal's security. The same can be said for issues such as abortion. Some are strongly pro choice while others feel it is the same as committing murder. In this case some would fight against laws that allow abortion while others will fight to allow the women to decide. In both scenarios, if everyone fought against the standing laws chaos would surely ensue.

To resist unjust laws could hold a very different meaning to each individual in society. Some believe that the best way to resist an unjust law would be to send letters to the capitol, quietly protest by putting up signs, or simply getting word out by holding town meetings out that these laws are not acceptable. Others take resistance to a totally different level by vocally protesting, holding sit-ins, and in some cases becoming violent. This being said, unless is there is a hard and fast rule describing what is considered unjust and what "resist" means, there needs to be caution when attempting to stand up for what one individual decides is unjust.

In the most extreme cases, such as allowing genocide of an entire race, there would be no question that citizens need to stand up and fight the laws put in place by the corrupt justice system. In such cases the line is drawn and it appears to be a black and white issue. Again, caution needs to be taken when disobeying the laws. If the resistance becomes violent, then their cause can become questionable. Are they not doing the same thing in retaliation, therefore committing unjust crimes to fix unjust rules? Tactful and effective methods that do not put society as a whole in more danger than they currently stand in would be acceptable. However, more often than not violence is used to fight violence, which essentially seems to contradict the cause and undermine the end goals of the resistance.

In the end it is critical that society follow just laws in order to keep society healthy and happy. It is in fact their individual responsibility to do so. As for disobeying unjust laws, there seems to be a large grey area. Depending on the means to the end, disobeying could potentially be beneficial to the entire society, yet with strong opinions leading the way there is potential for damage to be done to the entire society. In that case, "responsibility" is too strong of a term.

Reader Commentary

In addressing the specific task directions, this strong response presents a generally thoughtful and well-developed analysis of the issue. The writer does not merely accept the claim as stated but instead addresses it as two distinct assertions, which results in a fully reasoned response. While agreeing that "every individual in a society does have a responsibility to obey just laws," the writer takes a more pragmatic approach when evaluating the validity of the counterclaim that every individual in society also has a responsibility to disobey unjust laws. For example, in paragraph two, the writer presents a view favoring the obligation to obey laws and then, in the third paragraph, clearly signals a turn to challenging that view: "When it comes to unjust laws it is not such a black and white situation." To illustrate this point, the writer examines several reasons why it is difficult to make such a broad claim about unjust laws, including the differing views among individuals as to what constitutes an unjust law and what actions should be taken "to resist" such laws. The writer warns that engaging in resistance to unjust laws could justify extreme methods of retaliation which would undermine the goal of resisting (e.g., using violence to fight against violence). Examples are well chosen and reasoning is logically sound. Ideas are connected appropriately (e.g., "In these situations," "However," "In that case," "Again," "In the end"), and the response is well organized. However, it lacks the superior facility of a typical 6, and that keeps it from receiving the higher score. For its well-considered, thoughtful analysis and logically sound reasoning, this response earns a score of 5.

Score 4 Response

I disagree with the claim that individuals in a society have a responsibility to obey just laws and to disobey and resist unjust laws. I believe individuals are responsible to obey laws, whether they seem just or unjust. Promoting the idea that members of a society ought to disobey and resist any law with which they disagree is dangerous. We should encourage society members to use proper channels to challenge the laws which they believe are unjust.

Our society is based on democratic law. As such, our current laws represent the values and needs of our society as a whole. If an individual of our society disagrees with a particular law, we could all be in danger if that individuals belief conflicts with the greater good of our society. For example, if John believes he should be able to use methamphetamines, and therefore chooses to produce them in his home despite the current ban on methamphetmines in our country, this could put many other individuals in danger. Methamphetamine production creates many toxic byproducts, and faulty production can result in dangerous explosions, both of which put his neighbors in harms way. John may be justified in his choice to endanger himself by using methampehtamines, but he is not justified to endanger his neighbors.

Some might argue that obeying unjust laws only serves to reinforce those laws, but I disagree. Many laws in our country and been changed or modified over the years. An important example is abortion. Abortion was previously illeagal in our country. In resistance to the unjust laws, many women obtained illegal abortions. These abortions were not safe and were often performed under unsanitary conditions. Through out legal system, we have now ensured that women have the legal right to abortion. Seeking action through appropriate channels did not reinforce prohibition of abortion, but led to it's legalization. By following the proper legal channels, and obtaining legalized abortion, woman now have access to abortions at safe and sanitary medical facilties, and the unjust laws were changed.

As responsible citzens, we have the right to obey laws. The responsible response to unjust laws is to change them.

Reader Commentary

In addressing the specific task directions, this response presents both a position on the issue and a potential challenge to it. Disagreeing with the idea of resisting or disobeying laws, the writer argues that all laws should be obeyed or challenged through "proper legal channels." Using a democratic society to provide context and through the example of John the methamphetamine producer, the writer illustrates the potential danger in advocating disobedience to laws which one personally deems to be unjust. Next, the writer satisfactorily responds to a potential counterargument: "Some might argue that obeying unjust laws only serves to reinforce those laws, but I disagree." By comparing the consequences of disobedience to abortion laws (unsafe operations performed under unsanitary conditions) to the results obtained when legal channels were pursued (legal abortions in sanitary medical facilities), the writer successfully addresses the counterargument while reinforcing support for his/her own position. Although it is adequately organized and ideas are supported with relevant examples, the response lacks the breadth and depth required for a score of 5 or 6. For instance, while the example of John illustrates the point that there is a potential danger to society when individuals disobey laws which they deem unjust, it does not demonstrate any thoughtful consideration of the more complex aspects of the issue. The same is true of the abortion example which cites changes in the law but does not engage the thornier and more contentious aspects of that issue. Ideas are conveyed with acceptable clarity although there are some errors. For its competent analysis of the issue conveyed with acceptable clarity, this response merits a score of 4.

Score 3 Response

The purpose of stating the laws is to maintain law and order in the society. Without the laws there will not be any control on the behaviour of the individuals in the society. Laws are made for the welfare of society itself so it is the responsibility of each and every individual to obey the stated laws.

Obeying the laws is beneficial for the society, but then the question arises that what is the difference between just and unjust laws? It depends on the thinking of individual to individual. The law which is just for one individual may be unjust for another individual. For example in a country like India there is a law which gives reservation for backward class people in most of the fields like education, employment etc. This law is supported by those who are benifited by this law but the people who dont get reservation are resisting such laws. Or a theif does a robbery, when roberry is a crime according to law which is just law for normal people but may be unjust for the theif. So whether a law is just or unjust depends on individual perspective.

Take for example on the roads traffic signals every individual has to follow the signals or else there will be a lots of confusions, and also may result in to accidents. If each individual follows the laws there will be no confusions and the traffic movement will be smooth, thus every one in the traffic gets benifitted.

So it is the responsibility of each individual to obey the laws stated whether it may seem just or unjust to him. Even though the laws seems unjust the resistance can be shown in some different ways, but the laws must be obeyed. The best example of this is the recent movement in India about the Jan Lok pal bill which will soon become a law. Thus the laws can also be changed or modified by the contribution of individuals but the its necessary that the laws are obeyed.

Even though one can voice his opinion about the unjust laws the resistance also has to be done as per the law. The laws cannot be classified as just or unjust as per an individual opinion. Thus to conclude the laws are made for the welfare of the society as a whole and not only for an individual so it is the responsibility of each and every individual to obey the prescribed laws whwther he likes it or not.

Reader Commentary

This response demonstrates limited competence in addressing the task directions and analyzing the issue. The writer disagrees with the prompt ("it is the responsibility of each individual to obey the laws stated whether it may seem just or unjust to him") and supports this view by explaining why the claim is untenable ("the laws cannot be classified as just or unjust as per an individual opinion"). In accordance with the task directions, the writer also addresses implied objections to the prompt. The fourth paragraph, for example, centers on explaining that although the writer objects to disobeying the law, this is not necessarily an objection to all forms of resistance ("Even though the laws seems unjust the resistance can be shown in some different ways, but the laws must be obeyed"). Despite these strengths, the response is obviously flawed. An accumulation of frequent minor and occasional major errors interferes with clarity: "For example in a country like India there is a law which gives reservation for backward class people in most of the fields like education, employment etc. This law is supported by those who are benifited by this law but the people who dont get reservation are resisting such laws." Therefore, primarily because it has problems in language and syntax that result in a lack of clarity, this response merits a score of 3.

Score 2 Response

> At first glance it would seem easy to agree with this statement. Obeying laws that are just and resisting laws that are unjust helped build our nation. Our founding fathers resisted laws imposed by England such as taxation without representation. Rosa Parks sat in the front of the bus at a time when blacks were prohibited from doing so. We can now look back and see that these acts were heroic and beneficial to our country which at first sway me to agree with this statement. However, after further analyzing what the full meaning of this steament is I would have to disagree.
>
> My disagreement arises from two words, just and unjust, and creates more questions than answers. How does one determine which laws are just and which are unjust? Each individual in society has their own opinion about what is considered just and unjust, fair or unfair. Would it be wise for someone to radomly decided not to follow a law because they felt it was unjust? I think not.

Reader Commentary

While the language is relatively clear, with only occasional errors, this response exemplifies seriously flawed analytical writing primarily due to its lack of development and it is not fully addressing the specific task directions. In the first paragraph, the writer briefly considers the merit of the prompt's claim, offering a few unexplored examples of occasions in history when resistance to unjust laws was "heroic and beneficial to our country." The writer then abandons that line of reasoning and takes a different position, that the prompt creates "more questions than answers." Although questions raised by the writer have the potential to be developed into thoughtful analysis of the issue's complexity, they are left unexamined. Therefore, because it is seriously limited in presenting and developing a position on the issue, the response merits a score of 2.

Score 1 Response

> Generally speaking, every individual in a society has a responsibility to obey just laws and to disobey and resist unjust laws, it is important that obey the laws and it must be receive the agreement all of us.
>
> Firstly, the squence of the list like number, look like beautiful and vivid, at the same time, the behavior of human being in the society will be influence the other people, if

the attitude of recongizing the subjects is correct will added the confidence each other. For example the individual tax, if exceed the amount of salary the country proved, must be a feedback in the revenue in the finance government.

Secondly, we are surfing the web all day and all nitht, so the internet is ever so import ant to every person. The famous websit **www.taobao.com**, it involved0 the honest issue recently, the CEO Ma Yun insist on the law, announce the whole issue in the websit on public, receive the good goals in the mind of all over the world. On the contrary, if a person disobey and resist unjust laws,for example the drugs in good famous singer and good anthelte, will be give the children bad message, must be get to bad influence in the future in the children, include the mother and father, the brother and sister, etc.

Last but not the least, as human being not another animals in the world. Must be keep the good mind in the brains, resist the happence of unjust laws, don't like the Stock Indexes bounce around like yo-yo game on Friday, day after yesterday lost 4 percent in the value. Do the correct things in the end.

In sum, I firmly consider, receive the normal message, good message will influence more people, fininsed the harmony society, God wished. Friendly speaking, every individual in a society has a responsibility to obey just laws and to disobey and resist unjust laws.

Reader Commentary

The length of this response does not offset its fundamental deficiencies in analytical writing. In the opening paragraph, the writer repeats the prompt and appears to agree with the prompt's claim. From that point on, however, severe and pervasive problems in language and sentence structure interfere with meaning so persistently that it is impossible to recognize any potentially relevant analysis, as is shown in the following: "The famous websit **www.taobao.com**, it involved0 the honest issue recently, the CEO Ma Yun insist on the law, announce the whole issue in the websit on public, receive the good goals in the mind of all over the world." Following the introduction, transitions appear at the start of each paragraph, but the content of those paragraphs is largely incoherent. Due to the severe and pervasive problems in language and sentence structure and in spite of phrases from the prompt being sprinkled throughout the response, there is little or no evidence that the writer understood the issue and the task. For all of these reasons, the response must receive a score of 1.

Task 2

> Claim: The best test of an argument is its ability to convince someone with an opposing viewpoint.
>
> Reason: Only by being forced to defend an idea against the doubts and contrasting views of others does one really discover the value of that idea.
>
> Write a response in which you discuss the extent to which you agree or disagree with the claim and the reason on which that claim is based.

Essay Responses and Reader Commentary

Score 6 Response

The claim that the best test of an argument is its ability to convince someone with an opposing viewpoint is a compelling one. The reason given for this claim is that only through defending an idea against all possible criticism does the idea gain true and tested merit. Indeed, it is this very reason which forms the basis of academic scholarship: by debating and discussing opposing ideas in a collective discourse, we are able to home in upon those ideas which are truly of value. The concept that an argument should be based on sound principles that convince even those who are biased against it falls in line with the foundation of our post-Enlightenment society of reason.

Consider, for example, two disparate political parties with vastly different approaches to governing a country. If, in this tense political climate, a representative from one party raises an argument which she can defend openly in front of a group of her opponents, the value of the idea becomes clear. Say, perhaps, that a representative proposes a new strategy for increasing employment which falls much more in line with her own party's philosophy than with the other party's. By arguing with representatives from the opposing party, and by addressing each and every counterpoint that they raise to her new employment policy, the potential flaws in her idea are laid utterly bare. Furthermore, the logic and reason of her points must be measured in the balance against the biases and emotions of her listeners. If after such a conversation she is able to convince the opposing party that her proposal holds some merit and might actually be beneficial for the citizens of their country, then its value becomes far more evident than if she were a dictator who had merely administered her vision unchecked. It is apparent from this example that the ideology of convincing others with opposing viewpoints is pervasive in the way many governments and institutions are structured, such as our own—through checks and balances, public discourse, and productive disagreement.

The strongest reason for the excerpt's validity is found by comparing the claim to its reverse. Imagine a scenario where one is asked to present one's argument, but the group of people to whom one is presenting already espouse those very ideas: "preaching to the choir" is the ubiquitous idiom we use to describe this phenomenon. In this situation, it becomes irrelevant whether or not a particular argument holds those indicators of merit: logic and reason grounded in evidence. Even the most inflammatory or tenuous arguments would not be exposed for their true hollowness by a group who were unwilling or unable to question the speaker. The "choir" presents no challenge to the argument, and in doing so the argument's merit cannot be tested. In fact, it is this lack of challenge which can lead to stagnation both in the governing of nations—consider, as mentioned above, dictators who eliminate the possibility of dissent—and in academic discourse, where complacency with prevailing ideas can halt the creation of new and possibly contradictory findings. For this, we see that being forced to defend an idea against the doubt of others does indeed bring out its true worth; in the opposing situation, whether or not the argument holds intrinsic merit, this merit cannot be tested or discerned in any way.

There is, however, one modification which makes the claim more complete. The claim suggests that the best test for an argument is its ability to convince others, which may lead to the inference that an argument which cannot convince others holds no value. However, this inference is not true, and here lies the caveat to the claim. Throughout history there are ideas or arguments that are perhaps too modern, beyond their times, and in these situations those who oppose them refuse to believe an argument that is later on discovered to be entirely true and valid. Imagine, for example, Galileo's attempts to convince his contemporaries that the Earth revolved around the Sun, and not vice versa. In the scientific climate of his time, others simply couldn't accept Galileo's reasoned argument despite his multiple attempts to convince them. In this instance, the value of Galileo's argument actually could not be tested by defending it in front of others. The value only became apparent later on, when other scientists began to repeat and understand the insightful calculations that Galileo had made much earlier. So while convincing the opposition is certainly one mark of a good argument, it is not always the ultimate test.

In conclusion, the examples discussed reveal that the worth of an argument can be measured through its ability to withstand dissent and doubt. As long as an argument is not deemed invalid by the mere fact that no others are persuaded by it, it is reasonable to claim that the best way to test an argument is to attempt to convince those who oppose it.

Reader Commentary

In addressing the specific task directions, this outstanding response presents a cogent examination of the issue and conveys meaning skillfully. After stating a clear position in agreement with both the claim and its reason, the writer emphasizes the significance of the latter: "It is this very reason which forms the basis of academic scholarship: by debating and discussing opposing ideas in a collective discourse, we are able to home in upon those ideas which are truly of value." Skillfully, the writer demonstrates the validity of the claim by comparing arguments presented to different audiences. First, a political representative defends a proposal against the arguments of the opposing party. Here, the proposal is fully tested "through checks and balances, public discourse, and productive disagreement." In contrast, the writer considers a similar presentation of ideas to a like-minded group ("preaching to the choir") and concludes that, in the absence of discourse or dissent, the merit of an idea cannot be determined. Finally, the writer reexamines the claim and finds an exception to it (the rejection by his contemporaries of Galileo's reasoned argument), and modifies the claim as follows: "So while convincing the opposition is certainly one mark of a good argument, it is not always the ultimate test." Examples and reasons are both compelling and persuasive, and language and syntax are consistently precise and effective, as in the following: "In fact, it is this lack of challenge which can lead to stagnation both in the governing of nations—consider, as mentioned above, dictators who eliminate the possibility of dissent—and in academic discourse, where complacency with prevailing ideas can halt the creation of new and possibly contradictory findings." Because of its superior facility, fluent and precise presentation of ideas, and clear and insightful position, this response clearly earns a score of 6.

Score 5 Response

As an undergraduate college student, I have come to understand that many of my peers are very emotionally attached to their opinions and political viewpoints. While a gut reaction may tell you that what you believe is correct, that initial instinct is not sufficient in backing up an opinion or idea. In a court of law, or in a debate, one must use rational reasoning and clear, specific examples when arguing a side. Oftentimes, one does not realize how well (or, conversely, how little) one knows a subject until those ideas are challenged. It is through debate, and through the process of being challenged by an opposing viewpoint, that one really begins to understand why they believe what they believe, and how intellectually sound those reasons are.

Many times, over the course of my education, I have come into contact with those whose viewpoints differ from my own. I consider myself to be a person with an open mind, and I enjoy debate with others who value different sides of an argument than I do. In those conversations with others, it is easy to tell who is educated on a topic, and who has had a gut, emotional reaction to the issue being discussed. Those who know about the topic use specific examples to explain why they feel the way they do. Those who don't sometimes resort to more emotional persuasive methods, and sometimes the discussion can become heated.

It is through discussions such as these that I have been able to shape my own opinions and viewpoints on current social issues. I appreciate being challenged by my peers or someone who is "playing devil's advocate" because, through that process, I am able to really examine the motives behind my beliefs. Sometimes, I have encountered discussions that have led me to realize that I simply do not know enough about a topic to hold a valid discussion about it. Other times, I have realized that I am well-versed on the subject, and my opinion or viewpoint is logically sound.

While I agree that this process of challenge is valuable in the formation and upholding of personal viewpoints and opinions, I do not believe that a person should enter into a conversation with the specific purpose of persuading others to change their opinions. Opinions are highly personal, and each person has a reason to believe what they do. It is valuable to question beliefs and opinions, but it is not constructive to feel that your opinion is best and others need to believe what you believe or be considered wrong. I think that there must exist a balance between questioning the beliefs of others and being able to understand why other people believe what they believe. It is more important to be able to understand another person's perspective on a subject than it is to change their mind. In other words, you may disagree with someone, but it is important to be able to see why they believe what they believe. This promotes a well-roundedness that is important in intellectual discussion, and, indeed, in many areas of life.

Though the best test of an argument is challenge (and the subsequent ability to meet the challenge of defense or question the validity of the original opinion), I do not necessarily believe that the challenge must involve convincing someone with an opposing viewpoint that you are correct. You may challenge the idea of others—and be challenged—without feeling as though you must change the minds of others. While discussion of this type may result in changing someone's mind, I don't believe that that should be the goal. The goal of such a discussion should be to share thoughts and ideas, to uphold your own ideas, and to challenge ideas that may be based on emotion or instinct. In this way, we may grow intellectually in an amiable way without stunting the growth of those around us.

Reader Commentary

This response presents a generally thoughtful, well-developed analysis of the issue in addressing the specific task directions. The writer introduces the response's position by first addressing the reason given in the prompt, rather than the claim itself. Through generally thoughtful analysis of personal experiences, the writer agrees that challenges to one's beliefs by those with contrasting views play a vital role in shaping and testing the validity of one's convictions. Turning next to the claim, the writer rejects the assertion that the ability to convince someone with an opposing viewpoint is the best test of an argument. Instead, the writer argues that more is gained by understanding the views of others than by convincing them of the superiority of one's own position. Although a minor digression follows in the discussion of the importance of respecting the opinions of others, this does not detract significantly from the logical flow of analysis; it does, however, suggest that the response is generally thoughtful rather than cogent and compelling. The concluding paragraph demonstrates the writer's ability to formulate a cohesive position on all aspects of the issue. Also, ideas are presented clearly with appropriate vocabulary and sentence variety, as in this example: "I appreciate being challenged by my peers or someone who is 'playing devil's advocate' because, through that process, I am able to really examine the motives behind my beliefs." Overall the response demonstrates facility with the conventions of standard written English. For all the reasons above, the response earns a score of 5.

Score 4 Response

Whether valuing one's own ideas requires challenging them against the views of others is a contested position. This is problematic when we seek to choose the proper action, especially when it comes to religious beliefs and political ideals. It seems though that convincing those who have an alternative perspective on a specific topic will ultimately be what allows us to recognize the value of our own stance.

Some argue that the values of our ideas are realized without being discussed with those holding a different point of view. The proponents of this position claim that as long as we are convinced of our views, then there will be no need to challenge them by considering the ideas of others. For example, let us consider religious beliefs. One may argue that it will be unnecessary to establish any exchange of ideas between different religions, as such exchange will have no effect at all. Religious arguments are presented in the first place to be upheld by faith and not reason. Accordingly, such ideas should not be contested and contrasted with others, as that will only lead to religious tension. Religious tension in the first place is the outcome of dominant religious groups trying to force their views on others who hold different beliefs.

Nevertheless, it seems it is still necessary to challenge our positions against the critical arguments especially of those who have an opposing view. The main force of this argument stems from the claim made by John Stuart Mill of the fallibility of our ideas. This view has also been advocated by a number of contemporary philosophers, especially Jurgen Habermas. The recognition that our arguments are fallible will urge us to continuously consider alternatives while contesting our beliefs against those of others. In the case of international terrorism for instance, we do believe that considering the view of others is required. The destruction of the twin towers in New York possibly would not have occurred if there had been any dialogue between the two contesting parties. The notion of utilizing terrorism for arriving at particular political goals would be subjected to thorough criticism. Consequently, those who appeal to terrorism as a legitimate mean to arriving at ends will in the least recognize the fallibility of their position beforehand. This however can only be done through contesting it against those who hold a different view and not against those who are already convinced of the legitimacy of terrorism.

Ultimately, it seems that challenging our views against contrasting perspectives does appear to be the best way to test the soundness of an idea. This stems primarily for our recognition of the fallibility of our ideas. Therefore, we should always consider any argument we hold to be contestable. This will prompt us to discuss our ideas against people who hold opposing views first and foremost in order to see whether our beliefs are right or not.

Reader Commentary

In addressing the specific task directions, this response presents a competent analysis of the issue and conveys meaning with acceptable clarity. It begins with the writer agreeing with the claim: "convincing those who have an alternative perspective on a specific topic will ultimately be what allows us to recognize the value of our own stance." Before developing this position, however, the writer considers the views of others who assert that the value of a belief can only be determined by one who holds the same belief and acknowledges that circumstances exist when efforts to convince others of one's views can be futile, as in exchanges between those who hold faith-based beliefs. According to the writer, such efforts should be avoided as they have a greater potential to create religious strife than to ascertain the soundness of ideas. The writer then reaffirms agreeing with the claim and reason and suggests that they stem from and align with the views of Mill and Habermas: "The recognition that our arguments are fallible will urge us to continuously consider alternatives while contesting our beliefs against those of others." However, to rise to the level of a 5 or 6, the response must go beyond merely mentioning two philosophers to discuss in some depth the intersection of their theories with the writer's own position. Such philosophical under-pinnings of the response offer rich possibilities for exploration and development but they are left unexamined, and the writer even declines to elaborate on his or her own views. Instead, the writer offers an example, also unexplored, of the destruction of the Twin Towers on 9/11 and argues that the attack might not have occurred had the terrorists allowed their views to be challenged and the fallibility of their beliefs exposed. While this does not demonstrate thoughtful probing or insightful consideration of the issue especially because it seems to contradict what the writer has said earlier about challenging one's religious views, it does provide a relevant example to support the writer's position. Thus, the analysis remains only competent. In spite of some errors, the response generally demonstrates control of the conventions of standard written English. And as the following example shows, ideas are expressed with acceptable clarity: "Consequently, those who appeal to terrorism as a legitimate mean to arriving at ends will in the least recognize the fallibility of their position beforehand." For its competent analysis, relevant examples and reasons, and its sufficient control of language, the response earns a score of 4.

Score 3 Response

Everyone is entitled to their own opinion, and this can often lead to debates between parties with opposing views. Though some would describe debate as combative, it can be much more. Debate is essential to the development of well formed ideas because it forces the participants to more deeply analyze not only their viewpoint but also the opposing viewpoint. By defending you stance on an issue or idea you are naturally deepening your own understanding of it through deeper analysis and reflection.

When debating an issue the opposing sides puts up criticisims to cast doubt on ones stance. Naturally that person must not only discredit said criticisms but also attempt to weaken the opposing sides argument. This process naturally forces you to analyze the issue from both sides, both trying to anticipate and deflect the attacks from the opposition. A deeper understanding and apprectiation of ones ideas comes as a result of this reflection.

Another natural by product of debate is discovering the value and truth of said idea to you. Most often people choose to defend positions that they agree with and believe in. For example, some people would not defend a pro-choice stance because it is not something that personally believe in. When defending a stance it is often times critical to believe in at least part of what you are fighting for.

Many differing opinions exist in the world and the beauty is we can learn and enrich ourselves almost all of them. Defending your ideas against opposing views enables you to deepen your understanding of your ideas and those of others. Along with this deepened understanding comes a greater appreciation of your own ideas and values. This is truly the height of debate and discussion.

Reader Commentary

Demonstrating some competence in understanding the issue and addressing the task directions, this response presents a clear position best illustrated in its conclusion: "Defending your ideas against opposing views enables you to deepen your understanding of your ideas and those of others. Along with this deepened understanding comes a greater appreciation of your own ideas and values. This is truly the height of debate and discussion." The writer argues that debate can lead to a deeper understanding of issues as both sides of an argument are analyzed in order for a person to be able to defend ideas from criticism, weaken an opponent's position, and discover the value and truth of personal beliefs. While this is a valid line of reasoning, it is developed only superficially as the writer relies on unsupported assertions. The only example appears in the third paragraph, the "pro-choice stance," but it is left unexplored and undeveloped. Much of the response consists of slight modifications of the same idea, that of deepening understanding. Notice the repetition of words and phrases in the first, second, and fourth paragraphs: "deepening your own understanding," "deeper understanding and appreciation," "with this deepened understanding comes a greater appreciation." While the response exhibits some flaws in grammar, usage, and syntax, meaning is generally clear. Overall, the response earns a score of 3 primarily because of limited development and its reliance on unsupported claims.

Score 2 Response

I agree with the statement, "The best test of an arguement is its ability to convince someone with an opposing viewpoint." Often in school one has to debate an issue and is assigned a side to represent. I am no exception. One can find reseach to support almost any argument. The challenge is how well one can compose their thoughts and present them. If one can persuade another with an opposing viewpoint, whom in reality shares your same viewpoint, therein lies a victory.

> I feel that the reasoning statement does support the claim. One must have proof in order to back an argument. If one is conducting reseach for a debate, they may never have discovered some of the opposing thoughts. This provides the opportunity to make an informed decision when taking a side.

Reader Commentary

This brief response demonstrates serious weaknesses in analytical writing. Although the writer attempts to address the task and indicates clear agreement with both the claim and reason, the response is seriously limited in developing a position on the issue. The very few logical reasons or examples provided to substantiate its position are undeveloped. In addition, there are problems in language and sentence structure that seriously interfere with or even obscure meaning as in these examples: "If one can persuade another with an opposing viewpoint, whom in reality shares your same viewpoint, therein lies a victory"; and, "If one is conducting reseach for a debate, they may never have discovered some of the opposing thoughts." For seriously limited development, few relevant reasons or examples in support of its claims, and serious problems in language that frequently interfere with meaning, the response clearly earns a score of 2.

Score 1 Response

> I agree with the claime, I feel that any topic should have an an opposing viewpoint. Without having an opposing viewpoint, an individual does not get to truly understand two sides of any particular topic. (Value of that idea) It is only a fair fact that two different viewpoints are being presented, so that you have enpugh information to defend your beliefs.

Reader Commentary

Extreme lack of development of ideas in this response renders it fundamentally deficient. The response sketches an understandable position but provides little evidence that the writer can develop an organized response. For that reason and because it is extremely brief, the response merits a score of 1.

Scored Sample Essays and Reader Commentary for the Practice Analyze an Argument Tasks on Pages 207–208

Task 1

> The following appeared in a health magazine published in Corpora.
>
> "Medical experts say that only one-quarter of Corpora's citizens meet the current standards for adequate physical fitness, even though twenty years ago, one-half of all of Corpora's citizens met the standards as then defined. But these experts are mistaken when they suggest that spending too much time using computers has caused a decline in fitness. Since overall fitness levels are highest in regions of Corpora where levels of computer ownership are also highest, it is clear that using computers has not made citizens less physically fit. Instead, as shown by this year's unusually low expenditures on fitness-related products and services, the recent decline in the economy is most likely the cause, and fitness levels will improve when the economy does."
>
> Write a response in which you examine the stated and/or unstated assumptions of the argument. Be sure to explain how the argument depends on these assumptions and what the implications are for the argument if the assumptions prove unwarranted.

Essay Responses and Reader Commentary

Score 6 Response

> The magazine article concerns itself with a common worry in this day and age: health. It makes an intriguing connection, that of fitness and economic status, but engages it too many clear logical fallacies and fails to present enough factual evidence to be a truly compelling argument.
>
> The article itself is discussing the fitness level of Corpora's citizens, saying that half as many citizens meet the health standards today as did twenty years ago; standing alone, it is persuasive evidence that helps the article's argument. It is the article's own words that undercuts its efficacy. By clarifying that there are "current standards" and "standards as then defined," the writer questions his or her own connection without acknowledging the possible repercussions of that change, thereby assuming that the standards are similar enough for the difference to remain relevant. If that assumption is incorrect, that is, if the standards twenty years ago are drastically different than those today, it is possible that there has been no change in the citizens' fitness at all. It could just be that fitness standards have become more exacting and the citizens are failing to measure up the way they did before, under the more accepting fitness standards. If this were true, the article's entire purpose would be undermined. There would be no change in fitness levels at all, and therefore no cause for concern. This is a major flaw in the argument and should be at least acknowledged by the author, perhaps improved upon by defining the fitness standards, in order to improve the argument as a whole.
>
> The author of this article also makes a tragic assumption by supposing a correlation between high rates of computer ownership and computer usage. The author argues that areas with high computer ownership are also highly fit, and therefore computer

usage cannot result in lower fitness. That statement relies on the assumption that a home has multiple computers because the people in that home are using the computer. It is entirely possible that those homes are the wealthiest homes and own multiple computers, but no one in the home uses the computer. Similarly, someone in a poor neighborhood could not own a computer at all but still use a computer for a great portion of their day at a job and/or library. High ownership rates do not necessarily correlate to usage, and therefore the author cannot logically argue that the relationship between ownership and fitness automatically precludes a correlation between usage and fitness.

The above assumption has even deeper implications. As discussed, the homes with high ownership rates could very well, and even most likely, be the wealthiest homes in Corpora; therefore, the homes with the lowest rates could be the most poverty-stricken. Consequently, the high fitness levels in the high ownership areas may have nothing to do with their computer usage, for which we have no data, or their computer ownership, which we have no proof they own, but everything to do with their wealth and subsequent access to private trainers and gyms. If this were true, it could help strengthen the conclusion of the article's original argument by taking it on a slightly different, albeit still economy-concerned, course. It would nonetheless render the entire article's actual argument false and therefore pointless.

As evidenced, the article engages in three major assumptions, both stated and understated, which do a great deal of work in the author's argument as a whole. That is, if the assumptions prove true. The reasoning relies on data that isn't provided and correlations that may not necessarily exist. For that reason, the article fails to successfully defend its conclusion. If just one of these assumptions were to prove wrong, the entire point of the article would be thrown into question, and it is entirely possible that all three assumptions could be wrong. The author would have to get a great deal more data and add lengthy explanations of the standards upon which the article relies before the article could have any hope of standing successfully on its own.

Reader Commentary

This outstanding response clearly addresses the specific task directions and presents a cogent, insightful analysis by specifically detailing the erroneous assumptions of the argument and what the implications of those assumptions are on the argument. For example, the writer points out that the argument's author accepts the different health standards "without acknowledging the possible repercussions of that change [over time], thereby assuming that the standards are similar enough for the difference to remain relevant. If that assumption is incorrect, that is, if the standards twenty years ago are drastically different than those today, it is possible that there has been no change in the citizens' fitness at all. . . . If this were true, the article's entire purpose would be undermined." Similarly, the writer examines the argument's other points and concludes "If just one of these assumptions were to prove wrong, the entire point of the article would be thrown into question, and it is entirely possible that all three assumptions could be wrong." Throughout the response, the writer exhibits superior facility and fluency, as this example attests: "High ownership rates do not necessarily correlate to usage, and therefore the author cannot logically argue that the relationship between ownership and fitness automatically precludes a correlation between usage and fitness." The response does contain a few typos and minor errors, but these do not detract from its overall fluency, precise diction, and varied syntax. Because of its compelling and insightful development and fluent and precise language, this response fits all of the bullet points for a score of 6.

Score 5 Response

The study in which fitness levels of Corpora's citzens were examined states that the decline in physical fitness can be attributed to the economic downturn. It states that since spending on fitness-related products and services has declined, the most likely reason is the decline in the economy and that spending too much time using computers is not a factor in poor physical fitness. The conclusion drawn in this study needs to be reexamined due to flaws in its assumptions.

First, the study compares current rates of physical fitness with those that were measured twenty years ago. The study explicitly states that the "only one-quarter of Corpora's citizens meet the current standards for adequate physical fitness, even though twenty years ago, one-half of all of Corpora's citizens met the standards as then defined." Current standards for adequate physical fitness may have changed dramatically from the standards that were in place twenty years ago. The study does not state whether or not these standards are comparable. In addition, there is no information about how the previous study was conducted. The study conducted twenty years ago may not have been as rigorous as the current study. Results from the study twenty years ago may not be generalized to the whole population if its sample size was too small or if its methodology was flawed. Therefore, the article needs to include more criteria from the current study and from the previous study in order for readers to understand whether or not the findings from each can be compared.

Second, the high physical fitness levels in regions of Corpora where computer ownership is the highest may be due to other factors. Citizens in this region of Corpora may lead different lifestyles than citizens in other regions of Corpora. A healthy and balanced diet may be important components of everyday life in the region with high computer ownership. Also, income levels is an important factor in physical fitness. Residents of the region of Corpora with high computer ownership may have higher annual incomes than residents of other regions and may be able to afford healthier foods and health services, such as personal trainers. High physical fitness in this area can also be due to the geography and layout of the region. Perhaps there are more available parks where people can exercise. Authors of this study need to account for other factors that may explain why computer ownership is high in areas of higher physical activity.

Third, the study states that low expenditures on fitness products and services can be attributed to the decline in the economy and once the economy is no longer in a decline, expenditures will increase. This implies that expenditures on fitness-related products will increase once the economy improves but this may not necessarily happen. Even if the economy does improve, people may find other outlets in which to spend their money. In addition, this study assumes that in order for physical fitness to be high, people need to spend money on fitness-related products and services. People can attain physical fitness without spending money on products and services. For example, running outdoors is a physical activity that does not require people to spend money. Thus, if fitness levels do not improve once the economy improves, then the conclusion of the study would be regarded as false.

The article in a health magazine published in Corpora summarizes findings from a study and offers explanations for its findings. The conclusion drawn in the study cannot be regarded as fact until the stated assumptions are addressed.

Reader Commentary

In addressing the specific task directions, this strong response presents a generally thoughtful and well-developed analysis of the argument. It identifies key flaws in the argument and examines them in a generally perceptive way. Note, for example, the range of flaws analyzed in each body paragraph. First, the assumptions are identified, then analyzed; the analysis is next followed by a conclusion such as the need for accounting "for other factors that may explain" assumptions about the effects of computer ownership on health and fitness, or why "if fitness levels do not improve once the economy improves, then the conclusion of the study would be regarded as false." However, while this analysis is certainly strong, it never rises to the cogent level of a 6 as can be seen in this example: "Current standards for adequate physical fitness may have changed dramatically from the standards that were in place twenty years ago. The study does not state whether or not these standards are comparable. In addition, there is no information about how the previous study was conducted." This is neither compelling nor skillfully presented. Ideas are clearly and logically organized and clear transitions are employed both in introducing paragraphs and in connecting ideas within paragraphs. In addition, the response conveys ideas clearly and well using appropriate vocabulary and sentence variety: "Results from the study twenty years ago may not be generalized to the whole population if its sample size was too small or if its methodology was flawed. Therefore, the article needs to include more criteria from the current study and from the previous study in order for readers to understand whether or not the findings from each can be compared." In terms of writing skill and analysis, then, this response earns a score of 5.

Score 4 Response

The article suggests that the lagging economy of the region is to blame moreso than increased computer use for the decline of physical fitness for the population of Corpora. The article references that the levels of physical fitness is significantly less than it was twenty years ago, and computer use has drastically increased in that timespan. Yet it discounts computer use as a prime cause for the problem in stating that in areas of high computer use, physical fitness rates are also highest in the region. Then the article goes on to make a broad and unfounded claim that due to recent declines in physical fitness products, the poor economy of the region is most likely to blame. While it is true a lagging economy will tighten personal spending, there are many ways to stay fit. One would expect to see a reduction in physical fitness amounts during times of economic turmoil, but the drastic numbers mentioned in the article seem to indicate other factors are also responsible.

The problem here is that the article fails to take into account these other factors. It doesn't even address them. For instance, what other health issues have arisen in recent years? What about other forms of time consuming entertainment? Did television watching also rise considerably in recent years? What trends can be traced to a reduced emphasis on pysical fitness for the population? There are many factors that can affect how much people exercise. Although the economy might very well be a factor in declining physical fitness rates, is it the prime factor? The article should also take into account the neighboring areas and examine what effects the lagging economy has on measurable levels of physical activity. Did the same levels of physical fitness declines occur elsewhere in the region?

There is also another consideration to be made here. The article concludes that as the economy rebounds, fitness levels are most likely going to increase as well. Since the article fails to establish conclusively the economy is the prime culprit, there is no guarantee that fitness levels will rise. It also does not take into account the change in attitudes that might result toward exercise in the interim. In short, people can become lazy, and after all, there are many ways to stay fit other than purchasing equipment and utilizing gyms.

Although the article may be correct in its conclusions, there is no way to know that in the scope of given information. Most likely as the economy rebounds, levels will rise, but not to the levels expected. In conclusion, there are many factors left unanswered here.

Reader Commentary

This adequate response identifies some important features of the argument and presents a competent examination of it in accordance with the specific task directions. Following a rather lengthy summation of the argument, the writer approaches the task by asking relevant questions, but the writer does not answer some questions or develop answers to other questions beyond an adequate level. For example, in the second paragraph, the writer asks, "For instance, what other health issues have arisen in recent years? What about other forms of time consuming entertainment? Did television watching also rise considerably in recent years? . . . Although the economy might very well be a factor in declining physical fitness rates, is it the prime factor? . . . Did the same levels of physical fitness declines occur elsewhere in the region?" In contrast to this, a 5- or 6-level response would delve into the implications these questions raise, such as what specific other health issue the writer is alluding to, what the implications are of any other factors which affect levels of fitness, and why examining regions other than Corpora would be relevant and illuminating. Exploring implications such as these would result in the kind of thoroughness and thoughtfulness characteristic of responses that are better than merely competent. In addition, support for the analysis is uneven although, overall, development is adequate. Some transitions are present and ideas are conveyed with acceptable clarity. Because of its adequate control of language and syntax and its competent analysis, the response earns a score of 4.

Score 3 Response

Since the level of fitness has gone down and computer use has gone up, it is not sure that there is a causal relationship. The assumption that computer usage effects a Corpora citizens level of fitnessis somewhat valid, however there could be other factors. Since the level of spenditure on fitness-related products has gone down, maybe the standarded of living went down also or the price of fitness-related products went up. Since there can be many other factors which cause this decline researchers must examine them.

The level of fitness in Corpora could have went down do to th change in the standard of living. Yes, computer use his increased and people are stitting at the computer more instead of doing other things. Nevertheless, one can not be sure that these other things are fitness related. People could be spending more time in the workforce or spending more to in eductional institutions. Over time people have become more sedintary, but computers can not totally explain this decline in fittness levels.

The envirnoment may be to blame also. May be in Corpora there are not as many recreational areas for fittness activities. The price of joining a gym has increased or the amount of fittness centers in Corpora are deceasing. Poeple may want to be fit but since things are changing they are not able to, unlike before. Technology has increased across the world and if this is a causal relationship in Corpora, there should be a global effect. The assumption that computer use effects fittness level is somewhat valid. But, can not be totally to blame to the decrease in fittness in Corpora.

Reader Commentary

Although this response examines the argument according to the specific task directions, it is limited in development and in conveying ideas with acceptable clarity. In particular, the response contains occasional major errors and frequent minor errors that can interfere with meaning. A basic error in verb form ("could have went down"), errors in sentence structure (a comma splice and a sentence fragment), errors in usage ("it is not sure"), and problems with wording ("or spending more to in eductional institutions") among others combine to affect clarity and sometimes meaning. In addition to the problems with language and sentence control, the response demonstrates limited development by not identifying and examining most of the aspects of the argument and by accepting some of the argument's reasoning: "The assumption that computer use effects fittness level is somewhat valid." Relevant analysis is undermined by poor reasoning and the absence of explanatory connections between ideas: "The envirnoment may be to blame also. May be in Corpora there are not as many recreational areas for fittness activities. The price of joining a gym has increased or the amount of fittness centers in Corpora are decreasing." Because of its limited development, limited examination of the argument, and problems with language control that affect clarity, this response earns a score of 3.

Score 2 Response

How can the economy recent decline prove health and fitness of people? How can computer improve such thing? Well, how couldn't? Since this crisis, that all of us are going through, came up, people are restricting to themselves things that usually they did, so that money is enough to put food on the table and kids in school. No more cinema nigth, no more weekend vacation, ect. This things can really mess up with people's mind and therefore, some can drop into depression. Then, these persons, try to a refuge. SOme are drugs, Alcohol, gambling or food.

There is another aspect that we should count, anf it is the power of marketing and the ultra consumist society that we live in. With the decline of economy, companies try to gain more costumers in order to mantain business runnig. So big prices one side, and sales on the other, people go after the second one. And It's obvious that fast food industries are making a lot of money these days.

With depression and food, fitness is decreasing, of course. Only the rise of economy can undo this.

Computers are a method of information sharing. It's amazing how a headline of a newspapper in africa can be in India, and it only took one click.

Information abput obesity, heart deseases, statistics, rates and much more can be found on the wonderworld of the internet, aswell some diet recepies, or calories table, ect. There are even some videogames that persue this idea of health and fitness.

I have to say thta, of course, there are people who get fat in front of a screen. But that is because they are depressed and they find confort on the computer.

> With all of this said, I really think that the experts of that health magazine in Corpora areindeed mistaken. Computer can increase peoples health and economy can be the cause of people's lack of fitness. It's important to say that there is no rule without excepetion, so there can be rich unhealthy people, aswell poor and on shape people.

Reader Commentary

This seriously flawed response largely disregards the specific task directions and demonstrates serious weaknesses in analytical reasoning. Except for only three sentences, the writer discusses the supposed ripple effects of "the economy recent decline" by arguing that such phenomena as depression, substance abuse, gambling and consumption of fast food are consequences of economic contraction. The writer argues, "With depression and food, fitness is decreasing, of course. Only the rise of economy can undo this." This non-analytical approach continues as the writer marvels at the "wonderworld of the internet" and its power of information sharing: "It's amazing how a headline of a newspapper in africa can be in India, and it only took one click." Finally, the writer tentatively identifies a flaw in the argument by acknowledging that the health experts in Corpora are "mistaken" since there may be "rich, unhealthy people, aswell poor and on shape people." But this point is neither developed nor made analytically. Overall, language is weak, exhibiting a range of errors that interfere with meaning but which do not frequently interfere with or obscure meaning. Thus, primarily for its significant weaknesses in analytical reasoning and clear disregard of the task directions in discussing the writer's own views on the subject rather than examining the stated and/or unstated assumptions of the argument, the response earns a score of 2.

Score 1 Response

> this passage indicate the relation between the low expenditure on fittness and less physical fittness. In fact, many researches have proven that some of the inadequate physical fittness could be due to the sedentary life-style that humans are living nowadays.

Reader Commentary

This response is fundamentally deficient because it provides little evidence of the ability to develop an organized response. A reader cannot even tell if the writer understands the prompt and task since the response consists largely of a paraphrase of the prompt. Thus, because it is extremely brief and provides little or no evidence of understanding the argument, this response must receive a score of 1.

Task 2

Collectors prize the ancient life-size clay statues of human figures made on Kali Island but have long wondered how Kalinese artists were able to depict bodies with such realistic precision. Since archaeologists have recently discovered molds of human heads and hands on Kali, we can now conclude that the ancient Kalinese artists used molds of actual bodies, not sculpting tools and techniques, to create these statues. This discovery explains why Kalinese miniature statues were abstract and entirely different in style: molds could be used only for life-size sculptures. It also explains why few ancient Kalinese sculpting tools have been found. In light of this discovery, collectors predict that the life-size sculptures will decrease in value while the miniatures increase in value.

Write a response in which you discuss what questions would need to be answered in order to decide whether the prediction and the argument on which it is based are reasonable. Be sure to explain how the answers to these questions would help to evaluate the prediction.

Essay Responses and Reader Commentary

Score 6 Response

The prediction that life size sculptures will decrease in value relative to more abstract miniatures rests upon dubious inferences within its supporting argument. These inferences invite questions whose answers will assist in evaluating the argument, its relationship to the market for Kalinese sculpture, and hence the prediction of relative price movements.

One such inference appears to suggest that if the body sculptures are made via molds as opposed to the miniatures being made free-form by hand, then collectors will cease to value the body sculptures because they represent works of diminished artistic skill. For this to be true, we must first agree with the conclusion that the discovery of hand and head molds in fact means that the body sculptures are made entirely by molds. To evaluate this claim, we would ask if perhaps the molds could have in fact been used in artistic studies, for guidance, and then the body sculptures afterwards made by hand in observation of the models. If this were known to be the case, we would expect no impact on collector demand, as the underlying skill level of the sculptures would stand unchanged. Alternatively, we would ask where the molds are for the rest of the bodies. Without molds of back muscles, feet, limbs, and so on, could we truly conclude the entire statue to be a copy rather than an original creation? And if indeed the head and hand molds did produce parts of the statues, could we be sure that sculptors' skilled hands did not in fact join these aspects together to create a unified whole, exhibiting an adroit artistry worthy of appreciation and valuation?

Furthermore, we also wonder why the miniatures, by contrast, are abstract in nature. Could they in fact have been produced by different sculptors, perhaps belonging to a discrete guild or to a different age? If so, such revelations would differentiate the two art forms making their relative valuation less easily anticipated. We thus note that the prediction that the value of the miniatures will increase due to new information about the body-sculptures appears to rest on an inference that the two art forms are analogous. If instead they are made by different artists, in different eras, or of different materials, we would hesitate to assume such a relationship, and ask why, if they do not share an origin, would any decrease in the value of one form lead to an inverse change in its correlate?

Finally, and in a similar vein, we would ask why the Kalinese body-sculptures are prized in the first place. Could it be that they are prized because of their physical beauty, or due to the unique materials employed, like pied clay? Pied clay is shot through with various elements and colors. If in fact these sculptures' high valuation follows not from the perceived sculpting skill of the artisan but from the attractiveness or distinctiveness of the human forms themselves, or the high value of the material (could they in fact be made of clay infused with gold?), then we could anticipate a much more modest devaluation, if any, due to revelations about the technique or materials involved in their creation. In fact, were they to be made of gold, amid current climates of international financial insecurity and imminent inflationary pressure, we might well conclude that the most relevant questions by which to assess the argument's prediction would hinge on the financial context. For example, inquiries about the degree of monetary expansion planned by the Federal Reserve for the next fiscal year and the solvency of the Spanish Central Bank, rather than some remotely-supported questioning of sculpting technique on a far-off island of a bygone era, might be more relevant.

Reader Commentary

This outstanding response clearly addresses the specific task directions while presenting an insightful, cogent, and well-articulated examination of the argument. Throughout, the compelling analysis is supported by persuasive, fully developed, and nuanced discussion. For example, in questioning the logic of the argument regarding the relative value of the life-size statues vis-à-vis the miniatures—"Could [the miniatures] in fact have been produced by different sculptors, perhaps belonging to a discrete guild or to a different age?"—the writer concludes that the answers to the questions consistently undermine the argument's prediction: "If so, such revelations would differentiate the two art forms making their relative valuation less easily anticipated." Support is always thorough and compelling as in paragraph three when the writer asks, "If instead [the sculptures] are made by different artists, in different eras, or of different materials, we would hesitate to assume such [an analogous] relationship, and ask why, if they do not share an origin, would any decrease in the value of one form lead to an inverse change in its correlate?" Language is fluent and precise, exemplifying the superior facility typical of responses that receive a score of 6, for example, "adroit artistry," "relative valuation less easily anticipated," "current climates of international financial insecurity and imminent inflationary pressure." Organization is both clear and skillful with ideas cohesively linked not only by more obvious transitions ("Furthermore," "Finally") but also through embedded transitions ("Alternatively," "If so," "In fact, were they to be made of gold . . . we might well conclude . . ."). Because of its compelling and insightful development and fluent and precise language, this response fits all of the requirements for a 6.

Score 5 Response

For this situation, the word "beauty" in the common saying "beauty is in the eye of the beholder" could be replaced with "value." Who the potential buyer is of an ancient Kalinese sculpture will determine the value of the piece. To state that life-size statues will be worth less due to the way in which they were made is a presumptuous statement. The price of a piece of art has always depended on how much the buyer is willing to spend. More work must also be done to confirm the use of molds in ancient times.

First, the issue of molds must be addressed. Just because the ancient Kalinese artists used molds, does that make their art less valuable? Since we are not given a time period, it is possible that the concept of molds, their use, and how to make them had not been developed yet. If this is the case, then one could argue that the life-size statues from molds are more valuable than the ones made using sculpting tools. Molds could have been invented and implemented by Kalinese artists first. A creation using a tool that had never been seen before would be very valuable indeed.

Second, how can we be sure that the life-size sculptures will decrease in value? They are still ancient art and will be valued by modern society. While some experts in the field of ancient art may look down upon the use of molds, are they the main market? Some curators may have much knowledge in a field of study, but that does not mean they have the financial ability to purchase pieces. A wealthy individual may not have a great affinity for art, but they may desire to fill their home with seemingly important and expensive things. In that case, one would think that a larger piece would be more valuable to such a buyer than a smaller piece. The larger piece will declare its importance, while the smaller piece's value would most likely only be known by an art enthusiast. Another large market for ancient art would have to be museums. Museums are storehouses of all kinds of history and work to educate the public. Such an institution would be very unlikely to frown upon the life-size work just because it was made from a mold; a museum would most likely desire to obtain both life-size and miniature sculptures for its exhibit of ancient Kalinese art. Third, while the statement says they found molds, they cannot definitively say that molds were used to make all or even any life-size statues. It merely says molds have been found. Further research could provide a use for the molds that has not been seen before. If this was the case, life-size statues may have been previously sold for less their worth.

This statement could have been further strengthened by addressing the above issues as well as obtaining a poll from the target market as well as the everyday individual. Such a poll would yield a better idea of whether or not the mold-formed, life-size sculptures or sculpted miniatures would have more value in the market at the present time.

In summation, at present there are still too many unknown variables to be able to say with conviction which work of art would be more valuable. The use of molds, the effect that molds have upon the value of art, and the reaction of the market are all serious considerations that must be determined before conclusions can be drawn. What can be said is that regardless of the technique used, ancient Kalinese art has great value to many.

Reader Commentary

This strong response addresses the specific task directions and takes a generally thoughtful and well-developed approach to its examination of the argument, including, among others, such elements as the time period when the molds were developed and used, and how the relative value of the two types of figures is determined. While development is strong, overall it does not rise to the level of insightfulness and cogency found in responses that earn a 6. In the third paragraph, for instance, the response depends, at times, on the writer's own assumptions rather than on logical analysis: "They are still ancient art and will be valued by modern society," and "Such an institution [as a museum] would be very unlikely to frown upon the life-size work just because it was made from a mold." Also, while reasons are logically sound and examples well chosen, they are neither compelling nor utterly persuasive. In meeting requirements for a score of 5, the response demonstrates some facility with language though it does not convey meaning skillfully: "Since we are not given a time period, it is possible that the concept of molds, their use, and how to make them had not been developed yet"; and, "Third, while the statement says they found molds, they cannot definitively say that molds were used to make all or even any life-size statues." Overall then, the response demonstrates strong, not outstanding, writing skills. The response is generally thoughtful with ideas connected by clear transitions ("First," "Second," "Third," "In summation"), and exhibits appropriate vocabulary and sentence variety. It clearly earns a score of 5.

Score 4 Response

Kalinese art holds value to the collectors who recognize the significance of the piece. The article states that the human sculptures are a result of molding techniques and not the actual skill of the Kali. Does that mean that they're any less valuable? How do they make their determination? Is it certain the molded sculptures didn't carry any significance to their makers? It makes me wonder if the molded statues were cast from living or deceased individuals, or if the dead body is still contained within the clay. Would it make a difference in the value of the art? I think so. In the archeological community, there is a great deal of curiosity about ancient civilizations and their way of life. By studying those molded sculptures, scientists may be able to unlock a hidden clue about these ancient people, and potential value may increase.

The rarity of the art piece would also determine its value. Large items are more susceptible to damage than small ones, and if the number of "life-size sculptures" were to diminish, the price would probably increase. One could make a similar argument about the mini sculptures, as they could be misplaced over time. How small are the minature pieces? Is there any more detail in their form than the human statues that would make them worth more? If the intricate details are found on both types of art, the predicion about their true value may not be as simple.

What makes art valuable? Maybe it is its condition, how much money was spent on it, or maybe it is a sentimental piece passed down through generations. The value of art holds true to the ones who care enough to obtain it. As long as there are collectors who are willing to bid at auctions, the art will hold its value. As the interest goes down, maybe the value will too. The antique or collectors market can be precarious at times, and though emphasis on certain items may be a little swayed, only time will determine what happens to the value of the Kalinese art.

Reader Commentary

This adequate response presents a relevant examination of the argument with acceptable clarity and addresses the specific task directions. The writer identifies some questions central to evaluating the argument and its prediction, for example, "The article states that the human sculptures are a result of molding techniques and not the actual skill of the Kali. Does that mean that they're any less valuable? How do they make their determination? Is it certain the molded sculptures didn't carry any significance to their makers?" But while a response earning a score of 5 or 6 might have asked the same questions and thus identified the same weaknesses in the argument, this response does not develop its questions in a compelling or insightful way. For example, regarding the question of whether the molds carried "any significance to their makers," the writer says, "By studying those molded sculptures, scientists may be able to unlock a hidden clue about these ancient people, and potential value may increase." A more thoughtful response would engage in further discussion of what "a hidden clue" might reveal and how it might correspond to the sculptures' potentially increased value. In addition, speculation on whether the molds still contain bodies is extraneous since only molds of "human heads and hands" have been found. The writer does address the relative value of both the life-size sculptures and the miniatures, but, again, examination of these values remains only adequate. Language conveys meaning with acceptable clarity; sentence structure lacks variety. Thus, demonstrating adequacy in all aspects of the task, this response earns a score of 4.

Score 3 Response

The basic flaw in the arguement is that something that is made from a mold is of less value. The use of molds in sculpture was previously frowned upon in European Modernism. The public and critics alike feel that the artist must have a mastery of hand and tool and each piece must be original. Therefore, realistic sculpting is the prize of all sculptors.

This degredation of life-casting is a perticulary western approach to sculpture. One of the most famous examples of Chinese ceramics, is the life-size clay army in the tomb of the Qin dynasty emporer (I cannot remember the correct spelling of his name]. These clay figures are not astounding for their realisitic interpretation of the human figure, but of the sheer quantity. They were cast from life molds. There were several different molds for each part of the body, and the sculptors would simply piece together arms and legs etc. to make different figures.

Perhaps the purpose of the Kalinese life-size figures, is not the celebration of one master sculptor, but the number of figures created. There is obviously a pre-existing market for the larger sculptures, so there must have been many that were created. Perhaps the Kalinese people appreciated the ease of production so they could be available for everybody. They people obviously did not care for each object to be individually crafted. They would put their energy into something they cared for, which is the creation of large, cast figures.

The mis-use of the word 'abstract' is astounding. The minatures are different from what we know the human body to look like, but who can argue with the interpretation of the Kalinese artists. Their perception of the figure cannot be put into Western terms.

Also, the claim of "molds could be used only for life-sized sculptures" does not have any evidence to support it. The use of molds can be used at any scale.

Despite the flaws in the authors logic, the prediction of the value shift may be true, simply due to the western liking of 'original' art. This article claims, lacking any evidence, that the smaller objects are not made from molds and therefore inharantly more valuable. This could then cause the price to shift.

Reader Commentary

Although this limited response identifies some important features of the argument and presents some relevant examination of the argument, it is limited in addressing the specific task directions and its analysis generally deals with tangential matters. Much of the analysis is based on the writer's own assumptions, for example that "[t]here is obviously a pre-existing market for the larger sculptures, so there must have been many that were created"; and the "people obviously did not care for each object to be individually crafted. They would put their energy into something they cared for, which is the creation of large, cast figures." The fourth paragraph does approach relevant analysis in implying that the abstract nature of the miniature sculptures should not be questioned or dismissed, and the fifth paragraph likewise implies relevant analysis. But the analysis in both of these paragraphs is poorly reasoned, development is clearly limited, and the support offered is of little relevance to the overall task. In addition, the writer concludes by agreeing with a major logical flaw in the argument, that "the prediction of the value shift may be true," but bases this conclusion not on logical analysis but on another unsupported assumption, that the change in value is "due to the western liking of 'original' art." Overall, control of language and sentence structure is adequate although there are some minor errors. But because the examination of the argument does not rise to an adequate level, this response earns a score of 3.

Score 2 Response

Because the miniatures sculptures are the reason why the larger ones are there, people will buy things because they are important. They want the most expensive and most beautiful thing, yes the life-size sculptures are beautiful but they are not the real reason. They are also just too big, people don;t want to have to move big pieces of art all around the house. They want to move little things that can move easily. It is unbelievable that these artists really sculpted their art after human figures, it would make sense because they would have the acutally body standing right next to them and they could feel their legs and their arms to understand how to sculpt it. But for the miniature statues, they did not have as much luck. They needed to use their imagination for those. They could look at people and see how their bodies were but they could not actually mold the body of their statue like a human because it was much smaller. The Kalinese people should be proud of themselves for being interesting and imaginative people.

Reader Commentary

This seriously flawed response largely disregards the specific task directions and demonstrates serious weaknesses in analytical writing. Rather than presenting a critical examination of the argument, the response offers the writer's own views on the relative value and desirability of the two types of Kalinese sculptures. For example, in discussing the life-size statues, the writer claims that "[t]hey are also just too big, people don't want to have to move big pieces of art all around the house. They want to move little things that can move easily." In addition, there are problems in the writing that interfere with meaning, for example, "Because the miniatures sculptures are the reason why the larger ones are there, people will buy things because they are important." The reader can only conjecture what the writer actually meant. Writing problems appear throughout the response, but in general they affect clarity, not meaning, and are not the main reason for this response's score. It is because the writer accepts the argument's logic unquestioningly, without any attempt at analysis, that this response earns its score of 2.

Score 1 Response

his is all about "Kali Island" there was in the some satatues made my the human bengies in the olden days they are been described as collectrs prize the ancient (olden days) life size clay statues of the human fingures are been made on the "kali island there was more wounderful statues and more artist were able to depict the bodies with such a realistic percison there was be done.

There are also some are the important in the kail since there was archaeologists this people are been used as resuarch depatment thet where apionted my government this pepole had gone into the kali they found recenty they whetre discoved molds of the human heads and hands on kali, they where saying that we the depart of the archaeologists we can now conculde thet the ancient lalinese artist used, olds od actual bodies there maily use this body 2 where useing this bidies for molds of actual boides to prepare status

In the olden day there was no technology was used for making status there where using some techiniques to creat there statuses this showes how the olden day the artist where constructing the statues in the ancient period. This showes the discovert and explains why the kalinese miniature staues where abstract and entriety differnt in style there was so many style od statues there where usinf molds are maily use d for could be used only for life-size scuptures it also explining in the ancient kalinese suplting tools havebeen used this tools where found when the archaeologists depatment where doing rsearch work thet where been found some doffernt kind of tools that are been used in ceartion of statues in differnt models in the kalineses in this research they where found some kinds od tools. In the kali island there was a light of discovery they have been collected predict that the life size scuptures will decrease by seeing this statues when the human body there will be considering the hand and head by seeing that they can say that when this have been made has statuies there will be decrease in the value while miniatues increase in value.

i conclude that here in the kail island there was may statues where found by the resrach departement "archaeogists" this is the department to find out the art and find the year when it had made and who as been artist dtail infomrmation will be given by this dept. likely in kali island also they wher found many differnt life size statues in this island.

Reader Commentary

This response demonstrates fundamental deficiencies in analytical writing. Its pervasive errors in language, sentence structure, grammar, and usage render this response nearly incoherent. For example, "This showes the discovert and explains why the kalinese miniature staues where abstract and entriety differnt in style there was so many style od statues there where usinf molds are maily use d for could be used only for life-size scuptures. . . ." Note that the most intelligible parts of what is quoted rely on using the specific language of the argument. Since every sentence verges on the incomprehensible, it is impossible to determine whether the writer understood either the argument or the task. This fundamentally deficient response exhibits the full range of characteristics for the score of 1.